FRAGMENTS OF GOOD NEWS

FRAGMENTS OF GOOD NEWS

*Selected Lectionary Stories for Cycles
A, B and C from StoryShare*

David O. Bales

CSS Publishing Company, Inc.

Lima, Ohio

FRAGMENTS OF GOOD NEWS

FIRST EDITION
Copyright © 2021
by CSS Publishing Co., Inc.

The original purchaser may print and photocopy material in this publication for use as it was intended (worship material for worship use; educational material for classroom use; dramatic material for staging or production). No additional permission is required from the publisher for such copying by the original purchaser only. Inquiries should be addressed to: Permissions, CSS Publishing Company, Inc., 5450 N. Dixie Highway, Lima, Ohio 45807.

Library of Congress Cataloging-in-Publication Data

Names: Bales, David O., 1948- author. Title: Fragments of good news : stories on biblical texts compiled from StoryShare, a component of Sermonsuite / David O. Bales. Description: First edition. | Lima : CSS Publishing Company, Inc., [2021] Identifiers: LCCN 2021027106 | ISBN 9780788030383 (paperback) | ISBN 9780788030390 (ebook) Subjects: LCSH: Christian life. | LCGFT: Short stories. | Christian fiction. Classification: LCC BV4515.3 .B347 2021 | DDC 242--dc23 LC record available at https://lccn.loc.gov/2021027106

For more information about CSS Publishing Company resources, visit our website at www.csspub.com, email us at csr@csspub.com, or call (800) 241-4056.

e-book:
ISBN-13: 978-0-7880-3039-0
ISBN-10: 0-7880-3039-6

ISBN-13: 978-0-7880-3038-3
ISBN-10: 0-7880-3038-8   DIGITALLY PRINTED

> I would tell the tale
> as I have heard fragments of it
> in the Hall of Dreams,
> in the palace of the Heart of Man
>
> *Henry Van Dyke*

Acknowledgments

Always to Judy
Always to Katherine, Mary, and Lydia
    and to the sons they have chosen for us:
        Rodrigo, Zach, and Nathan

Earl Burkholder
Chris Gebauer
Dave and Lois Haag
Stephen Hedlund
John and Sydne Linggi
Barbara "Mom" Miller
Wesley Runk

Trinity Presbyterian Church, Seattle, Washington
Calvary Presbyterian Church, Enumclaw, Washington
First Presbyterian Church, Myrtle Point, Oregon
First Presbyterian Church, Miles City, Montana
Miles Community College, Miles City, Montana
First Presbyterian Church, Klamath Falls, Oregon
Stephen Ministries, St. Louis, Missouri
CSS Publishing, Lima, Ohio
Bethany Presbyterian Church, Ontario, Oregon
College of Idaho, Caldwell, Idaho

Table Of Contents

Chapter 1: Most Improved   19
A Proper 6 (11) Genesis 18:1-15
C Proper 11 (16) Genesis 18:1-10a

Chapter 2: Mumbling Hope   23
A Proper 9 (14) Genesis 24:34-38, 42-49, 58-67

Chapter 3: Jake's Limp   26
A Proper 13 (18); C Proper 24 (29) Genesis 32:22-31

Chapter 4: Moses Prepared   29
A Proper 17 (22) Exodus 3:1-15

Chapter 5: Great-Grandma Hazel   32
C Thanksgiving; C Lent 1; Deuteronomy 26:1-11

Chapter 6: Incident In Jericho   36
A Proper 26 (31) Joshua 3:7-17

Chapter 7: Blessings Of Unconventional Marriage   39
B Proper 27 (32) Ruth 3:1-5; 4:13-27

Chapter 8: Of Prophets And Heifers   43
B Proper 6 (11) 1 Samuel 15:34-16:13

Chapter 9: How It All Started   46
A Lent 4; 1 Samuel 16:1-13

Chapter 10: Prophetic Jitters   49
B Proper 13 (18) 2 Samuel 11:26-12:13a
C Proper 6 (11) 2 Samuel 11:26-12:10, 13-15

Chapter 11: Sequence Of Service   52
B Transfiguration Sunday 2 Kings 2:1-12
C Proper 8 (13) 2 Kings 2:1-2, 6-14

Chapter 12: O'Henry's "The Last Leaf" — 55
A Proper 25 (30); B Easter 7; B Proper 20 (25);
C Epiphany 6 (6); C Proper 18 (23) Psalm 1

Chapter 13: Angel's Feet — 58
ABC Holy Name; ABC New Year's Day; AC Trinity Sunday;
B Proper 22 (27) Psalm 8

Chapter 14: Prairie Lessons — 62
ABC Easter Vigil; A Easter 2; B Proper 28 (33);
C Proper 8 (13) Psalm 16

Chapter 15: Answer! — 66
B Proper 6 (11) Psalm 20

Chapter 16: Abandoned? — 70
ABC Good Friday; Psalm 22; B Proper 23 (28) Psalm 22:1-15

Chapter 17: Vows — 73
B Easter 5 Psalm 22:25-31

Chapter 18: Valley Variation — 77
ABC Easter 4; A Lent 4; A Proper 23 (28); B Proper 11 (16) Psalm 23

Chapter 19: Sainted Mother-In-Law — 81
B Lent 1; C Advent 1; Proper 10 (15) Psalm 25:1-10
A Proper 21 (26) Psalm 25:1-9

Chapter 20: If It's Worth Telling — 84
A Proper 21 (26) Psalm 25:1-9

Chapter 21: Gloriously Stormy Worship — 88
ABC Baptism of the Lord (1); B Trinity Sunday Psalm 29

Chapter 22: In The Heart Of The Sea — 91
ABC Easter Vigil; ABC Reformation Day; A Proper 4 (9);
C Proper 29 (34) Psalm 46

Chapter 23: Mark Twain's "The War Prayer" — 94
A Easter 7 Psalm 68:1-10, 32-35

Chapter 24: Prayer For Righteous Government   98

   A Advent 2 Psalm 72:1-7, 18-19

Chapter 25: New Christmas   101

   ABC Christmas Day 3; ABC Easter Vigil; B Easter 6; C Proper 27 (32), Proper 28 (33) Psalm 98

Chapter 26): No-Matter-What   104

   A Proper 6 (11), Reign of Christ (34); C Thanksgiving Day Psalm 100

Chapter 27: Self-Serving   108

   C Proper 17 (22) Psalm 112

Chapter 28: Control   112

   A Epiphany 6 (6); B Proper 26 (31) Psalm 119:1-8

Chapter 29: A Good Night's Sleep   116

   B Proper 27 (32) Psalm 127

Chapter 30: Fish And Flowers From The Depths   120

   A Lent 5; B Proper 5 (10); Proper 8 (13); Proper 14 (19) Psalm 130

Chapter 31: Unity   124

   A Proper 15 (20); B Proper 7 (12), Easter 2 Psalm 133

Chapter 32: A Capable Woman, Past And Present   127

   B Proper 20 (25) Proverbs 31:10-31

Chapter 33: Less Than A Peaceable Kingdom   130

   A Advent 2 Isaiah 11:1-10

Chapter 34: The Perfect Candidate   133

   A Baptism of the Lord (1); ABC Monday in Holy Week Isaiah 42:1-9

Chapter 35: Beyond Comparison   137

   ABC Passion/Palm Sunday; ABC Wednesday in Holy Week; B Proper 19 (24) Isaiah 50:4-9a

Chapter 36: Bearing Our Infirmities   140

   ABC Good Friday Isaiah 52:13-58:12

Chapter 37: A (Really) Free Lunch — 144
A Proper 13 (18) Isaiah 55:1-5

Chapter 38: The Old Egyptian — 147
C Proper 17 (22) Jeremiah 2:4-13

Chapter 39: Remember Their Sin No More — 151
B Lent 5; ABC Reformation Day Jeremiah 31:31-34

Chapter 40: Lonely Prophet — 154
C Proper 10 (15) Amos 7:7-17
B Proper 10 (15) Amos 7:7-15

Chapter 41: No Matter What, Yahweh's Word — 158
A Proper 26 (31) Micah 3:5-12

Chapter 42: Thorough Temptation Of The Thoroughly Human — 161
A Lent 1 Matthew 4:1-11

Chapter 43: Pup — 164
A Epiphany 4 (4); A All Saints Matthew 5:1-12

Chapter 44: Called And Freed To Serve — 168
A Proper 6 (11) Matthew 9:35-10:8

Chapter 45: Mustard Seed Yard — 173
A Proper 12 (17) Matthew 13:31-33, 44-52

Chapter 46: If You Don't Forgive — 177
A Proper 19 (24) Matthew 18:21-35

Chapter 47: The Other Wise Man — 180
ABC New Year; A Reign of Christ Proper 29 (34) Matthew 25:31-46

Chapter 48: Serving Light — 190
B Proper 9 (14) Mark 6:1-13

Chapter 49: Failures For Jesus — 194
B Resurrection Sunday; B Easter Vigil Mark 16:1-8

Chapter 50: A View From The Very Top — 197
ABC Nativity of the Lord I Luke 2:1-14

Chapter 51: A Messianic Message? — 200
C Epiphany 6 (6) Luke 6:17-26

Chapter 52: The Way Jesus Would Have Told It — 204
C Proper 13 (18) Luke 12:13-21

Chapter 53: Second Cutting — 207
C Lent 4 Luke 15:1-3, 11b-32

Chapter 54: Aunt June's Thanksgiving — 213
A Thanksgiving; C Proper 23 (28) Luke 17:11-19

Chapter 55: Further Visions To Follow — 216
B Epiphany 2 (2) John 1:43-51

Chapter 56: Lord, Where Are You Going? Domine, Quo Vadis? — 219
ABC Holy/Maundy Thursday John 13:1-17, 31b-35

Chapter 57: The Spirit's Guidance — 222
C Trinity Sunday John 16:12-15

Chapter 58: Pilate's Point Of View — 226
B Reign of Christ (34) John 18:33-37

Chapter 59: Claustrophobia — 229
A Pentecost John 20:19-23; ABC Easter 2 John 20:19-31

Chapter 60: Second Chance — 233
C Easter 3 John 21:1-19

Chapter 61: The Soles Of Jesus' Feet — 237
ABC Ascension Acts 1:1-11

Chapter 62: A Way To Meet Jesus — 241
A Easter 2 Acts 2:14a, 22-32

Chapter 63: Helena's Touch   247

    B Easter 5 Acts 8:26-40

Chapter 64: Patternless Suffering With God   251

    A Proper 6 (11) Romans 5:1-8; C Trinity Sunday Romans 5:1-5
    A Lent 3 Romans 5:1-11

Chapter 65: One Man   255

    A Lent 1 Romans 5:12-19

Chapter 66: Paul's Innards   259

    A Proper 9 (14) Romans 7:15-25a

Chapter 67: Honest, Not Courteous, Prayer   262

    B Pentecost Romans 8:22-27

Chapter 68: Too Deep For Words   265

    A Proper 12 (17) Romans 8:26-39

Chapter 69: A Christian From Nowhere   270

    A Proper 19 (24) Romans 14:1-12

Chapter 70: God's Weakness   273

    A Epiphany 4 (4); ABC Tuesday in Holy Week 1 Corinthians 1:18-31

Chapter 71: Wired   277

    B Epiphany 2 (2) 1 Corinthians 6:12-20

Chapter 72: Blissful? Agnosticism   281

    C Epiphany 6 (6) 1 Corinthians 15:12-20

Chapter 73: Everything Has Become New   286

    C Lent 4 2 Corinthians 5:16-21

Chapter 74: Enveloped Into Jesus' Life   289

    ABC Ascension; A Reign of Christ 29 (34) Ephesians 1:1-15

Chapter 75: Those Who Know What Armor Is For   293

    B Proper 16 (21) Ephesians 6:10-20

Chapter 76: A Freshman Experience   298

C Advent 3 Philippians 4:4-7

Chapter 77: First Of All   302

C Proper 20 (25); B Thanksgiving 1 Timothy 2:1-7

Chapter 78: Confidence Corrective   305

B Proper 23 (28) Hebrews 4:12-16

Chapter 79: Priests For Whom?   309

B Reign of Christ (34) Revelation 1:4b-8
C Easter 2 Revelation 1:4-8

Chapter 80: And Under The Earth   313

C Easter 3 Revelation 5:11-14

Index Revised Common Lectionary A   317

Index Revised Common Lectionary B   319

Index Revised Common Lectionary C   321

Introduction

All the stories gathered here have been published in the CSS on-line publication "StoryShare." As such, each story ended with a preaching point. These preaching points aren't the only focus of the story. They remain here to help people utilize the stories in ministry.

I have included a **Discussion Guide**. Scholars are positive that all biblical stories were first told orally and that most certainly they were discussed after the telling. If you read these stories aloud for others, don't waste the story. Discussing a story is an excellent way to aid people in their life with God.

At the end of the book is a **Index to the Revised Common Lectionary** for all three cycles, noting the chapters that apply to which preaching events.

Discussion Questions

People respond differently in a group discussion. The first guidance for after you ask a question is: Pause and wait. Don't get jittery and feel you have to answer it yourself. Silence doesn't mean the question doesn't make sense. Some people need time to think. Of course, others have minds ready to pop out their instant thought. Then there are some who will wait until someone has answered first before they venture to speak. And often groups will include a member who will be mentally preparing a summary of the group's views.

Even though this page doesn't do it for you, be ready to phrase the question in different words. Which leads to: coming up with questions that you believe will lead your group into deeper discussion of the story. One good question in ministry for Jesus Christ can be worth a dozen sermons... or stories.

1. What immediate responses do you have to the story?
2. Do you identify with a character in the story? If yes, how and why do you identify with the person? If no, why don't you identify with anyone in the story?
3. Would you like to have a conversation with a character in the story? What would you say, ask, or suggest to the person? Why?
4. Does the story bring the biblical text into clearer focus for you? How? Why or why not?
5. How would you improve, modify, retitle, or completely rewrite the story? Why?
6. What further depth of meaning, symbols, connections with or applications to the biblical faith do you find in the story?
7. Since Jesus Christ has risen from the dead and is alive among us through his Holy Spirit, what of this story would you like Christ to activate in your life?

A Proper 6 (11) Genesis 18:1-15
C Proper 11 (16) Genesis 18:1-10a

Chapter 1: Most Improved

In the teachers' lounge at South Middle School, the morning gossip and general world critique turned to Darrell Schmeling. "Old prune face," one called him.

A teacher getting a soda from the refrigerator turned and said, "I saw him smile once, but I think he was being paid to do it."

The assistant principal said, "Have you ever seen a squarer jaw?" to which another responded, "No, but this one is always clamped shut."

"He's just serious," his history team-teacher said. "He's always concentrating on something and he doesn't hurt anybody. He just doesn't know how to be any other way."

"Well, by fifty," the physical education teacher said, "you'd think he'd found something to do instead of reading giant tomes. He just plods closed-lip through the halls with his big books."

Another teacher leaned into the group, "And I'll bet if he were here …heard everything you said …he wouldn't utter a word."

The door knob turned and they all looked guiltily toward it; but, it wasn't Darrell Schmeling, just Melanie from the office staff, talking with someone behind her as she slowly opened the door.

At Darrell's church they were talking about him too. The ministry committee convened to sift through the church membership list to determine which gifts members had and which ministries they were performing. Pastor Sharon repeated her usual introduction, "I don't care if they define their ministry as farmer, stockbroker, or parent, as long as they understand that Christ has given them gifts in order to serve the church and the world."

"Yes, we all know that," James said as he took the copies of the membership list from the pastor's hands. "Let's get going."

Fragments of Good News

The six members and pastor studied the list the secretary had prepared. Person by person they discussed and suggested how people were serving or might serve. They narrowed the list to Darrell Schmeling. Ten minutes' discussion brought no good idea for Darrell. "He's so quiet," Jan said.

"So brainy," another said.

After a long pause, James puckered his lips and said, "Let's pray and wait for an answer." So they did. The prayer was their usual practice: each silently meditating and speaking to God in their own heart. Soon Ceciline said, "I've got it: middle school youth group advisor."

"What?" the rest said in unison.

"No, I don't think so," James said.

"Yeah," another said. "He's so distant. I can't imagine him with a youth group. It would take a miracle."

Pastor Sharon said, "Let her talk. Let her talk."

Ceciline stated that, if Darrell were convinced to work with the middle kids, it would be for his sake as well as the group's. "Serving others fulfills us," she said. A couple still shook their heads and one sighed, but the idea had come from prayer and they all were willing to follow the Spirit's leading — whether they understood it or not.

James was delegated to visit Darrell that night, and Darrell agreed. No discussion, just a quiet, "yes" to James' request. He did blink and give a small gasp, however, when James told him that his first service would be with the middle school retreat next weekend. James reassured him, "It's all planned at a dandy retreat center. You'll have a bed."

Throughout the retreat Darrell proved a quick learner — for being such an old person, as the middle school kids said. He took directions well and, even though the other leaders were concerned about his joining the organized craziness of the games, he did. Samuel, the youth pastor, had explained, "We play dignity destroying games. Everyone's dignity is shattered in a silly way, old and young alike, and we become just people together. It's more than team-building. It's getting closer to the image God put on us."

In the learning groups Darrell shared, just as the students were asked to share, answering about what the Bible said and what it meant and how they felt God working in their lives. At fifty — and with thirty extra pounds — he usually lost at the game Scoot, Scoot! He was obviously embarrassed, but squeezed in with everyone when they played Sardines. He was huffing and puffing, but he held his own at Round Robin Ping Pong. He won hands down, however, at If You Love Me, Honey, Smile. No one could approach him in the circle and say to him, "If you love me, honey smile" and provoke him to smile. With the coolness from deep within him he answered, "I love you, honey, but I can't smile."

Samuel watched Darrell wipe sweat off his face in the round robin tournament. At lunch he nudged him and said, "You're doing great."

During worship the next Sunday, Samuel reported to the congregation about the middle school retreat. The middle school kids and their advisors sat in the three front rows and he announced that they would now bestow awards for the weekend. The students each received outlandish awards: longest in the bathroom, worst morning hair, most tears in the jeans. The congregation enjoyed the antics as much as the kids.

Then Samuel announced one more award. "Would Mr. Schmeling come up here." The kids all cheered. He stood stone faced before the congregation. Samuel said to him, "Please turn sideways and face Joleen." He did, and the middle school girl held up to the congregation a large page with the word, "SMILE." She handed it to Darrell and said, "Mr. Schmeling, I give you this award as Most Improved. Everyone laughed. "Now," she said, looking grimly at him and leaning forward, "If you love me honey, smile."

Darrell, without a missed breath, answered, "I love you honey, but I can't smile." Then Darrell Schmeling, fifty-year-old history teacher of the square jaw, thirty pounds overweight, and second runner up in the round robin ping pong tournament, laughed out loud.

Preaching point: *How do God's miracles come into our lives — especially if we seem too old to change?*

A Proper 9 Genesis 24:34-38, 42-49, 58-67

Chapter 2: Mumbling Hope

Phabi and Nahum rode obediently behind Eliezer, tossed rhythmically side to side on their camels. They glanced to one another with knowing looks. Eliezer was mumbling again. "I suppose I could've told them the whole story. They were certainly interested. A display of wealth will do that, especially to a fellow like Laban."

Phabi and Nahum had listened to Eliezer's rambling for two months. It was a joke among the men who accompanied him. Nahum spoke quietly sideways, "It's like anything he thinks just trickles from his mouth."

Phabi responded, "Not only does Eliezer repeat his own thoughts and actions. He starts with a redo of the master's instructions and dribbles on: 'Insisted on my solemn oath. Scared me to death, like the destiny of all human life on my shoulders.' He tells himself again about the situation, 'Poor old Abraham's thinking …getting more sketchy every day and, instead of dispatching his son to scrutinize the Canaanite lasses, insists I head off a month north to Aram-naharaim. Have to keep asking directions; and I'm no spring sparrow either. Aches are in my knees, hips, back, and shoulders. And this camel-rocking jars me step by clomping step.'"

Nahum gave a snigger to Phabi, "Old Eliezer can't even enjoy 95% of success. Never known a guy who worries this much, even when everything's working out. All the way to Aram-naharaim he kept mumbling, 'O LORD, God of my master Abraham, please grant me success.' Had to sleep by him sometimes and the muttering continued until dawn. While we were traveling north he'd roll over in his sleep whispering, 'Where's the angel? Where's the angel?' Then, after we've gained the women, his sleep talk is, 'Heaven and earth, heaven and earth.'"

"I calculate three days at the most until we're home," Phabi said. "He delivers the young princess and he's done. Anybody else would be ordering older and older wine day by day. But he can't relax. He's so jittery that if he had feathers he could fly."

The two servants rode in silence through the morning. Then Phabi screwed up his face as though he was thinking hard. "Know what it is?" he asked. "The oath. He can't shuck the seriousness. Not as though the master sent him to market with a flock of sheep and said, 'Sell all you can and get the best price possible.' No, he hung all of heaven and earth on his senior servant's shoulders with the oath. Anybody ever make you put your hand under his thigh and take an oath?"

Nahum shuddered and answered, "Yes, yes," he stuttered. "I mean no, no... I see what you mean. I guess I'm just anxious to get home too. At least we recognize the trail in this direction. That's a blessing."

The caravan entered a woodland and Eliezer called a halt for a rest. He rushed to Rebekah and her maids' camels and made sure they knelt slowly for the women's safe dismount. He left them and worked his way down the line of other camels, looking at each animal to confirm its healthy condition.

Standing by his camel now, Nahum said to Phabi, "Treats her like a queen." Phabi laughed and Nahum continued, "I admit she's a looker all right."

The two tied their animals to tree limbs and sat in the shade. Eliezer came by inspecting each servant with a nervous glance up and down. "Just checking," he said, then he went back to the women, to see if they needed anything.

"This Rebekah is Isaac's cousin," Phabi said, picking up what he'd been thinking before Eliezer walked by, "and she gets along with everybody. Might be just what the boy needs." He ran his hand through his beard and said, "With Eliezer it's about the boy, not just his oath. Eliezer's been around Abraham's son a long time."

"I'm always with a different herd. Don't really know the son," Nahum said.

"Eliezer has always been protective of him," Phabi said. "The boy seems like a slightly crooked arrow that'll never comes off the string right. Spends a lot of time just walking around. Started when he was a kid. Shouldn't happen to anybody's son. You know what I'm talking about?"

"No."

"A couple years before you hired on, the old man took Eliezer and me and traveled with his son three days to the land of Moriah. This is his only child by Sarah and born late in life. He left Eliezer and me and went off with the boy. Over the years, I've put pieces together from what the boy and his mother have said. The old man built an altar there, set wood on it. He bound his son and laid him on top the wood. Had his knife raised to kill him as a sacrifice when he's struck from heaven by an angel and told instead to sacrifice the goat caught in yon thicket. Let me tell you, that boy was shook up when they came back — having seen his father hovering over him with the knife pointing down. To my mind he hasn't been lively since. It's no wonder the master doesn't trust him to find his own wife."

"I don't know the son," Nahum said, "but I know Eliezer and he's been good to us. I hope at least for his sake that all works well when we finally deliver the bride. I pray that the destiny of heaven and earth be lifted off his shoulders. And," he shook his head, "I hope for a quiet night's sleep after we get home."

Preaching point: *Feeling responsible for heaven's future on earth.*

A Proper 13 (18); C Proper 24 (29) Genesis 32:22-31

Chapter 3: Jake's Limp

No one knew if Uncle Edwin would be able to travel. He too had been seriously ill; but he made it to the church social room on a cane. After a few hugs and hellos he sat and began to talk, "West Virginia in the late '40s. Coal — everything was coal."

On this evening before the funeral, no one expected a speech. Edwin, however, went right on, as though speaking to no one and everyone. "You either worked in the mine, the railroad, or in the yard on the tipple. After high school Jake and I both wanted to go to college, though we had no good reason to think we could."

By now all twenty-plus adults in the church social room, the relatives, were listening. Those who knew him well were surprised; because Edwin was the twin who seldom talked. He was a doer. "Only when I had children of my own did I truly understand our parents' anguish. They'd tried. They just hadn't been able to save much. This was before student loans. Jake and I'd both applied to Curells College and were accepted. We petitioned for every cent, but received only a promise to me of work in the campus laundry and Jake to be assistant to the women's softball coach. Yet, in the days and weeks after high school it became obvious we both couldn't attend, not then, not at the same time."

"I can't remember who suggested it or even how Jake and I agreed to it. It was such a strange arrangement. Word went around what was up — to neighbors and, especially, relatives. We'd play a tennis match to see which of us got to start college that fall.

"Seemed every other person in the state was our relative — cousins strung out like a mile long coal train. And you know how the family telegraph is faster with news than any television station." He waited until the laughter ended. "Two cousins, Uncle

George and Aunt Effie's daughters Betsy and Ann, when they heard, they got right on the bus, traveled half the day and found me as I walked home from work that evening. Wouldn't even let me clean up. Grabbed me and pulled me around the woodshed before Jake got there. And here's what they said....

"But first you need to know Betsy and Ann were religious. Boy howdy were they religious. Our family was religious enough, Jake the least. His prayers tended to be, like most kids, 'Oh God, get me out of this mess and I'll....'

"My two cousins were convinced. They'd been praying again and had a vision or something. They told me their good friend Rose from their church would also be a freshman at Curells College and she was going to play softball."

The younger people let out an "Oooh."

"Yup, they were sure, as only adolescent girls can be sure, that, if Rose and Jake met, they'd marry and she'd make him into a decent Christian man — decent by late '40s West Virginia standards. They wheedled and whined at me, one on each side with their God-given absolute certainty. Tears and reminding me that I hadn't always been kind to my brother, or even fair. They wanted me to throw the game. I was the older of the two, they said, and as the older I must take responsibility for my younger twin. Such logic!

"I'm sure Jake told you he wanted out of coal country even if he didn't know exactly where he wanted to go. He at least wanted to go to college and he'd play his heart out in a tennis match to go. We set the time after our day shift in the mine. Betsy and Ann, other relatives, and a few people from the mine and the neighborhood showed up.

"Jake played with all his might, but he played tennis like he was fighting a bear with a club. I determined, if he was going to win, I'd make him battle for it. I'd win a game, then he. I'd win a set, then he. Until we'd strung out the match for over a couple hours at least — and after a full day's work.

"It was getting dark. Could hardly see the ball. He'd get me to ad in and I'd take him back to deuce. Ad in, deuce, ad in. Until I figured he was about to pass out and I hit a drive two inches out. The cousins circling the court and the dozen or so others who'd come screamed and yelled. Jake, simply exhausted, fell to the court. That's when he hurt his hip. Bothered him, but reminded him, the rest of his life.

"He went to college. He met Rose and married and became a comparatively fine fellow. He never knew it was all arranged …never knew. His whole life thinking he'd won. But it was the strangest kind of winning. Betsy and Ann told me my defeat was a triumph of grace.

"I made it here tonight to tell you. First time to anyone. To let you know God's grace made Jake who he was, God and Rose made him — your dad, granddad, great grandad. And you children, descendants of Jake and Rose, are recipients of Jake's limp, a secret plan of grace. I wanted you to know before the funeral."

One last deep breath and Edwin slowly stood and steadied himself on his cane. "Now you all enjoy being together. I'm going to hobble back to the motel to rest up for tomorrow. As usual, I'll probably dream about Jake and our childhood in coal country."

> **Preaching point**: *Even when we seem to succeed by our own efforts, it is also somehow God's victory.*

A Proper 17 (22) Exodus 3:1-15

Chapter 4: Moses Prepared

Moses can almost consider his situation as fortunate. The Egyptians aren't concerned enough about justice to tramp ten days across the desert for one murderer — especially to a place so bleak that it's named "Desolation." No, best for Moses that he concentrate on the positive: safety from Egypt's revenge, plus a wife, family, job, and social stability as the son-in-law of a priest. A shepherd's nomadic life isn't as flashy as Egypt's palaces; but in a reduced way it has its perks. No crops means no enemies driving their livestock into your fields to feed on your toil. And if you don't have a house, no one can covet it.

Yet, when he's alone out here with the sheep — these crafty, stupid, needy sheep—he remembers and wonders. He remembers the years in Egypt. Servants leaping at his whisper, the land's luscious food, clothing that emanated royalty — besides the obeisance everywhere as the adopted son of Pharaoh's daughter. Walk down a street and everyone bowed and he saw awe and envy in their faces.

Awe and envy. Awe and envy. And all past. Moses walks now behind the flock. He sees on the rise ahead that he must hurry to get there before the speckled ewe crests. He calls, but she doesn't respond. If she gets out of sight, that ornery sheep will turn and lead the rest to last month's graze. She's smart enough to remember her last month's sustenance but stupid enough not to remember that it was consumed a month ago. If she gets her way, Moses will lose half the day rounding the flock and leading them to their new pasture.

Best for everyone if Moses settle his thoughts into this daily plodding and not dwell on his old life or wonder what might have been if he'd curbed his rage. One senseless act. He could've done differently. He had the Pharaoh's ear. He could've complained about the treatment of the Hebrews, even suggested that he help solve the problem.

No, he took matters in his own hand, and took a human life with that hand. Now, even if he'd flee as far as possible, trudge through the desert's shimmer of last night's dew until he can't think another thought, he'll still see the Egyptian. The man had been doing what he was ordered to do. Nothing extraordinary about the taskmaster. He was trained to beat laborers. But no matter how long ago it was, a dozen times a day Moses sees the man's face as he twitched his last. The memory touches him like the strap of the shepherd's bag over his shoulder. Again, he hefts the knife is his hand, and the warmth of blood spurts from the man's chest, and the man's legs seem to resist him as he drags the corpse into the sand's shallow grave. Moses looks toward the sheep, quickens his pace, and sees the Egyptian's face again.

He's never spoken to Zipporah about this. She doesn't deserve to worry about him. She has enough to do to guarantee survival of the family and clan. He's never talked to anyone about it. He has only his thoughts growing grotesquely and blooming into poisonous plants in his dreams, waking her and the children again, yet shaking his sweating head and saying, "Nothing. It's nothing."

Then the walk outside the tent under the stars to calm himself. Again last night, most of the night, until he tiptoes into the tent before dawn, hoping he's been gone long enough for all to return to sleep. Zipporah touches him gently and, as she's learned during these strained years of marriage, says nothing.

He thinks of Zipporah, her dark, trusting eyes, and wonders what he can say that would help her without telling all the truth. He can't stand the idea of revealing everything to her. She's always been impressed by his educated, Egyptian ways. What would she think or do if she heard it all?

That ewe, the speckled one. Moses has lost sight of her again. And, being exhausted from lack of sleep, he's wandered into thorns. Maybe he's been sleep walking. He certainly hasn't been vigilant for his flock, his father-in-law's flock. He tries to run but stubs his toe on a pyramid of rock. Not only have the sheep wandered over the rough ground, Moses has, as though in a dream, found himself encircled by bushes like a fence around him. He halts and looks to the broken ridge before him, wondering at the same time if he'll ever find the sheep or his peace of mind.

Only a few more steps and he'll meet another bush that will sweep him above the regret of any memory and beyond any wonders he's ever had.

Preaching point: *Moses, and each of us, is somehow prepared for God to meet us with a task much larger than ourselves.*

C Lent 1; C Thanksgiving Deuteronomy 26:1-11

Chapter 5: Great-Grandma Hazel

It shouldn't be this hard, Kayly thought. Seemed simple when Mr. Harmon assigned it to his college prep English class: "'I did not get here by myself.' Each of you," he said, "is the living fringe of a long genealogy. Certainly you have received some disabilities from your family," to which most students chuckled. "No family's perfect. What I want you to write about is that you're just the wave as it meets the shore. Your life energy started way out to sea — generations ago."

The assignment was to interview a current family member about an older family member already dead and write how a generation in the past affects those living today. "If you're adopted," he said, "you can use your adoptive parents to tell you about someone who's gone before you. If you don't seem to have any relatives in the world, talk to me. I'll hook you up with some friends of mine who'll be your surrogate parents for a while. But don't ask to borrow their car keys for prom night."

Why the resistance? The first time Kayly mentioned it to her mother, she watched her mother's lips thin. She didn't consider interviewing her father. Her parents were divorced and she seldom saw him. "It's about your grandma, Mom. Just tell me some things about her, especially what she handed on to you."

Both times Kayly brought it up again her mother's face tightened. The best Kayly could get from her was, "Why don't you talk to your Uncle Zach? He's a year and a half older than me. I was only eleven when Grandma died."

"But you lived in the same town and saw her a lot, didn't you?"

Her mother spoke while facing away from Kayly, "Get Zach in on this."

That evening Kayly phoned her Uncle Zach and left him little time to think as she explained her assignment, saying her mom was willing — which was not exactly true — to help if Uncle Zach would join. For his usually being bright and ready to jump into anything that included his nieces and nephews, there was a long pause on the phone. Kayly almost had to beg him. She wheedled him into coming to their home on Saturday afternoon.

Whenever Kayly's mom and uncle got together, the noise level rose and Kayly almost had to raise her hand or step between them to get into their conversation. Today they sat silently with her in the living room as she again reported the assignment, reading word for word from her tablet. She soon pictured herself as a dentist trying to pull teeth. All she could extract from them about their grandmother was: "She was a nice person... Yeah, but we were pretty young... Took real good care of her kids... For the first years of your grandpa's business she worked on the books at the shop on Friday and Saturday nights."

Kayly was frustrated. "What else?" she said with force. "As a human being, what else? What do you most remember about her?"

"Well..., she was charitable," Zach said as he shook his head slightly while glancing at his sister. Her mother's face muscles tightened. Kayly peered at her and waited. Finally, as her mother looked squarely at Zach, she said, "She was very charitable. Grandpa's electronics shop became a financial success. Your uncle and I have benefited from that business. Wouldn't you *agree*, Zach?"

Kayly had always felt that her mother and uncle were wonderful people. What was going on here? Did they bury Great-grandma Hazel under the garage or something? The sister and brother sat beside one another looking down. Kayly realized that she was gaping at them. Then her mother nodded to Zach and said, "Yeah. Tell her."

Zach blew out through his nose as he grimaced, and, speaking to his lap, he said, "Grandpa, your great-grandpa, had died when your mom was in kindergarten. Grandma, your great-grandma, was almost beyond charitable. She lived to give money away.

We knew that as kids and, even after she was dead, our parents talked about her giving.

"The one thing Grandma told us every Christmas — as she told our parents before us — was about when she was a child in Oklahoma in the 1930s. She called them 'the dirty thirties.' Dust Bowl, the truly great depression. She was old enough to know what was going on. She said most farms were already repossessed by the bank. Some people had given up and surrendered to life on the county poor farm. A few men had hopped freight trains heading west in hope of a job to send money home. Her family had sold their last milk cow. That money was gone and by December there wasn't a potato left in the root cellar. At every meal in December her father repeated that he couldn't stand his family's going on relief. All five of the children knew there'd be no Christmas presents. Then word came that a Salvation Army truck would arrive in town. Grandma Hazel didn't remember exactly how the Salvation Army provisioned her family, but they did, at least for a while. And she remembered their giving her a rag doll she kept for years.

"So every Christmas when we were children, Grandma Hazel led the family in giving to the Salvation Army. She helped us and our brother and sister to save money for the Salvation Army 'pail,' she called it. And she gave us money to go with her to put in the pail. Up to a couple Christmases before she died, she still came with us. When she wasn't able to leave her house anymore, she gave us the money and sent us."

He looked to his sister. She nodded, "Go on."

"I'm sorry to be the one to tell you this, Kayly, about your mom and me, I mean."

Kayly couldn't figure out what he was talking about but she faced them attentively.

"It was even in her will for Dad and his brothers and sisters, the request that, since they were receiving a great deal of money from that little business on Second Street that was the first in town to sell transistor radios, they should be grateful and give to others, especially the Salvation Army at Christmas." He paused, looked at his sister next to him, then began speaking again focusing over Kayly's head, as if addressing someone behind her. "Of Dad's generation, one of his brothers and one sister lived by Grandma Hazel's example and advice. Two other siblings didn't. They didn't have to. It was just Grandma's request in her will. And, as you can surmise, in our generation, your mother and I haven't either."

"We've talked about it," her mother said quickly. "We just never got around to it. We've enjoyed the inheritance that came to us when we reached 21. But by that time we'd pretty well forgotten Grandma." Tears formed in her eyes. "*But*," she said, "it's been a long time…, but I'm going to start now. Don't you dare write what we told you about us. But I'm going to start today with a check to the Salvation Army. Zach?" She looked at him sternly.

"Me too," he said. "It's a relief. Maybe sometime, as Grandma said, it will become a joy."

Kayly fiddled with the tablet, upon which she'd written nothing, and looked back and forth at her mother and uncle. She wanted to say something to assure her mother and uncle that she loved them. But the event was so out of the ordinary that she just said what she'd heard on television, "Thank you for the interview. I'll only write about my grateful great-grandmother and me. That's more than enough."

Preaching point: *Directing gratitude.*

A Proper 26 (31) Joshua 3:7-17

Chapter 6: Incident In Jericho

On July 11, 1927, fourteen-year-old Andrew was up a tree in Jericho. He thought this must be something like Zacchaeus did in order to see Jesus. He'd been there four hours. His arms were aching. He peered steadily to the east, intent on the trail. All Andrew could do was watch and wait... and think. Along with the whole village he was excited when the earthquake struck and the news came that an entire cliff fell into the Jordan, damming it — just as for Joshua. If his father hadn't forbade him to leave the village, he'd be on the trail there himself. But lately Jews, Christians, and Muslims had been experiencing friction in Jericho, so Andrew wouldn't see Jordan's cut off waters. He'd accept the witness of Father John, who waved to him as he'd departed for the Jordan.

After Father John left, Andrew shinnied up the tree and pondered the situation in Jericho as well as Joshua's crossing the Jordan on dry ground. His group of Christian boys had been studying with Father John; and Father John encouraged his students to reason about their faith. Andrew, he said, had the mind and temperament to serve God as a priest — if he had the faith. His mind now was swirling with Jordan's cut off waters, because he thought about how, after crossing the Jordan, Joshua invaded the land and slaughtered everybody. How was that different than when armies later did the same thing? In Father John's history class, he'd learned it happened many times in Palestine.

Over the hill, he finally spotted the top of Father John's hat bouncing rhythmically from the road to the Jordan. He bounded down and dashed toward him jumping and yelling, "Was it really cut off? Was it really cut off?" Father John smiled from afar, waving and yelling back, "Yes, Andrew. Yes."

David O. Bales

When Andrew met him, Father John explained that the cliff wall had sloughed off and dammed the stream perfectly.

"A miracle, like Joshua," Andrew said.

"Yes," Father John said, as he continued to walk to the village. In July's heat he was dripping with sweat and caked with dust.

Andrew drew in beside him, jumped once more and said, "Miracle!" then he stretched his legs to match Father John's steps, "I've been thinking," he said.

"That's what you're supposed to do," Father John gave a tired smile.

"The miracle's so great I can hardly stand it; but…" Andrew paused, "Joshua slaughtered innocent people and the Bible says God told him to do it."

"Yes?" he tipped up the word in a question.

"Really?"

"Yes," Father John said, "that's really what the Bible says. But the Bible is the Word of God and the word of man. We have to remember it's genuinely human, and thus in the Bible humans wrap a lot of what they want around what God wants. The Bible's as human and divine as Jesus was human and divine. So, many heresies, you remember, tried to make Jesus only divine. Took hundreds of years for the church to get it right. People try to do the same with the Bible."

Andrew shook his head, "You mean the Bible's wrong?"

"No, I mean we get to, we must, ask questions of the Bible. What's the eternal message bound up with the people and time it was written? Like Psalm 137, about blessing those who smash enemies' babies on the rocks, or David's daily slaughtering every living being in 1st Samuel 27. That's clearly not what God wants. One difference that Christians and Jews have from Muslims is that we get to question and even argue with the Bible. Muslims have to believe their Koran dropped to them word for word. We believe God came here into people's lives, just as in Jesus, really here in people like us, that's why I say the Bible is the word of man as well as the word of God."

"What about Joshua and the Jordan being cut off?"

Fragments of Good News

"We sure know today that it's possible, don't we?" He smiled to Andrew. "Thing is, we can't prove it. That's what faith's about. God gives us enough from around us, so that the Holy Spirit inside us helps us believe. But it always takes faith."

They were approaching the village and others were coming to meet Father John to hear his report. Andrew rushed to ask another question before Father John was surrounded for the rest of the day telling and retelling what he'd seen. "Then what can we believe in the Bible?"

Father John stopped and looked down at him, "We believe it all, that through it all God speaks to us; but we believe that some things are much more important than others. That's what Jesus was about. He's the center of our faith and of our Bible. He helps us realize what's most important and how to live. His resurrection, by the way, is so much more important than the cutting off of Jordan's waters that the Jordan's flow doesn't even rank." He looked up to receive the people running to him and added to Andrew, "You won't understand everything, Andrew. But get used to trusting Jesus who once before in Jericho looked up a tree to choose a servant."

Preaching point: *The center of the Bible's faith is not the slaughters or just the miracles, but the heart of God seen in Jesus Christ.*

B Proper 27 (32) Ruth 3:1-5; 4:13-27

Chapter 7: Blessings Of Unconventional Marriage

Melanie was on the sidewalk, approaching 429 Oak Ridge Drive. She'd spent an evening at the church discussing and role-playing how to call upon new worshipers. This was now her first visit for the congregation. Prayer, she thought. I'm always supposed to pray before calling. I suppose I could pray no one's home. She knew that was silly; the church secretary had phoned ahead and Joel and Kyla Rue had agreed to a call. The secretary told Melanie, "They were the couple sitting by the senior high drama group. They seemed to enjoy the kids a lot."

With a shapeless wave of prayer toward God, she repeated to herself: Prayer and listening, prayer and listening. She punched the doorbell and a couple of about retirement age greeted her with toothy smiles. Melanie noticed that Kyla showed more of her gums than Joel.

"You must be Melanie. We've been looking forward to your coming," Kyla said. Joel was gesturing toward their couch, "Come and get comfy."

As Melanie was being seated, she blurted out, "We're really pleased you worshiped with us," which she instantly regretted as seeming too forward. Also, she realized she hadn't done any listening yet.

"We're glad we visited your congregation on drama Sunday," Joel said, "I used to teach drama. I thought your casting director did just right with the choice of actors. And the script allowed the freedom of the actors to flow through."

"I'm glad you feel that way," Melanie said. "Nothing like my high school drama teacher. At our rehearsals, she pointed with a yard stick and hovered around us repeating lines and calling beats."

"Here? You grew up here?" Joel asked.

"Not exactly, I moved here in eighth grade and been here ever since. Sometimes it feels like all my life."

"So you have longterm friends here," Kyla said. "In the church?"

"Plenty. Yeah. In lots of ways, a bunch of us are still dealing with the sad things of high school."

"Sad?" Kyla asked.

"Well, in high school, an inordinate percentage of our parents died. In what I call my large circle of girlfriends, a third of the parents died or were killed by the time we graduated high school and in my close group of three one of each of our parents was dead."

"That must have been terrible," Joel said. "Any of your three stay in town?"

"All of us, eventually. We all attended the community college and two of us became dental hygienists. Our third member went on to dental school and we work for her."

"That's amazing," Kyla said, with her gums at maximum smile.

The three chuckled as Melanie realized she'd talked instead of listened. Hadn't asked a single question or reflected any statements.

She was just opening her mouth to ask, she knew-not-what, when Kyla said, "How about some coffee and cookies? I put a pot on fifteen minutes ago, decaf, and the cookies are fresh from Safeway."

"Sounds great," Melanie said.

"She's as good at making cookies as she is at making coffee," Joel said as Kyla left for the kitchen.

"Oh," Joel said. "You take cream or sugar or one of those fake sugar-things?"

"Cream's fine if you've got some," Melanie said.

"Ruth," Joel spoke loudly over his shoulder, "bring some cream too." He turned to Melanie, "So you've always been a member of this congregation?"

Melanie must have answered, though she didn't remember doing so. Her mind hooked on Joel's saying "Ruth." She'd been sure that the church secretary had told her "Joel and Kyla." That's what Melanie had written on the note with their address. But she distinctly heard Joel say "Ruth." She started breathing regularly again when she recalled that many people go by their middle names with relatives and friends.

When Kyla brought the coffee and cookies, Melanie was determined to ask some questions, hoping the answers could lead naturally to talking about faith and church. She sipped from the cup, "Mmm, that's good. Now, you know, ah, I'd like to hear about you two, like where you from?"

"I'm mostly from Michigan," Joel said, "A lot of moving around, but Kyla spent her life in Atlanta."

Melanie looked from one to the other of their friendly faces, "You said 'Kyla'; but, you called her 'Ruth' when she was in the kitchen."

They smiled at one another with more gums than Melanie thought possible; Melanie waited as they giggled. Kyla continued chuckling and Joel let out a happy sigh, "I admit, I called her 'Ruth;' most always do, when I'm talking to her."

"And I call him 'Boaz,'" Kyla said. They grinned. Melanie looked at them with a question locked on her face.

"Book of Ruth," Joel said.

"Okay, sure, yeah," Melanie said, nodding in confusion.

"Goes back to when we got married," Joel said.

"How we got married," Kyla said.

They were just out of high school and wanted to marry, but their parents refused because they were too young. So they lied, said Kyla was pregnant, and that got the parents' permission. The rest, Joel said, "was history."

Melanie realized her mouth was open and maybe they could see her older, amalgam fillings. She closed her mouth with a thump.

"I know," Joel said, "rather dramatic," and they all laughed.

"So to me," Kyla said, "Joel has always been 'Boaz' and I've always been 'Ruth' to him; because, we had a strange marriage to match their strange marriage in the old Hebrew world."

Melanie was mute, so Joel said, "We shouldn't have done it, but we've never regretted it. We think it's part of the way God rewrites the usual script in order to bring something good into the world. We've certainly found that life doesn't always turn out the way you plan or expect, but God can bring about wonderful things through, shall we say, unusual circumstances."

Melanie still didn't speak. For the rest of the evening, she listened to Joel and Kyla (Boaz and Ruth) tell about their lives and faith, their jobs, the churches they attended, and their daughter, named, as they said, slightly out of order, Naomi.

Preaching point: *God blesses strange marriage situations.*

B Proper 6 (11) 1 Samuel 15:34-16:13

Chapter 8: Of Prophets And Heifers

Samuel would be safer if he'd begun before dawn; but, Yahweh's word didn't come to him until after the morning sacrifice and then he still had to secure a heifer before he could leave. His greatest risk in his southern trek was to pass Gibeah, Saul's fortress hill. Samuel had to go right by it, almost under it, fully visible to Saul's soldiers. Saul's men were loyal to their master to the point that they'd kill the prophet Samuel just as he himself had executed Agag, king of the Amalekites. With the late start, Samuel couldn't get to Bethlehem in one day. And here he was dragging this heifer. "Come on, little heifer," he said. Always her slow *clip, clip, clip,* two steps behind him.

Yahweh gave no explanation, just that he'd rejected Saul and Samuel needed to fill a horn with oil, travel to Bethlehem with this heifer, and anoint one of Jesse's sons. No one could guess what Saul would do if he captured Samuel on this mission. What a horrible position: caught between Yahweh and the king. In this case, between Yahweh and two kings, the second of which Samuel didn't even know yet.

Samuel wiped his forehead. The day wasn't warm enough to sweat, but sweat he did. He could make better time if he didn't have to tug this heifer — funny little cow, white speckled nose and the rest of her dun to the tail. Samuel kept trying to yank her faster, but she wanted to nibble every third clump of grass, now digging in her hooves to stop and urinate. He looked into her huge brown eyes and felt a kinship with her. As he led her along, Samuel believed that he too had a halter around his neck. She had to do what Yahweh commanded, all the way to sacrifice, and so, if commanded, must he.

What had he gotten himself into? Or, as he peered at the problem more accurately, what had Yahweh gotten him into,

Yahweh that zealous God who'd adopted the Hebrews and led them out of Egyptian bondage two hundred years before? Samuel was bounced back and forth between a wild God and a wild king — Yahweh, using Samuel to choose Saul as the Hebrews' first king, then Yahweh rejecting him, and Saul, whose ups and downs were never predictable. In it all, what choice did Samuel have but to obey Yahweh? He was Yahweh's servant, a prophet, selected long ago to speak for him and to do his will. But Samuel would be more at peace if Yahweh's actions made more sense to him.

He pulled the heifer. She kicked up dust with every step of her hooves. She seemed more submissive now, having eaten a few bites along the way. Perhaps Samuel was simply calmer, having passed Saul's Gibeah without detection. Late in the day he made it by Jerusalem, but he was less worried by Jerusalem's Jebusites than by Saul. The strap holding the horn of holy oil dangled across his shoulder, reminding him every step of the danger of his mission: Off to Bethlehem to anoint another king for Yahweh. Couldn't Yahweh get the right one the first time? he wondered. Isn't he all powerful? And if he didn't succeed choosing a king the first time, how will he get the right king the second try? He consoled himself that the people needed a king. In the past he'd questioned whether the Hebrews should have a king, but he'd conceded that they needed a central authority to organize their defense.

He gritted his teeth and said, "Further, young cow." She let out a moan, but she followed. He spent a cold night on the trail before arriving in Bethlehem. By then he'd gotten used to the heifer, explaining, "I don't like this any more than you do."

Before midday he crested the last low rise toward Bethlehem and even at that distance, someone spotted his approach and immediately a crowd ran out to him. "Where'd they all come from?" he asked the heifer. "Isn't anyone working the fields?" Now, whereas he'd been fearful while sneaking past Gibeah, he faced others who were frightened by his presence. "I've come in peace," he told the cohort of elders who trembled before him. They knew that he didn't always bring peace; and news had spread quickly that he and Saul had parted. The Bethlehemites didn't want to become involved in a power struggle between king and prophet. Plus, they'd heard that Samuel could grab a sword and hack an unarmed prisoner to pieces — and do it for Yahweh! "All I want to do is to hold a sacrifice," he said.

The men still looked at him uncertainly, but Samuel gathered them for the sacrifice. He made sure Jesse's boys were consecrated along with everyone. Afterwards he latched onto Jesse and told him he wanted to inspect his sons, quite an honor. Finally, Samuel thought, I'm getting this over with.

Jesse lined up the lads and Samuel approached Eliab, the oldest, thinking, here he is. My search is over and I'll go home now. Maybe I can evade Saul again and get some peace. Yet Yahweh didn't indicate Eliab, but spoke within Samuel, "I don't see as mortals. They evaluate by outward appearance, I scrutinize the heart." So Samuel continued with the rest of Jesse's sons, one by one, and Yahweh acknowledged none of them.

When he'd gone through the lineup of the boys, Jesse told him of another, a younger son, working the flocks. When they brought David from the pasture to Samuel, Yahweh confirmed him as the one. Samuel could finally yank the plug from the horn. With the brothers watching, he put oil on David's head. The rest was up to Yahweh.

Samuel was done. This pink-faced boy was God's favorite. What would happen next, he didn't know. He got out of Bethlehem as quickly as possible. Who knew what Saul would do when he learned of Samuel's deed? Walking back, he found himself frighteningly alone. A common problem for a prophet. He'd have felt better to be accompanied by even a complaining heifer; but she had to die to get the rope off her neck. Samuel wondered what would happen if he no longer felt tugged by Yahweh's halter.

Preaching point: *God has purposes that God's servants need not understand, but they must obey.*

A Lent 4 1 Samuel 16:1-13

Chapter 9: How It All Started

Every evening King David's three oldest brothers gathered in Jerusalem's inn for wine with other retired soldiers. Tonight they met after news arrived to David's city announcing another great victory over the Philistines. Soon David would return with the Hebrew army in glory. The brothers and their friends, too injured or enfeebled now for combat, stretched out their evening repeating stories of the battles of old they'd fought in.

Joah joined them in drinking at their table. He was newly handicapped from the Hebrew army and trying to learn how to walk with a staff and half of his left foot gone. He appreciated the effects of the wine numbing his battle aches. David's brothers spun their tales of bravery and sacrifice in King Saul's service and how they then followed David until he was acknowledged as king. Joah asked, "Were you at that famous cliff battle where the slaughter followed down past that little spring?" They all nodded. "But," Eliab said, "that was service under Saul. David was nowhere on the scene yet." Joah set down his cup, wiped the drip off his chin with the back of his hand, and said. "I've always wondered: How in this Lord's world did your youngest brother take Saul's place and end up as Israel's king?"

"Well," Eliab said with a wine enhanced drawl, "started right after the barley harvest. Grandfather Obed always managed to arrive during the barley winnowing. You want to hear a story, you just turned Grandfather Obed loose. Loved to tell how his parents met and every year it got more elaborate until it wasn't just a matter of one family in Bethlehem, but nearly an international affair — involving Moab too."

"Wasn't the barley harvest," Abinadab said. "Wheat harvest. I've told you before. And Grandfather wasn't there. He'd been dead four years. I think time's either rotting your memory or the wine is ruining it."

"Barley harvest," Eliab said and banged his hand on the table.

Abinadab took a deep breath, "Say what you like, as many times as you can. Won't change when it really happened. Wheat harvest."

Eliab rubbed a hand on his forehead scar and stuck out his lower lip, "Barley."

Joah looked back and forth between the brothers, enjoying their dispute.

Shammah sat farthest from his older brothers who argued at the end of the table. He caught Joah's eye and said, "Starts with the prophet Samuel arriving in Bethlehem. Scares the gizzards out of everybody. Young fellow runs out to where we're working and announces 'Samuel's come to Bethlehem dragging a heifer on a rope. And a horn of oil.' Couldn't scare us more if a thousand Philistine warriors crested the next hill unopposed. What's the Lord's prophet doing here? He's the guy who will grab a sword and whack you to pieces. We start asking, what have we done? Worse maybe, what haven't we done? Especially, what's he going to pronounce or do?"

With Joah listening to Shammah, Eliab grumbled a little more, took another drink, and stopped bickering with Abinadab.

"All we'd heard about Samuel lately was that he's peeved with Saul and holed up in Ramah. But he must be here for something major. We wonder if he's mustering troops from the south for another foray against the Philistines. But all he says is he's come for worship, even bringing the sacrifice.

"He gets our family off to the side. Awkward as can be. Villagers all gawking at us. Starts fiddling around in his funny way of praying and says we're now 'sanctified.' We look at one another in question, but don't say a word to him. You ever around Samuel?" he asked Joah.

"Never saw him."

"Let me tell you, no matter who else is around, when he's there, he's in charge of everything. We haven't the slightest idea what he's doing. Makes us boys parade before him, like he's sizing us up to send us into battle. Stares at us, working his way down the line of us. Expectant with each of us and then frustrated. I can tell he's let down when he passes me up. Makes me feel like a failure. Talk about a mix-up of thoughts and feelings."

Eliab yells for a servant to bring more wine; but, when the servant comes, he looks first to Abinadab who smiles and waves him away from Eliab.

"Obviously none of us meets his standards," Shammah said, "and he asks if Father has more sons. More! He has more sons than any father in Bethlehem and Samuel wants more! So Father tells him. 'The youngest, but he's tending the sheep.' Samuel won't settle for anything less than a full lineup of all the family's males and we have to stand around waiting while a servant lights out to see if the flock's in the same place today as yesterday.

"Soon the kid comes trotting in from the field wondering what's going on. He's a cute little guy. You can catch the contrast between the tall Saul and the short David. So …so, Samuel goes from looking as though he's going to vomit to acting like he's been reprieved from a death sentence. Takes out his horn of oil, puts some on David's head, then drops everything and he's out of here without an extra breath. David too. He takes a little jump and runs back to the sheep."

"Fortunately," Abinadab said, "none had wandered off while he'd been away."

"Samuel departs," Shammah said. "David's back to the flock. We're left standing there, like the party's over and we missed it. We couldn't be more confused if the moon landed on our housetop. We don't know what's happening and can't guess what might come of it — for the whole family." He wagged his head slowly with wonder on his face. "Or for the nation."

"Or the world," Eliab said. But by that time he was nearly asleep with his head on the table and no one listened to him.

Preaching point: *Momentous royal selection process.*

B *Proper 13 (18) 2 Samuel 11:26-12:13a*
C *Proper 6 (11) 2 Samuel 11:26-12:10, 13-15*

Chapter 10: Prophetic Jitters

"Hey! Watch out," the man had leaped up and almost threw himself in Nathan's way. Nathan stopped and stood rigidly upright. One more step and he'd have mashed the merchant's persimmons piled so neatly on the cobblestones. The fellow wasn't angry, just concerned. For five heartbeats Nathan remained still, realizing that he was in the marketplace. How did he get here? It was as though he were sleepwalking. He shook his head vigorously and thought how much better if he truly were asleep. Then this all might be a dream, the worst he'd ever had.

Nathan thought, so this is what it means to be Yahweh's prophet. He carefully maneuvered his way out of the market, walked right by fresh cucumbers, his favorite, and didn't even smell them. He was on his way to confront King David because word was out about the whole ordeal. As in any royal household, there were no secrets among the servants in David's palace. A few servants knew these pieces, and some knew other pieces, and then some figured out the whole despicable story: Uriah's wife taken into the house for David's pleasure while Uriah was fighting with the army. Then her message to the king that she was pregnant. Next, the sordid events as David summoned Uriah from the battlefield and contrived to send him home to have sex with Bathsheba. Finally, word was out that David not only planned Uriah's death, but had the faithful Uriah carry the message to Joab to arrange it.

Nathan had first dealt with the king when he was consulted whether David should build a temple for Yahweh. His inclination was to agree, yet that night Yahweh's word changed Nathan's advice. So Nathan had delivered the message that David wasn't the one to build the temple. His prophetic oracle wasn't only

Fragments of Good News

negative. He also reported Yahweh's promise of David's perpetual dynasty. However, this time Yahweh had placed in Nathan's heart no good news along with the bad. Now while publicly David was praised for marrying the wife of a distinguished war hero, Nathan knew the truth and his task was to face David with his crimes.

Why can't Yahweh's prophets be like the prophets of Baal, just dancing in ecstasy, agreeing with all the king's policies? Kings need dozens of such religious promoters to maintain their grip on the people. And David's grip is firm. He's every boy's idol, every priest's example to worshipers — the pious David, darling of the people with his growing collection of psalms. Everyone forgets he was a turncoat, having fought for the Philistines. They conveniently don't recall how day by day and settlement by village he and his raiders murdered every man, woman, and child, stripping them and taking their clothes and goods back to his Philistine master. Whereas David, not a Philistine, enriched the Philistines, Uriah, not an Israelite, fought for Israel to the death, one of Israel's thirty great warriors.

How much easier if Nathan didn't know about David's past, so much easier if he were just dragged along with the royal desires. But his mind wouldn't rest on his own tenuous position as Yahweh's prophet. Not for a moment did he plan to get out of his duty, for every time he thought of another reason why Yahweh's directive was difficult, he called to mind the righteousness of Yahweh's decision.

He continued up Zion's hill toward the royal dwelling. He was completely defenseless in David's private city. The whole place belonged to David. He'd won it in battle. Everyone in Jerusalem was his subject and must obey him. Yet here was Nathan, ascending the steps toward the royal dwelling with seriously disagreeable news.

He would confront David. Nothing could stop him. Yet he hadn't considered how to phrase Yahweh's indictment. All he desperately prayed about was how to begin speaking. If he received an audience with the king and could choke out the first few words that he was sent by Yahweh, he could keep talking. He would get it done though it could mean his death. But how to start? With each step farther up the hill he rehearsed another approach, "Your excellency, King of all of Israel and Judah, Savior of your people, Judge among the nations." Too grand. "King David, a word with you, if you please." Too chummy. He was now at the king's gate. He requested audience and, as the prophet who promised David's dynasty eternal reign, the guards hustled him right into the king.

The doors swung open to the king's reception room. David stood to greet him, a rare honor. Nathan stepped forward, his mind a muddle, no idea how he'd phrase Yahweh's charge against the king, only wondering how to start. The only solid thought was his determination to do Yahweh's will. Without knowledge of what he'd say after a first word, he began, "There were two men in a certain city, the one rich and the other poor...."

Preaching point: *What it's like to be inspired and compelled to speak God's truth to power.*

B Transfiguration Sunday 2 Kings 2:1-12
C Proper 8 (13) 2 Kings 2:1-2, 6-14

Chapter 11: Sequence Of Service

1915 was not a good year for Giustina. Beppe became more violent by the day. He came home every evening to beat her because she'd lost her wedding ring down the sink. He'd punched her before, but now it was as if he'd gained a license for cruelty. Giustina took the blows while she crouched between him and the three children. The old woman in the next apartment heard the screams. She stationed herself to meet Giustina in the hall and offered sympathy but told her the law seldom prosecuted men for violence against wives. Giustina's relief came when Beppe was arrested and held without bail for attempted murder of a fellow worker at the slaughter house.

She'd been totally, desperately dependent upon him for the few dollars he brought home after spending most of his weekly pay at the tavern. Now at 22, Giustina held 34 cents to her name and her rent paid for nineteen more days in her crime and disease-ridden Chicago tenement. She'd immigrated with Beppe from Italy early in 1914 in order to escape the war in Europe. She didn't know how Beppe arranged it, but she feared it wasn't done legally.

She balanced her infant on her hip and with her free hand tried to herd her two and a half year old twins. She walked Halsted Street door to door asking for work or at least for help from people with the olive colored skin she'd grown up with in Italy. The best she could secure was a few hours in the evening scrubbing floors in a theater while keeping her children with her. It didn't work. In a week she was on the street again, but this time someone directed her to Hull House.

The staff of Hull House settlement house — creation of Jane Addams and Ellen Starr — took her in. No one in America had treated her with such kindness. Minnie Steadman, a single woman in her thirties with an adequate grasp of Italian, became her mentor. Minnie was also a nurse. She immediately placed the children into Hull House childcare and got Giustina a job in a garment factory with the promise that she'd find better work for her.

After a year of staggering labor, with Minnie's tireless help and Hull House resources, Giustina could see that she and her children had a future. She spent an hour every evening after work there polishing her English and garnering skills to survive in America. One evening in February 1917, when she dragged herself to Hull House to get her children — long after dark — Minnie met her. Minnie looked more overworked than usual. She said, "I wanted to talk with you before I leave."

Giustina was so exhausted she didn't at first comprehend what Minnie said.

"I'll depart for France on Thursday morning," her voice trailed off tiredly, "the next ship."

"France?"

"I've volunteered as a nurse."

"But you're against the war."

"I'm not going to help the war but to help the wounded."

"People killed there," Giustina said, "millions." She grabbed Minnie's wrist, "For you it's not safe. No Americans there. Why you do this?"

"I don't want to talk about why. I simply must go and help."

In less than a minute Minnie told her the terms she would serve under and what she expected to do whether for civilian or military, French or English, German or Turk. Giustina wasn't listening. She'd only survived the year with Minnie's help. For her, Minnie was Hull House. What would Giustina do?

Minnie sighed as she looked into Giustina's sorrowful eyes and said, "Now, about you."

Giustina managed, "What about me?"

"You'll take my place at Hull House."

Giustina coughed and gulped at the same time, "Me? Me? But

I'm not… nurse. I'm nothing."

Minnie looked confidently at her, "You're a great learner. The staff will train you in some things, but they can't give you the compassion you've already got. And people who've just learned can often teach others best. When I show you something or tell you something, you grab it and keep it and use it. That's what you'll do for others. People taught me. I taught you. You'll do what I did for you but in new and different and probably better ways."

"I hardly speak the English," she said.

"There's plenty of Italians for you to help and you've learned English as fast as anyone." She chuckled as she said, "Your twins will perfect your English." Minnie smiled and said, "It's set. Tomorrow morning someone will introduce you to the other workers." Minnie hugged Giustina, and left.

On a morning a month later as Giustina arrived, a large poster appeared on Hull House door. Minnie's photograph was in the middle. People gathered to it weeping. A person read it for Giustina. It reported that Minnie's ship was torpedoed mid-Atlantic. There were no survivors. A service in Minnie's memory was scheduled for July fourth at noon. The final lines stated: "You are now Minnie's heritage. Carry on her work of compassion."

One of the twins tugged on her dress, "Mommy, Mommy." Others were crowding around. Finally Giustina had to move.

Preaching point: *The decision has already been made for us: We are to serve as we have been served.*

A Proper 25 (30); B Easter 7; B Proper 20 (25) C Epiphany 6 (6);
C Proper 18 (23) Psalm 1

Chapter 12: O'Henry's "The Last Leaf"

William Sydney Porter, known to us as O'Henry, wrote at the turn of the twentieth century. His flowery writing style isn't currently the fad and may never be again. His name, however, is forever stamped on stories with a surprise ending (a twist, a "snapper" as he called it). When one reads his work untroubled by his ornate and breezy style, the substance of his stories is truly worthwhile. He wrote about common people in their own world — often forgotten by the rich and powerful — who performed admirable and extraordinary things. Psalm One's depiction of a faithful ("blessed, happy") believer as a tree nourished by God can't be improved, but it can be amplified by a retelling of O'Henry's story "The Last Leaf."

* * *

At the turn of the twentieth century the Greenwich Village neighborhood in Manhattan, New York City is a refuge for struggling artists — rooms with good light and at low cost. Two of the artists are young women who room together on the third floor: Sue from Maine, and Johnsy from California. Two stories below them another painter lives on the ground floor, a sixty-year-old German: "Old Behrman," who always talks of painting his masterpiece, but has yet to accomplish it.

When winter comes to the village it strikes many people with pneumonia. Johnsy also becomes ill and she immediately loses hope that she'll live. Lying in bed without moving, she merely looks through the window at the wall of the house across the alley. The doctor visits and warns Sue that Johnsy doesn't hold any strong hopes for the future — projects, travel, or even romance. The doctor states that, if people have something to live for, plans or hopes for the future, their chances of recovery double. Sue tries everything she knows to pick up Johnsy's spirits, aiming her toward the future. However, Johnsy lies in bed, refusing to eat, staring out the window at the tree between the houses. Sue hears her now and then counting backward, "Twelve... eleven... ten."

Sue asks what she means with this countdown. Johnsy says, "Leaves. On the tree. When the last one falls, I must go, too. I've known that for three days. Didn't the doctor tell you?" No matter what Sue tries or how she reasons that the number of leaves on a tree makes no sense (and lies that the doctor said Johnsy would get well), Johnsy is convinced she'll die when the last leaf falls.

In Sue's search for help, she decides to summon "Old Behrman" to come up to their room upon the ploy that she needs him for a model in her current painting. An evening rain and snowstorm is brewing when Sue goes downstairs to get Old Behrman and explains Johnsy's state of mind. He finally returns to sit for Sue's painting, grumbling and asserting to Johnsy that the number of leaves on a tree means nothing. He departs late in the night and Sue, who has pulled the cover over the window, dreads the morning.

Morning arrives and Johnsy is wide-eyed and looking toward the window. "I want to see," she tells Sue. Yet, no matter that the rain and wind haven't stopped all night, one leaf remains against the wall, twenty feet above the ground, still dark green near a branch, its edges turning yellow with age.

The day passes and with the night the wind blows again and beats against the window. Morning comes and the leaf remains. It's what Johnsy needs to say she's ready to eat something. By the afternoon she even mentions a scene she wants to paint. The doctor visits again and agrees that Johnsy is recovering. He can't stay long but must visit another person in the building much sicker whom he'll arrange to get to the hospital in order to help him die in some comfort.

The following day the doctor confirms that Johnsy is safely on her way to health and needs only food and care. But that afternoon Sue comes and puts her arm around Johnsy to tell her that Old Behrman has died. He'd been ill for two days. Two mornings before, the janitor found him in his room helpless with pain. His shoes and clothing were wet through and icy cold. No one knew where he'd been that night until they found a lantern, still lighted, and a ladder that had been dragged from its place, and some scattered artist's brushes next to a palette with green and yellow colors mixed on it.

Sue says to Johnsy, "Look out the window, dear, at the last leaf on the wall. Didn't you wonder why it never fluttered or moved when the wind blew? Ah darling, it's Behrman's masterpiece — he painted it there the night the last leaf fell."

Preaching point: *Nature cooperates as a channel for God's love.*

ABC New Year's Day; AC Trinity Sunday;
B Proper 22 (27) Psalm 8

Chapter 13: Angel's Feet

Kate reluctantly came home for the summer — for her mother's sake. She'd rather be back combing through Europe's art galleries and inching a step closer to her master's degree. Instead, she was back in Mill Town and these three weeks had nearly sent her packing: smelling the sawdust and steamed lumber from the kilns and hearing the constant siren of the saws along with the roaring forklifts and chugging log trucks. Her mother recognized her desperation for intellectual stimulation and aimed her to the newspaper's story about the walking pairs website. Her mother explained that the website was run by three elderly Unitarian ladies promoting world peace two walkers at a time.

Kate signed up for the classification of "younger adult," which erased the majority of walkers. She realized after her first two tries that motivation for the "younger" group tended to be therapy. Her first partner was recovering from a leg broken after tripping on uneven carpet. The second was fighting boredom as her bandaged left arm healed from an exploding espresso machine.

Kate tried to study in the mornings. She made little progress, however, because the heat of the summer necessitated the windows being open at night and the sounds of the mill's second shift invaded her sleeping. She signed up for the next late afternoon walk with the same spurt of energy with which she began preparing her escape from Mill Town in two weeks.

She waited on the courthouse steps at four in the afternoon for Lawrence, guaranteed to be a "younger" person. When a cleanly shaven young man stepped beyond a group of bearded fellows Kate flicked her long brown hair out of her right eye and over her ear. She flung her head to the side and said, "A young man.

Not many on this circuit." The group of bearded fellows he was speaking with laughed and left.

"I'm Lawrence," he said, holding out his right hand but not looking her in the eye. Those guys just got off first shift. They stopped to tell me what's going on at the mill."

"You don't work there?"

"Not anymore."

Lawrence pointed east and then west as a question. Kate chose west and they were off. They took a brisker pace than her previous walks. It was difficult for her to determine which of them was or was supposed to be leading. She said, "I'm home from college for the summer. You?"

"I quit four years ago after sophomore year. Quit. Didn't flunk out," he said as he walked looking straight ahead.

"What was your major?"

"General studies. Didn't declare. Came home to decide if I wanted to manage the mill. If so, I'd be the fourth generation Harper to do so." He let only a fraction of a second lapse before asking, "Your major?"

"I'm doing a masters in art history, kind of art history mixed with psychology and religion." Lawrence continued to walk facing forward so Kate went on, "It includes dreams, the unconscious, art and religion. It's how nature and our social contacts first penetrate our minds and then emanate from us reminted in dreams, art and religion." She wanted to stop and face him as she explained her work, but he didn't slow or look at her arm or hand gestures. Kate wondered if the conversation must now sink to naming favorite NFL teams.

Without a stutter step, or a look at her, Lawrence asked, "Who's work is leading you in this direction?"

"Jung. You know about him?"

"A few paragraphs in Psych 101."

"He's really the first source for how dreams can express the depths of human life into art and religion. So when I study religious art, I spend as much time scrutinizing the artists as their work."

"Like Fra Angelico?" he asked as he marched next to her, looking directly ahead.

"Yes," she said, surprise in her voice. "You know the angelic brother?"

"A couple pages in the art appreciation textbook. So you study his faith too?"

"That's as important to me as the art he produced." After a few steps she asked, "You religious?"

"An inherited Episcopalian from my great great-grandfather on down. All bosses at the mill instantly become Episcopalians: snooty, reserved, enjoying all the Catholic bells and smells but not the guilt."

"You religious now?" Kate asked.

"Yes and no, on and off, right now off."

"Does that bother you?"

"Yep," he answered instantly and seriously. "Does it bother you — my being bothered?"

"No," Kate said, "that's fine with me."

They walked another half block away from the noise of the mill and toward the silence of the open fields.

"What I'm studying is that nature and humanity contribute to dreams which help inform and create art and religion. Sometimes a dream or moment in nature seems to assault us, strike us as an event whose meaning is almost beyond words. You dream?"

"Yep. About the mill."

"Yet you're not working there."

"But I carry it around with me."

"You think someday you'll take over the mill? Not everybody has such a thing handed to them."

"I'm not sure. Some days yes, some days no."

They were now west of the town on a graded gravel path next to the road. They stopped talking when log trucks swooshed past them like mobile earthquakes.

"When you get your degree, you going to teach?"

"Probably. I've also thought about being a priest, Episcopalian, Catholic lite, sophisticated and reserved."

Lawrence laughed and turned to look at her for the first time since they began walking. They laughed for half a minute. When they'd finally stopped and started walking again they giggled in fits for another couple minutes.

When Kate could finally speak without chuckling or hiccupping, she said, "I'm drawn to the Episcopal church because of a tradition that's open to God around us in nature and within us in the Spirit. Along with the biblical data, they turn the messages from around us and within us into all kinds of art, including the dramatic liturgy and highfalutin music."

Lawrence had returned to his forward-only stance but Kate could tell he was listening intently. "When I'm worshipping in an Episcopal church it's like my favorite painting in the National Gallery of Scotland in Edinburgh. It's Tintorello's *Christ Carried to the Tomb*. Early reproductions of the work had an arched top with an angel overhead. But somebody cut off the top and now there's just two small angel feet above the subject. It's like God's just hanging over us all the time, ready to break in."

It was nearly dark and with a common gesture between them they decided to turn around. They stopped abruptly. The moon, now fully and gloriously risen, hung directly over the mill. They stood stunned, startled to silence. After a moment Lawrence asked slowly, "Angel's feet?"

Kate shot open her arms, "Yes!" she proclaimed. "Angel's feet!"

Preaching Point: *God's natural world above us can strike the deepest within us.*

A Easter 2; B Proper 28 (33); C Proper 8 (13) Psalm 16

Chapter 14: Prairie Lessons

In late April 1919, Arnold had just turned thirteen. His mother didn't think he was old enough to be guiding Reverend Hunter, but most of the homesteaders agreed with Arnold's father that Reverend Hunter would be lost in no time if he drove any farther onto the Montana prairie alone. A gust shoved the car to the side. Reverend Hunter wrestled with the steering wheel to hold straight.

The windows had to remain open a few inches to keep the windshield from freezing, so Arnold and Reverend Hunter wore all the clothes they could get on, blankets around their shoulders and half a buffalo robe stretched across their laps and tucked under their legs. Arnold yanked the buffalo robe closer. It was as heavy as a lead blanket and as clumsy, but warm. For Arnold it seemed a touch of the old west. His father would never say where he finally sold it. For years after the family had fled their homestead (with the newspaper recording their name on the list of tax defaulters) Arnold wondered what became of it.

"Over the next rise," Arnold said, "some terrible gumbo ruts last fall." However, as the Model T rolled down the incline, evidence of last fall's few puddles had already been pounded to frozen dust. Half an hour later a few pin pricks of snow hit the windshield. Yet within a hundred yards, any sign of precipitation vanished, the sky again offering only a burning intensity, a strange match to the freezing drought.

"Not enough moisture to make snow," Reverend Hunter said, shaking his head, as he did at every empty homestead he saw, where wind was already flapping tar paper off abandoned buildings.

"The Bonners lived there," Arnold pointed. He'd gone to school for two months in the winter with the family's four children.

Last winter was so severe that school was cancelled for a month when the temperature didn't rise above zero. The Bonner family became so desperate that they yanked out their newly tamped fence posts for firewood. Trees near the house had been cut half a decade before. Arnold's father had said, "They've gone back to Madison on the same train that brought them." Then he'd turned to Arnold's mother a little too loudly, "We'll probably be next." His mother covered her eyes with her forearm and dashed into the bedroom.

An unexpected hole hit the Ford and bumped Reverend Hunter out of his head shaking. He took a breath as though trying to inspire himself, "We'll pray for rain in worship. At least it's too cold for grasshoppers yet," and gave a forced chuckle. His attempt to be encouraging failed both of them. Arnold couldn't tell how old Reverend Hunter was because he wasn't tanned and wrinkled like the farmers. Arnold watched his driving and his every glance from the road to the prairie was like he was seeing it for the first time. He spoke as if by proclamation, trying to convince himself and Arnold, "We must have faith." Arnold's mother had faith, though not like the Reverend's. Arnold promised himself that to his dying day he'd remember her on her knees every night crying, praying for rain.

"See the tangle of tumble weeds up there on the fence wire." Arnold pointed ahead. "Left."

As Reverend Hunter turned he spoke, "The cursed railroads. Spreading their lies not only across the continent. Their pamphlets even snookered people in Europe. I've collected a few. Gorgeous. Everything looks wonderful. Way to start a new life for anyone willing to work."

They jostled for a quarter hour beside a low ridge fissured with ravines before they arrived to the schoolhouse. It was the only one in eighteen miles with a piano. Two buckboards, three wagons, and a car rested on the ground stamped hard around the building by children's games. A man stuck his head from the door. The wind blew his hair up. He closed the door quickly when he identified the car as today's preacher.

Fragments of Good News

Reverend Hunter stepped in ahead of Arnold and shook hands as he moved toward the claw-footed stove in the middle of the room. As Arnold followed, he noticed a couple friends from school, but he too moved to the stove as fast as was courteous. Everyone had arrived early to get the room warm and talk with neighbors. Most people hadn't seen anyone beside family for a week. Their thin faces manifested their desire, or maybe their doubt, about a word of hope from God.

No one looked pleased with who the preacher was today. Arnold had never been around Reverend Hunter but had heard his father's disgust. His mother tried to persuade his father to take a better view of Reverend Hunter and honor all pastors, no matter their denomination. His father said, "He looks down on us honyockers. Why can't I look down on him?"

Worship proceeded as Arnold had known it: the piano dragging along the singing, prayers for rain, and the tall lady with the high forehead and black hair offering, "Precious Jesus" after each hymn. The preacher, in an obvious attempt to touch the homesteaders' lives spoke from Psalm 16, "The LORD is my chosen portion and my cup; you hold my lot. The boundary lines have fallen for me in pleasant places; I have a goodly heritage."

He compared the psalm to a land grant. For half an hour he tried to convince the homesteaders to be grateful, beginning with Israel crossing the Jordan on dry land. A man sitting in the back near Arnold whispered loudly to his wife, "See, the world's been drying up for a long time." He droned through the battles smiting the Canaanites, and then to the distribution of the conquered land. "Behold," he said, "land given to them who would take it. Just as to you. That's God's grace way back in the Old Testament. A gift. Just like in the New Testament with Jesus."

By that time, the preacher had lost almost everyone's attention. He must have realized that his message wasn't hitting the spot he was aiming for because he hurried to wind down. Arnold assumed he wanted to finish and flee, much as the homesteaders were winding down their era of drought on the prairie and about to escape to what they used to call "home."

Reverend Hunter's last idea seemed spontaneous and spoken slightly in defense of the congregation that wasn't accepting a sermon that called this land of disappointment "free." He mumbled quickly, "For me, like Israel's priests who wouldn't receive a portion of the promised land, I have only the Lord. 'The Levites who reside in your towns have no allotment or inheritance with you,' Deuteronomy 12:12."

That ended worship and Reverend Hunter hustled Arnold quickly to the freezing Model T. No discussion about remaining for the shared meal. Arnold wondered if they were leaving now in order not to eat food that the congregation dearly needed. He had only to tell Reverend Hunter a few turns on the drive back to his family's sod-thatched dugout house. Reverend Hunter said little to Arnold's parents, just that Arnold was home safely and he appreciated the directions. He gave a half smile and vanished from their lives.

Within six weeks Arnold's family too abandoned their claim. It hadn't rained. The wheat didn't germinate in the spring. Prayers didn't seem to be answered. Their family joined the reverse migration back east to former regions now unfamiliar. Such moves strained family solidarity as the hoax of free land disturbed faith. Many times when Arnold's parents discussed their farming failure and questioned God's part in it, his mother said, "I don't know. Just don't know. But we still have the Lord." Arnold was bothered — disoriented — for years by the move. All he held to from the experience was what his mother and Reverend Hunter agreed on: They might not have land, but they had the Lord. It took decades, however, for him finally to be reconciled to never knowing what happened to that buffalo robe.

Preaching point: *Life within God's grace no matter the tragic outward circumstances.*

B Proper 6 (11) Psalm 20

Chapter 15: Answer!

Arnie never spoke to Pastor Buck face to face. He turned his head slightly away. Eyes toward Pastor Buck, yes, but head cocked to the side. "The God thing I can take. Someone put this all together," he said as he rolled his arms toward the universe, "but not prayer. Doesn't work."

"Arnie's scientific," Ellie said. "He experiments." She smiled at Arnie and the pastor as if what she said was as pleasant as it was important.

"Ellie goes along with anything anyone believes," Arnie said. At which Ellie, to prove him right, smiled to the pastor.

Pastor Buck gazed affectionately at this teenage brother and sister. They seemed to know one another extremely well and feel comfortable describing one another to someone else.

The two had been sent by their mother to Pastor Buck for an off schedule, as he called it, confirmation class. The Harus family had moved to town and the mother and two children had immediately showed up at worship. Pastor Buck could hardly get in a word to introduce himself at the door after worship. Mrs. Harus had blurted, "These are our two kids, Arnie and Ellie. We need them to join the church."

Pastor Buck had stumbled all over his tongue as he tried on the spot to remember the names: Arnie, Ellie, wife Klara and husband, not present, Alfred. People were backing up behind Mrs. Harus and Pastor Buck felt pressured to get his pocket calendar, write their address, and make an appointment to call on Wednesday after school.

When he'd arrived at their home, Mrs. Harus leaped into conversation, telling about Mr. Harus's job, the plumbing that remained to be fixed in the house, her cousin suffering badly in her fifth pregnancy, and somewhere in the unpacked boxes she had Bibles for both children.

After a tour of the house and a commentary on each room, Mrs. Harus with Arnie and Ellie had sat with the pastor in the living room. Ellie had no chance to talk. Arnie, looking sideways, appeared to have little to say. Mrs. Harus said, "They need to join the church. Alfred and I've put off a lot in the last few years," she gazed sadly at the wall before she returned to the conversation, "and we decided this move is where we start over." Pastor Buck opened his mouth to ask what else they were going to start over, but Mrs. Harus went on to tell him about how they'd packed her grandmother's pottery, the willow tree in their front yard when she was a child, and the torn up lottery tickets they'd swept out of the basement before they installed their washer and dryer. By that time Arnie and Ellie had been excused and Mrs. Harus negotiated times for Pastor Buck to meet with the children in an abbreviated confirmation class.

So Pastor Buck now sat with Arnie and Ellie in the pastor's office, as a no-assignments, get-to-know-one-another time. He responded to Arnie's opening statement, "You're bothered with prayer?"

"Just don't believe it. Tried it," he said with his quarter turned head. "Okay if others pray."

"Arnie's broad-minded," Ellie said, nodding in agreement to her own statement.

"Prayer's pretty central to our Christian life," Pastor Buck said. "And you said you *have* prayed."

"Yes, didn't work."

"How about you, Ellie? You prayed?"

"Sure," she chirped.

"Tell me about your praying."

"Ah… with mom …when I was a kid, by the bed."

"How about lately?"

"Not much…, except when Dad kept driving way too fast coming here — especially on the mountain curves." She looked to Arnie.

"Sure was," he said. "Worse mood than usual, and Mom was

tugging on his sleeve, 'Alfred, Alfred, Al!'"

Pastor Buck was smiling and praying for what to say or do next for these two interesting, intelligent teenagers who so easily told the truth about themselves and others. He asked about their former high school and what they thought of their new high school; he mentioned what high school was like for him when he was trying to work out what God wanted with his life. Ellie listened to him courteously, as did Arnie in his slanting way.

"I'll tell you what's on my mind," Pastor Buck said. "We're scheduled to meet on Wednesdays after school for two months. When we get into the study more thoroughly, I'll have you read some parts of the Bible and we'll discuss them as well as talk about some high points in 2,000 years of Christian history. For now, what's on my mind is my sermon for Sunday. To prepare a sermon I read over and over the part of the Bible I'll preach on and I pray about it and meditate on it. You know what I mean by meditate?"

"Think it over," Arnie said, "seriously."

"That's a good part of it," Pastor Buck said. "For me it means I try to let it get into me. I'm preparing a sermon on Psalm 20 and I'm thinking about it all the time — especially about prayer. I'm focusing on the part of the psalm that's expecting, hoping, and even insisting that God answer our prayers. For this week, all I ask is that you pray about you and Jesus. It's okay if you doubt when you pray, Christians have been doing that a long time and God still wants us to pray. I want you to pray about you and Jesus. You know enough about Jesus to pray this. Just be asking Jesus to be like him. That'll keep you busy. You can beg God or yell at God. God can take it. But, as honestly as you can, hold what you know of yourself next to what you know about Jesus and ask God to get the two of you together. Make sense?"

Arnie nodded, sideways. Ellie said, "I'll try."

"Good, that's enough for all three of us to pray about. Now, I'll offer a prayer to end our first session together: Lord Jesus, thank you that Arnie and Ellen and I can be together here with you. Trusting your love for us, I pray that day by day each of us become more and more like you. We pray in your name. Amen."

After Mrs. Harus picked up Arnie and Ellen from church, and told Pastor Buck she'd found a good radio station, and that her dad had been a farmer in Kansas, and that she was growing to like dark chocolate, Pastor Buck set himself to pray: "Lord Jesus I pray that you answer the prayers of Arnie and Ellie. Answer them in a way they can understand. Answer them when they're alone or with others. And, Lord, please answer this prayer which I ask in your name. Amen."

Preaching point: *Prayer can include the urgent request that God answers.*

ABC Good Friday Psalm 22
B Proper 23 (28) Psalm 22:1-15

Chapter 16: Abandoned?

Curt walked half a block with his arms stiff at his side, not realizing that with each step he was clenching his fists by his hips. He used to clench his fists by his hips when he was angry with Noel, but not anymore.

Why am I doing this? And why do I even ask? And who am I asking? And how long do I go on asking toward the silence?

Without noticing, he'd walked the first block from home. Seven to go. Sharp's Neighborhood Grocery had butcher paper signs taped in the window advertising t-bone steaks and gala apples. He was close enough to touch the glass, but he passed without noticing, concentrating and asking why he even concentrated. It was Sunday morning and this is where he always walked on Sunday morning, to worship at Second Presbyterian Church.

His heels tapped rhythmically on the sidewalk, but he didn't hear them. He'd now walked the second block. In the past, which seemed as indistinct as a forest in a fog, he walked to worship with Noel and their daughter Karie and son Robbie. The walk was special then. Every Sunday, except in the most miserable weather, they walked to the church. He looked forward to that family time every week. If something was wrong in any of their relationships when they left home, it was better, if not settled, by the time they arrived to church. He'd felt the family's Sunday stroll to worship was a procession, a joyous parade to meet God. The kids grew up treading this street and because of this street had moved away from home, ready enough to face life.

He halted at the stop light beside Judd's pharmacy. He didn't notice the familiar door he'd entered more and more frequently in the last nine months to pick up medicines for Noel. Curt had watched Noel's strength fluctuate, sometimes even increasing for a few days, but inevitably decreasing. He'd shared her desperate, then hopeful, then desperate faith. They'd celebrated each felt recovery and mourned each notch down on the blood count numbers they received in the clinic month by month and then week by week.

He and Noel chuckled and wept in prayer. Their pastor and congregation prayed. The congregations of relatives and friends prayed. For weeks Curt felt as though beside Noel he was also side by side with Jesus. The presence felt like a halo of love. What happened to all that? He marched beside the school's playground where both his children had attended. The swings, monkey bars and the wooden skeleton of a castle didn't catch his eye.

It seemed we were cooperating with God. Seemed we were working together. We followed the doctors' treatment, but we thought God was the most help. Then all help was too late, unnecessary, futile. For all that Noel went through — pain and confusion, hope and fluctuating faith — she never said she felt abandoned by God. Now I, on the other hand....

He saw the steeple three blocks straight ahead.

We always went straight to church. That was our half mile walk. Helped us think we were going directly to God. Now I don't know why I'm doing this, marching to doom. Where's God now?

He threw his arms out in a semi-circle in front of him while he spoke his silent words. He was running out of distance to the church. The building loomed only a block and a half away.

Why am I spending the mental energy? Maybe all the talking to invisibility wasn't really prayer, wasn't anyone on the other end of our begging... or of our joys. Maybe it's just been my brain cells tangling and untangling in a cellular mess that means less than nothing.

He stepped off the curb, crossing the next to the last street before the church and aimed one more effort toward a question: Why am I doing this?

Mid-street, he remembered that for the last six months, whenever possible, he stopped at Mrs. Stilmann's house to walk their eight-year-old Jocelyn to worship so that Mrs. Stilmann could have the last few minutes to get her two-year-old ready. Curt had seen her at the funeral. She was trying not to weep and he felt the one thing he could do for her was to speak up and tell her he'd be there Sunday morning as usual.

He turned around and walked the half a block back, stepping carefully over a sidewalk tipped up by the root of a red oak tree. He looked at his watch and saw he was already late. The doorbell hung by wires. He had to hold it with one hand and press it with the other, but somehow it worked. Mrs. Stilmann was waiting and shuffled Shawnalee out the door with a grateful smile. Curt took Shawnalee's hand as she showed him her new pink dress. "Look," she said, "it has a belt. My friend Landy has a dress with a belt too, but these aren't the kind of belt that actually holds anything up, just kind of holds it in. Hers is blue, though not the blue like the sky, or the Bibles at church, a little like the swimming pool at the Y, but more like our school bus." She continued to talk about things that were blue and began to skip next to him. Curt walked faster to keep pace with her and because the church bell was already ringing.

Preaching point: *Wondering if God has abandoned us.*

B Easter 5 Psalm 22:25-31

Chapter 17: Vows

Mary-Alice Killingsworth drummed her hands impatiently on the arms of the wheelchair. Wished she could get up. Wished she could walk out by herself. But she still rated a hospital chaperone, one of those rainbow attired "health professionals" who'd been turning, poking and bathing her for eight days. She was more than ready to leave the smells of hand sanitizer and industrial cleaner. Ready to return to the diesel fumes and factory smoke of the life she knew.

Her yellow clad wheelchair pusher halted and they waited inside the hospital's main door. The hospital door had become the silent and secret obsession of the singsong voices in her mind. It was the direction that her most intent plans now led. To Mary-Alice, it was a gate into new life. Yet the giant wall of plate glass loomed with terrifying uncertainty.

She'd been goal-oriented for 58 years, concentrating her life and energies as if in competition. Pushing aside extraneous matters, even extraneous people, centering on what she aimed for, even coached herself for. Now her last eight days of mental labor situated her in new territory. It started with her heart attack. Raul, her administrative assistant, bent down to look in her eyes. "Miss Killingsworth? Miss Killingsworth!" She could hear him. He needn't speak so loudly. But she found herself unable to answer.

Now she looked at her hands and arms, bandages covering black and blue spots. Well, at least she'd come out weighing less from all the blood they sucked from her, and the food tasted only three degrees better than wretched.

She knew Raul was coming to get her. Todd and Eleanor were both at work. They'd phoned and came to see her on a schedule: Each day one visited, one phoned. Her two children — adopted, because she didn't have time to be pregnant — had followed her patterns. Their college educations added little to what their mother taught them about business. They'd grown up manufacturing and marketing pickup bed liners, floor mats and always more automotive accessories. No one in America knew more about the bed of every pickup and the floorboards of every car sold in the US in the last thirty years. They knew, well, everything to survive in business. They could fend for themselves now. Mary-Alice had decided not even to go to the next corporation meeting. Let the kids do it.

Raul had come on the last three days for her to dictate answers to employees' questions. She recalled standing outside the office door six months before as Todd and Eleanor interviewed him for her administrative assistant. They rattled off their pat routine. They performed it on average every sixteen months. Todd said, "If Mother says, 'Jump...'" Eleanor said, "You ask 'How high?'" Raul brought a get well card signed by all 41 employees. She assumed some signatures were obtained under duress. The first time Raul saw her in the bed, the young man fumbled with his tablet and dropped his pen. On that first visit he fidgeted more than usual and, when she became too tired to speak, he nearly injured a housekeeper as he raced from the room.

She peered out the hospital's glassy main entrance. Out there was the edge of new life. Beyond the hospital door she would live out the results of the tussle within her. She hadn't asked for or expected such a thing. She'd been caught up in it, trapped by it. Everything within her circled to question what direction she'd follow when she exited the hospital. Lines of thought straightened and then twisted. But her mind toiled on, gathering all her energies into this struggle.

The doctors prescribed a course of therapy. She didn't know if she'd take their advice. Had to think about it. She'd never followed someone else's plan; but, whatever she'd chosen to do, she'd been a success, except of course, in human relations. Two divorces. Her children relating to her as though employees reporting. No one to drive her from the hospital except Raul. And where was he, anyway? Said on the phone he'd be here eleven sharp.

She needed to let such matters go now. Outside the doors awaited a new management system and operational procedures. And relationships. Because lying in bed on the fourth day, trussed up with tiny plastic hoses, she'd faced herself and, though she wasn't ready now to recount it to just anyone, she'd met God. For all her disciplined church attendance, as she was disciplined in everything she did, she'd never gotten close to the God that faith was about. Her service on the altar guild meant no more than her serving on the United Way campaign. It hadn't equipped her for a near fatal illness. She didn't know that others before her had edged near to the same foggy, numinous, dangerous location she'd approached — that holy, searing light surrounding the region of God.

Even though she'd heard the word and understood the concept, she'd never made a vow to God. She didn't use the word now, but she did vow. She promised that if this shiny, burdensome chair could get her out the door, she'd take a different direction, her life rotating 180 degrees. 58 wasn't an unrealistic age to do such a thing.

But could she? "What time is it?" She asked the yellow clad person behind her.

"About eleven," came the answer.

"I mean *exactly* what time is it?" Catching herself, she said, "Please."

"Ah, eight after eleven."

"Thanks," she said. It was going to be hard, if she couldn't even be civil with someone trying to help her. "Didn't mean to snap."

Exercising her new-found relationship with the divine, she whispered, "God, can I do —"

"Miss Killingsworth," Raul sounded frantic, scurrying toward her, wringing his hands. "Sorry I'm late."

She silenced him with a hand gesture, then turned and looked up at the young woman who held the wheelchair handles. She patted the young woman's arm. "Would you please relate my thanks to the staff of the cardiac care unit?"

Turning to Raul she said, "I'm glad to see you, Raul. Thank you for coming to get me." She pointed toward the exit. "I desperately need to get out that door."

With eyes wide in amazement Raul looked over her questioningly to the young lady pushing the wheelchair.

Preaching point: *Personal crises can lead to vows to live faithfully with God.*

ABC Easter 4; A Lent 4; A Proper 23 (28); B Proper 11 (16) Psalm 23

Chapter 18: Valley Variation

Pastor Trevin realized after two years in ministry that when he called on new people, he became nervous and talked too much about the church and himself. Through advice of a fellow pastor, he reined in his runaway anxiety by having a pocket full of questions to ask people when he met them for the first time. His favorite with couples (although not the first he asked) was "How did you meet?" and if that was a success, he asked, "What was your first date like?"

The questions not only broke the ice, he enjoyed hearing about people being attracted to each other; and they usually liked telling him. But when he called on Ryan and Deanna — who'd worshiped in the congregation for the first time on Sunday — nothing he said, did, asked, or suggested generated any sparks in the conversation. Even his question, "how did you meet?" brought a ho-hum response that they'd worked together in Walmart for a year, didn't date others, and never considered the other as an interesting person. They admitted with nearly blank expressions that they basically got together for dinner and a movie just to have some practice in dating, no real expectations.

Pastor Trevin in desperation pulled out his last resort: "What was your first date like?" He thought it was sure fire, because he'd heard a long line of interesting answers: Got in a car wreck, dyed their hair, visited grandparents, dove into a swimming pool with clothes on, started writing a novel, strung toilet paper on their algebra teacher's hedge, fell asleep in a play, picked strawberries, broke up a bar fight.

Ryan and Deanna stated flatly, "Dinner and a movie." Trevin felt like he'd ordered a cream puff and was served a brick. "Uh," he said, "good movie?"

"Not really," Ryan said.

"Not at all," Deanna said.

"Obviously," Trevin said, shifting on the sofa, "the date went well enough you got together again." He decided to go for the center of their relationship, "So, why did you?"

Deanna looked at Ryan like she was confirming it was okay. She said, "We shared our dreams."

"Makes sense," Trevin said, "you're young and planning for the future."

"No," Ryan said, "we shared our real dreams. Each of us, for some reason. Maybe we were searching for something to talk about, just started telling the other what we dreamed the night before."

"Then we went on relating our usual dreams," Deanna said, "and some of our worst nightmares. Still do. Every morning."

"It's become the center of our marriage," Ryan said and laughed. "After three years, we can't do without it."

"When Ryan's out of town," Deanna chuckled and said, "he can usually phone in the morning and we share while we still remember what swirled around in our heads during the night."

Trevin was intrigued when Ryan stated, "It's a part of our faith."

Trevin had never heard such a thing. He tipped his head to the side in a question. Deanna was eager to continue, "We've worked out a lot, just by listening to ourselves. I don't mean a selfish kind of thing, but a little like therapy, and definitely as a way to trust God."

"That's very interesting," Trevin said. "Something specific?"

They glanced to one another again and Deanna said, "By our listening to some constant pictures and themes in my dreams, it's how I came to faith."

Trevin leaned closer to her. She said, "Over the years — and Ryan doesn't mind my saying this — Ryan's dreams are pretty pedestrian. Certainly more Disneyland than Jurassic Park: Day before rehashed, worries about tomorrow previewed, old friends, old jobs, old sports. Only a few shocking flashes through the brain. He goes months without a dream stabbing him. Right, Ryan?"

"Pretty well on the nose. I don't mind. My dreams seldom bother me. They entertain me. Yet, they don't offer much challenge or direction. Not the same with Deanna. She flies and dives, dances and dies in her dreams; and, by telling her dreams to me, she takes me with her. We travel together. Haven't said this to others."

"I'm pleased you'd share that with me," Trevin said, which was a go-ahead for Deanna.

"Even that first night when we sat chatting after the movie, I mentioned the dream that recurred the most — and bothered me most." Deanna began speaking as though reliving the dream, "It's messy and dark. Ryan's dreams are bright and splashy. Mine's in the shadows. In this one, always a spray of darkness looming. A month would flow by smoothly and then the dream leaped out to grab my mind." She clenched her hands together. "I'm going somewhere important, but without really understanding direction or goal. Always narrower, and the darkness growing against me like I'm being squeezed into a tunnel. Yet, I always feel a presence and I ask, 'Who's there?' The way's constantly more and more cramped, sides pressing in. I have to step onto a slant on the right, then onto a slant on the left to stay upright in the textured darkness. But always, whoever is with me is friendly. Out there beyond me is a benevolent somebody …something that cares about me and what I'm passing through. I don't know who."

She stopped and breathed deeply. Trevin's chest was tight for having followed along in her dream, "That's pretty heavy to dump on your first date!"

The couple laughed with him. Then the three sat quietly for a few moments. Deanna said in a soft voice, "We shared that dream, in all its variations, through our courtship, engagement, and marriage. We weren't worshipping then. Didn't think much about faith. Every few days we fiddled with what it meant, *if* it meant anything. Then Ryan's great aunt died and we went to the funeral. A year ago; a year on March 22. At the cemetery the pastor read the Psalm 23rd and when he said, 'Yea, though I walk through the valley of the shadow of death, I will fear no evil: for thou art with me,' I turned to Ryan and we both understood. We wanted to leap, laugh and scream at the same time. After the service, we could hardly speak to anyone. We were overwhelmed. We knew, both of us, deep within us: God was accompanying me through the valley of the shadow of death."

"Might not mean that to anyone else," Ryan said, "but when Deanna's dream intersected with the psalm, we instantly decoded what God had been saying to her."

Deanna's face almost shined. "I never experienced that dream again. We finally understood what God was telling me."

The three looked back and forth to one another for a moment, then they laughed and cried with joy; because they trusted that Deanna's was a strange journey, but God's goodness and mercy would follow her all the days of her life.

Preaching point: *God's caring presence through life's dangerous valleys.*

B Lent 1; C Advent 1; Proper 10 (15) Psalm 25:1-10
A Proper 21 (26) Psalm 25:1-9

Chapter 19: Sainted Mother-in-Law

On Gwen's right, her husband Jerome sat beside the center aisle and was closest to his mother's casket as serious dark-suited men rolled it to the front of the sanctuary. Gwen's three children sat on her left. She thanked God that the children had grown old enough to realize that their grandma Sarah hadn't been normal. Each grandchild had been confused and hurt by her as young children. Before Sarah died, her borderline paranoia was obvious to anyone near her. Anything negative triggered her anger.

When Gwen had met Jerome and fallen in love, they were living in New Mexico. His strong faith, nurtured by his lifetime in the church, had led her to a deepened faith. She was heartened that after they married she'd be part of a Christian family, since her family was religious in word only. Gwen hadn't taken seriously what Jerome had warned her about Sarah. She was used to college friends complaining about crazy parents with hilarious stories. Yet, each meeting with Sarah was damaging.

Years later, after Gwen and Jerome had moved to Eugene, Oregon, their young children were condemned to the tension of visiting their widowed grandmother often. On the drives home from the in-laws', Gwen calmed the children after they'd seen their grandmother stamp her feet and heard her say things like, "The Grueyars are absolutely the worst neighbors in the world. They park in front of my house just to annoy me." A mention of a brother or sister brought an outburst about her siblings, which the children mimicked to one another, "They always left me to do the work." Mention of someone's moving to a new home prompted anger at Jerome, "That was the most perfect house and yard in Corvallis — and my garden — but no, your dad insisted on taking the job in Ashland and then we had to put up with snooty neighbors."

Gwen didn't arrive at the funeral overcome with grief. Primarily she was relieved. She guessed and even hoped that, because the pastor had only recently met her mother-in-law, he wouldn't talk much about her.

"Sarah was wonderful person," the pastor said and Gwen sat up straight and began to listen to what was going on. She'd heard the pastor read his text, Psalm 25: "Lead me in your truth, and teach me, for you are the God of my salvation." She'd heard the obligatory obituary in which the pastor emphasized that Sarah had professed her faith and joined Christ's church 52 years before. "She was one of our most faithful members," he said. "An inspiration and an example to us all with her serene Christian life."

Gwen cocked her head to the side. Was she hearing the pastor right? "A friend to all, charitable, comfort to the suffering, with an open hand to the needy. A selfless wife, blessed sister, mother, mother-in-law, and grandmother." Jerome ducked his head and seemed to be contemplating the memorial folder in his lap. The children: twelve, thirteen, and sixteen, looked as stunned as Gwen. "Side by side with her Christian brothers and sisters, a stalwart and devoted servant upholding the ministry of Christ in this town, a testament to gracious living."

Gwen wanted to shout, "Are you out of your nut? She gave teeny gifts to her grandchildren and, if they didn't shower her with exaggerated gratitude, within the day she found a way to squash them with a word or gesture."

"Sarah will always be remembered as a blessed saint who lived by the prayer of David, 'Lead me in your truth, and teach me, for you are the God of my salvation.' In life, she prayed that she be led further into God's truth. In death she leads us still to the great and gracious God —"

Then Gwen figured it out. The new pastor didn't know her mother-in-law. He probably pulled out a funeral service he'd performed for someone else in a former pastorate. How obvious! Seemed like blasphemy. "'Lead me in your truth,' sure," Gwen thought. "Lead me to the mental hospital." She glanced at Jerome and his pain radiated to her. She turned to the children: tears and sniffling. She put her arm around Laura her youngest. She resolved that for her family's sake she must, more than ever, refrain from complaining about her mother-in-law.

In desperation she prayed, "God, help me explain to the kids that the pastor got everything backward about Sarah." She rolled the scripture over in her mind, "Lead me in your truth and teach me." As completely wrong as the pastor was about Sarah, Gwen took the Bible seriously. "Lead me in your truth and teach me. Lord, you know what the pastor said about Sarah wasn't true." Then among the swirling thoughts in her mind she heard — was it from God? — "But she's glorified in God's full presence, and it's true now."

Gwen remained silent, wide-eyed and rigid to the end of the service. Jerome had to jostle her when it was time for her to exit with the family.

Preaching point: *God's truth brings further understanding and gracious changes in our lives.*

A Proper 21 (26) Psalm 25:1-9
B Lent 1; C Advent 1; Proper 10 (15) Psalm 25:1-10

Chapter 20: If It's Worth Telling ...

"Let me tell you a story."
"No, no, no. That's not the way to start a story. Try again."
"I've got a great story to tell you."
"You're still missing it badly."
"But I just introduced the story."
"You don't have to introduce a story. You need only the story's beginning. Don't waste time — and your listener's patience. Just pause and tell the story. Trust that once you state, 'Three men walk into a bar: a priest, a minister, and a rabbi,' no one needs a green light flashing the story sign. The human mind has a built-in receptor for stories. You tell me a story and in my mind I see it, perhaps feel it, even smell or taste it. Just because I'm listening to it, it's real. Real enough to make people laugh or cry, or to change lives. This goes for scripture's stories too. You know, like Jesus' parables. Stories and scripture don't always need introductions or long conclusions about what they mean and how they apply. Listening takes us into the world of scripture, helps us lean over the gate to God's backyard and glimpse what's going on in that next door world of the Spirit.

"A story offers a 'for instance' to get people to think, just by sprinkling in front of them the few sentences that comprise a beginning, a middle, and an end that has something to do with the beginning and the middle. It doesn't have to be fiction. History is packed with interesting and meaningful events; and the human mind is designed to receive that information best when it's expressed with a beginning, a middle, and an end that has something to do with the beginning and the middle. Less than that is confusing or at least unsatisfying. Maybe you've heard sermons with a beginning, and a beginning, a middle, and a beginning? See what I mean?

"Scripture's story can pierce the human mind when it's laid beside another story: Here's scripture and here's a story, and the listener's thinking gets to grab both and make one new thing out of the two. We don't always need many details. It's natural to us. We're storytelling creatures.

"Consider this example: Take two lines from Psalm 25: 'Do not let my enemies exult over me' — that's near the psalm's beginning. And: 'Therefore he instructs sinners in the way' — that's near the psalm's end. Let those two lines sit together in the mind for a while."

* * *

In WWII Rome the Irish Monsignor Hugh O'Flaherty worked in the Vatican. The Vatican had been recognized as a sovereign nation in 1929. As such, it was a neutral in WWII. One of O'Flaherty's tasks was, in partnership with the International Red Cross, caring for Allied prisoners in Italy's prisoner of war camps. That was when Allied soldiers populated the camps. The Axis powers (including Italy at the time) were fighting against the Allies' forces. Then, along with a British diplomat interned safely within the Vatican's borders, O'Flaherty naturally fell into taking care of Allied soldiers who managed to elude German and Italian forces and show up at the Vatican. The illegal and highly dangerous Rome Escape Line came into existence. The network of faithful friends found safe houses for the escapees in Rome and the countryside.

The escape line became more hazardous and hectic in July of 1943 after the Allies invaded Sicily and Italians knew that the Allies would soon be fighting their way north through the mainland. By September, their dictator Mussolini had been arrested and a new Italian government signed an armistice with the Allies. But the Germans, who the day before had been Italy's ally, then invaded Italy. The Italian soldiers were hustled into the POW camps they'd built for Allied prisoners. Escape was slightly easier for the Italian soldiers because they knew the language and the geography. Along with downed Allied airmen and escapees from their earlier POW camps, the Italian soldiers arrived one by one in Rome seeking shelter. The network of lifesavers grew to thousands of people willing to defy Nazi law and hide an innocent person — Italians, British, Americans, Jews, and others from nearly every Allied country.

While this web of rescue grew, the Gestapo operated in Rome to stop it. They found some escapees and arrested a few of O'Flaherty's accomplices. But the safe houses had an intricate system of communication that usually delivered word of a raid in time for prisoners to flee.

Herbert Kappler was the head of Rome's Gestapo. The man was efficient and violent; and he became obsessed with catching O'Flaherty in the act. For the nine months that the Germans ruled the city of Rome, they knew what O'Flaherty and his comrades were doing, but they never caught him. Kappler set traps, some creative and expensive, some merely using thugs. None worked, but soon O'Flaherty had to stay behind the white stripe the Germans painted on the pavement around the Vatican. He was warned that if he stepped over he would be arrested — and certainly tortured and probably killed. O'Flaherty would walk up to the white line, knowing that Kappler's men watched his every twitch, hoping they could snatch him into Gestapo custody. From behind that white line, he co-directed the escape organization until the German army was expelled from Rome in June, 1944. By the time the Germans finally evacuated the city, the organization was sheltering 3,500 people in and around Rome. Altogether they'd assisted 6,500 people at that point.

When WWII ended, Kappler was arrested, tried, and sentenced in Italy to life imprisonment for war crimes. In a year or two, he wrote to O'Flaherty. He wrote back. After a few letters, O'Flaherty began to visit him regularly in prison. The two became friends. After Kappler's trial, during a silent moment in the jail, Herbert Kappler's request of Monsignor O'Flaherty was granted. He was received into the Roman Catholic Church.

* * *

David O. Bales

"Just lay that story of WWII Rome next to those two verses from Psalm 25: 'Do not let my enemies exult over me,' and 'Therefore he instructs sinners in the way.' As you don't have to introduce every story, so you need not tack on a moral. Let the listener's mind latch onto the story; because, people will often make a more meaningful connection for themselves than anyone else could suggest."

Preaching point: *Scripture speaks through story.*

(Stephen Walker, Hide & Seek: The Irish Priest in the Vatican Who Defied the Nazi Command)

ABC Baptism of the Lord (1); B Trinity Sunday Psalm 29

Chapter 21: Glorious, Stormy Worship

"No one could remember such a windstorm," Abuyah said. "Two days. Occasionally a shower of rain, but mostly just gust after gust, like the weather was playing a game and each blast fighting the last. Anyone who dared step outside to traverse a Jerusalem street found themselves leaning. Little children were blown over. I was just a boy, but my father had taken me along to help the other priests." Abuyah rested on his ragged cushion and gazed at the old men he'd invited to his home for this early evening meal. It was the thirtieth anniversary of the Jerusalem temple's destruction by the Babylonians. The guests resembled the land they lived in. Jerusalem and Judah were in ruins and the Babylonians left few people living in the area. This remnant of Judah's population was at wits end trying to survive, let alone to figure out what their nation's destruction might mean for their religion's future.

"The priests and Levites heard the storm all night," Abuyah continued, "Hoped it would abate, but this morning they faced even worse weather than yesterday. The cold was one thing, froze your dripping nose red; but, the hardest was to keep the fires burning under the sacrifices. Made you wish the temple court had a roof.

"You'd think those bedraggled priests would push along the sacrifices as quickly as possible and get out of the tempest. Pray their prayers, let the Levites chant their quickened praise. Maybe tomorrow's worship would feel more meaningful. But right there the most awesome thing happened."

His elderly friends, dour and hopeless, perked up whenever anyone talked about the temple. Most of them had seen it before it was destroyed. His telling them was like their being able to experience with him the heartbeat of Judah, which had stopped when worship on Jerusalem's temple mount halted.

"This tottery priest with his robe flopping in the wind was suddenly in ecstasy. He'd always been strange, bug-eyed and bandy-legged, but he was born a priest and that's what he did, stumbling around, talking to himself, fiddling with this or that, getting in everyone's way. This morning, everyone else is dashing around, hand over an ear to stop the wind's stabbing pain, and he's got his arms up in the air, face to the sky, blabbering: 'Ascribe to the LORD, O heavenly beings, ascribe to the LORD glory and strength. Ascribe to the LORD the glory of his name; worship the LORD in holy splendor.' He's talking to the angels, like he knows they're mixed up in this storm and they're delighted with it.

"The rest of the priests are doing their best to complete their tasks. He turns to them and shouts with a rumbling sound we'd never heard from him, 'The voice of the LORD is over the waters; the God of glory thunders, the LORD, over mighty waters,' like at that moment he actually saw through all this uproar and perceived the LORD above heaven's ocean.

"The temple servants are squinting against the wind and here he is: eyes wide and glazed over, facing into the force of it, dancing with glee. Lightning smashes the north side of the temple. Thunder lifts us off our feet and he yells, 'The voice of the LORD is powerful; the voice of the LORD is full of majesty. The voice of the LORD breaks the cedars; the LORD breaks the cedars of Lebanon.'"

Abuyah talked louder and faster, tipping his head up and turning his eyes above his guests. "The rest of those holy servants in the LORD's court finally drop their duties. Everyone moves toward him, like he's at the bottom of a funnel that's dripping the LORD's message upon them. He turns and points to the north, 'The LORD makes Lebanon skip like a calf, and Sirion like a young wild ox.' Another lighting slams its thunder on us and he shouts, 'The voice of the LORD flashes forth flames of fire.' He points south, 'The voice of the LORD shakes the wilderness; the LORD shakes the wilderness of Kadesh.'

"Everyone's drawn into heaven's activity swirling around the old man. The LORD's presence permeates the court of the priests. The old priest shouts like an announcement, 'The voice of the LORD causes the oaks to whirl and strips the forest bare.'

"The other priests and Levites are gasping, some laughing, some crying, some doing both. By that time I've gotten behind my father. Then, like the voice of a lion, the old man roars, 'Glory!' Everyone flinches, and the old guy shrieks again 'Glory!' shaking us all. Then he shouts again and again with every breath, 'Glory, Glory, Glory!' and soon everyone is shouting with him, such glory as you'd think could join with the wind to topple the temple. On and on for an hour.

"Then as abruptly, he stops. Stops. So, do all the others, though each eye is upon him and everyone's trying to catch their breath to see what might come next. At that moment, the winds cease, like they were a taut rope cut with a sword's one sweep. Everyone's wobbly, stunned and weeping.

"He turns to his fellow servants and states simply, like giving a report, 'The LORD sits enthroned over the flood; the LORD sits enthroned as king forever.' Then that old man, seemingly back to his right mind, spreads his arms to us, as at every priestly blessing, and states, 'May the LORD give strength to his people! May the LORD bless his people with peace!' and he walked away as though he didn't even remember what just transpired."

Abuyah takes a deep breath and speaks quietly to his gathered friends, "I thought that as we recall the day of the temple's ruin, we should hold to this memory of our LORD's glory." Then he stands and says, "Glory." After a pause he speaks louder, "Glory." Then he bellows to the group, "Glory!" at which all the old men struggle to their feet as quickly as they can. Jumping and throwing their arms to heaven, they leap around shouting together, "Glory! Glory! Glory!" until the sun sets and these remnants of the LORD's defeated nation of Judah finally fall over in exhaustion.

Preaching point: *Remembering the LORD's glory even in the worst circumstances.*

A Proper 4 (9); C Reformation Day; C Proper 29 (34) Psalm 46

Chapter 22: In The Heart Of The Sea

Martin should have figured it out earlier. He couldn't believe how obtuse he'd been. For three weeks after March 12, 2011, he'd thought that Katie's morose mood was because of their children's problems. Katie knew herself better than anyone Martin had ever met. She could speak of herself with scientific accuracy: "I'm as well as my children." It had been that way as long as she'd been a mother and especially now, with their son Roger between jobs and their daughter Amy, as she put it, "above the averages" in the ratio of miscarriages to a full term baby. But it was obvious now to Martin that the children's difficulties weren't Katie's only worry, not even her primary problem.

From where he sat in the car, Martin gazed at her as she stood silently among spring's final flowers on the Montana plains beside the little church balanced atop the rise. It had a few shingles blown from the roof and trim hanging ajar beside a window. Katie held her hands on her elbows. A breeze swept wisps of her grey hair across her face as she surveyed the landscape around the near ruin of the church. Martin waited in the car. He finally understood.

Katie had grown up with "nomadic parents" as they labeled themselves. In Katie's childhood they'd lived in half a dozen cities and towns, all of them in the western US. Yet, in the 35 years they'd been married, Martin and Katie never traveled to the west. Katie was an only child and her parents had died. The west held no relatives and only long forgotten friends; but on the evening of March 12, 2011, Katie had wound her way into the garage between the Snap-On tool cabinet and the Shop-Vac. She found Martin bent over a carburetor on the workbench. He dropped a piece of wiry metal into solvent in an ancient coffee can his father had used for the same thing. He turned to her to hear why she'd come to the garage. She didn't speak for a moment, then almost stuttered, "I'd like to take a vacation in late spring or as early in summer as possible …to eastern Montana."

Martin had neither complained nor questioned. "Fine," he'd grinned. "Your choice this spring. I'll have the old Corvette back together and we'll travel in style. Too bad we can't take Route 66."

On the Montana hillside he watched her from the car, this beautiful woman who still consumed his life as she'd filled his last three and a half decades. She'd told him pieces. He should have known. She was seven and living in Crescent City, California, when a tsunami from Alaska devastated the place. She and her parents were eating supper when water crashed through three windows and swept them across the dining room. "The tablecloth floated off right into my face. It was the plastic one with daisies." The family was fortunate to live at the farthest reach of the wave. The monster soon swept out again, but it had pushed the house off its foundation and, as Katie said, "didn't do much for my foundation either." She begged her family to move away from the sea. They didn't need much convincing. Their house and her father's commercial fishing boat were wiped out.

Within two weeks they'd rented a car and with their few recovered possessions departed Crescent City and never returned. As he drove away, her father had said to her, "the mountains shook in the heart of the sea. We'll go where we can't even see a mountain." Three days driving landed them seventeen miles outside Circle, Montana, where for five years the family had worshiped in this small community church on the plains. When Martin set himself to recall Katie's stories of her youth, those were her happiest years.

If Martin had been more alert, he'd have remembered how stories of earthquakes disturbed her. If the television showed the results of an earthquake, she either turned it off or left the room, often clutching her arms around her and squeezing her lips tightly. She didn't want to bother others with her fears. Obvious to Martin now, the news of the March 2011 tsunami had undone her.

Although he yearned to leap from the car and rush to her, he knew her well enough to leave her alone out there with her Montana memories. He watched her and suffered for her and turned his thoughts to this ramshackle church festooned by flowers already shriveling in summer's approach.

Katie glanced toward him and saw him staring with her at the church. She looked down and began dragging each footstep through the grass as she walked to the corvette. Martin didn't move when she got in and sat. He waited for her to reach her hand onto the console. He placed his on hers. She said, "That building and I haven't weathered well, but I really needed to come here again. Can't even see a mountain."

They sat silently for half an hour, then with a roar, Martin drove them away, starting toward eastbound I-94, relieved to be traveling home, even if not on Route 66.

Preaching point: *God strengthens believers in this uncertain world.*

A Easter 7 Psalm 68:1-10, 32-35

Chapter 23: Mark Twain's "The War Prayer"

January 1942 was a difficult time for the Society of Friends in the United States. What was one's Christian responsibility when Christ commands that we be peacemakers, yet our nation was attacked and war declared? For 300 years, Quakers had practiced as well as advised peace toward all. One congregation's prayer group felt that in the middle of a new world war, a message for peace must somehow be proclaimed again. But how to get people caught in fear, anger, hate and hysteria to consider Christ's peace now? They realized they couldn't affect the greater US, and they were sure of abuse to come their way, but they sent to all congregations within their city a copy of Mark Twain's *The War Prayer*. They wrote:

Samuel Clemons' ***The War Prayer*** can instruct us whenever we reason in this war that — as all sides in the Civil War and World War I reasoned — God is on our side. As difficult as it is now to believe, God is on the side of peace. We cannot recommend one particular and absolute way to bring peace, but with slight omissions and punctuation changes we offer ***The War Prayer*** for your contemplation:

* * *

It was a time of great and exalting excitement. The country was up in arms, the war was on, in every breast burned the holy fire of patriotism; the drums were beating, the bands playing, on every hand and far down the receding and fading spread of roofs and balconies a fluttering wilderness of flags flashed in the sun. Nightly, the packed mass meetings listened, panting to patriot oratory which stirred the deepest deeps of their hearts, and which they interrupted at briefest intervals with cyclones of applause, the tears running down their cheeks the while; in the churches the pastors preached devotion to the flag and country, and invoked the God of Battles, beseeching his aid in our good cause in outpouring of fervid eloquence which moved every listener.

Sunday morning came — the next day the battalions would leave for the front; the church was filled; the volunteers were there, their young faces alight with martial dreams — visions of stern advance, the gathering momentum, the rushing charge, the flashing sabers, the flight of the foe, the tumult, the enveloping smoke, the fierce pursuit, the surrender — them home from the war, bronzed heroes, welcomed, adored, submerged in golden seas of glory!

The community's worship service proceeded first with a war chapter from the Old Testament read; the first prayer said; it was followed by an organ burst that shook the building, and with one impulse the house rose, with glowing eyes and beating hearts, and poured out that tremendous invocation —

"God the all-terrible! Thou who ordaineth!
Thunder thy clarion and lightning thy sword!"

Then came the "long" prayer. None could remember the like of it for passionate pleading and with the pastor's moving and beautiful language. The burden of its supplication was that an ever-merciful and benignant Father of us all would watch over our noble young soldiers and aid, comfort, and encourage them in their patriotic work; bless them, shield them in the day of battle and for the hour of peril, bear them in his mighty hand, make them strong and confident, invincible in the bloody onset; help them to crush the foe, grant to them and to their flag and country imperishable honor and glory —

At that, an aged stranger entered the church and moved with slow and noiseless step up the main aisle, his eyes fixed on the minister, his long body clothed in a robe that reached to his feet, his head bare, his white hair descending in a frothing cataract to his shoulders. He made his silent way without pausing next to the preacher's side and stood there waiting. With shut lids the preacher, unconscious of the old man's presence, continued with his moving prayer and at last finished with the words, uttered in fervent appeal, "Bless our arms, grant us the victory, O Lord our

God, Father and protector of our land and flag!"

The stranger touched his arm, motioned him to step aside — which the startled minister did — and took the preacher's place. During some moments he surveyed the spellbound audience with solemn eyes, in which burned an uncanny light; then in a deep voice he said:

"I come from the throne — bearing a message from Almighty God!"

The words smote the house with a shock.

"He has heard the prayer of his servant your shepherd and will grant it if such shall be your desire after I, his messenger, shall have explained to you its import — that is to say, its full import. For as with many of human prayers, it asks far more than he who utters it is aware of.

"You have heard your servant's prayer — the uttered part of it. I am commissioned of God to put into words the other part of it — that part which the pastor — and also you in your hearts — fervently prayed silently. And ignorantly and unthinkingly? O God grant that it is so! You heard these words: 'Grant us victory, O Lord our God!' That is sufficient. The *whole* of the uttered prayer is so compact into these pregnant words. Elaborations were not necessary. When you have prayed for victory, you have prayed for many unmentioned results which follow victory — *must* follow it, cannot help but follow it. Upon the listening spirit of God the Father fell also the unspoken part of the prayer. He commandeth me to put it into words. Listen!

"O Lord our Father, our young patriots, idols of our hearts, go forth to battle — be thou near them! With them — in spirit — we also go forth from the sweet peace of our beloved firesides to smite the foe. O Lord our God, help us to tear their soldiers to bloody shreds with our shells; help us to cover their smiling fields with the pale forms of their patriot dead; help us to drown the thunder of the guns with the shrieks of their wounded, writhing in pain; help us to lay waste their humble homes with a hurricane of fire; help us to wring the hearts of their unoffending widows with unavailing grief; help us to turn them out roofless with their little children to wander unfriended the wastes of their desolated land in rags and hunger and thirst, victims of the sun flames of summer and the icy winds of winter, broken in spirit, worn with travail, imploring thee for the refuge of the grave and denied it — for our sakes who adore thee, Lord, blast their hopes, blight their lives, protract their bitter pilgrimage, make heavy their steps, water their way with their tears, stain the white snow with the blood of their wounded feet! We ask it, in the spirit of love, of him who is the source of love, and who is the ever-faithful refuge and friend of all that are sore beset and seek his aid with humble and contrite hearts. Amen."

(*After a pause.*) "Ye have prayed it; if ye still desire it, speak! The messenger of the most high waits!"

It was believed afterward that the man was a lunatic, because there was no sense in what he said.

Preaching point: *The danger of equating our enemies with God's enemies.*

A Advent 2 Psalm 72:1-7, 18-19

Chapter 24: Prayer For Righteous Government

Josh parked his Department of Transportation dump truck in the row of others for the night. He didn't look at Chas in the passenger's seat, nor did Chas turn toward him. They got out and walked separately to the shop to punch out for the day. Inside the shop, half a dozen men waited at 4:55 PM to punch out. They all, quite obviously, greeted Chas and didn't look in Josh's direction.

As had become his habit in the last three months, Josh waited while the others punched out before he grabbed his timecard from the rack. At least today it was here. Twice in the last week he'd found it on the floor tracked on by muddy boots. He pulled it out and grit his teeth as he pressed it into the clock.

He'd been ostracized for three months. No matter how maddening it was for his foreman to see him every day, the foreman knew the union's lawyer was ready to leap to his defense if Josh raised an eyebrow. Josh's job was safe …relatively. Three years yet even to early retirement. Could he endure it?

At his car, he checked the tires. Once he'd found them flattened. He was angered and hurt by such things. These had been his friends, yet they refused now to look him in the eye and turned their backs if he spoke to them about anything other than official tasks. The union's lawyer said that in the past such irritations were the prelude to violence; but those methods had been dead for half a century — he hoped.

If Josh had realized how far the money trail stretched, would he have reported the diminished quality of the asphalt? He thought he did what was right, although he hadn't guessed that the scheme even lined the governor's pockets. Now the consequences of his letter to the state's Department of Justice dogged his every step. At work it felt like buzzards were circling him. Outside of work it felt like gravity had doubled.

He didn't tell Lois because he didn't want to worry her. Consequently, his own worrying increased perilously. He'd planned to inform her after his deposition; but, when nothing came of it, he still lagged, as he put it to himself, "in reporting to the other half of his marriage." The union's lawyer told him, "Thoroughly hushed at all levels. Flushed right down the toilet. Been this way in living memory. Always has been and expect it always will be. Every administration appoints its own and they make sure everyone down the line is dribbled enough dollars to keep them cooperating. Expecting any administration in this state to be honest is like planning to teach first grade on Mars."

The next morning at breakfast, Josh was looking at the newspaper's front section. He wasn't reading, just fingering the edges of the front page. Lois commented on a couple of articles she read in the downstate section, to which he grunted a response. Then she became insistent. She held a cinnamon-raisin bagel and he noticed that her fingernails were bitten to the quick, a habit she'd broken fifteen years before.

"A two-inch article on the back page says the Office of the Attorney General announced an investigation dismissed in the Department of Transportation Southern District." She stared at him. He didn't respond, but looked back at his newspaper and grunted. She persisted, "'No reliable leads' it says. Know anything about that?"

He turned his head slightly toward her, "Yeah, but I don't think anything will come of it."

She leaned nearer, "It's our district," and left it hanging like a question and a challenge.

He coughed and spoke quietly, "Nobody talks about it," hoping that his near-honesty would end the discussion. He feared she'd ask him point blank if he were involved, so he folded the paper as calmly as possible but caught his foot on the table leg as he stood. She said nothing further, but touched her fingers lightly to her lips like she wanted to ask more.

He left the house quickly, but he realized what had happened to him. The false faces of his fellow workers had now caused his false face to his wife. Others weren't speaking to him and he wasn't speaking to Lois, and about this most important matter! He reviewed the massive kickback scheme of switched invoices and subcontractors with subs to subs, bribed inspectors, tanker trucks pulling off the interstate after the scales to pump into private tanks before delivering to the state depot. Shorting the mix one tenth of one percent yielded hundreds of thousands of dollars.

He'd spent a lifetime driving truck, yet in the driveway he fumbled with the car's shift, as though he were driving a clunker dragged from the state's mothballed relics. He tried to steady himself, didn't want to risk driving while he was so bothered by Lois's reaction. He banged the dashboard with his hand and shouted, "Are we living in Russia? Tentacles of corruption winding around everybody?" He pressed his fists to his temples. Lois must be picking up on his emotions. He could endure about anything except how he was affecting Lois.

He'd tried to bull through the situation, but he'd failed again. And because he'd put off telling her, each day that passed made it harder to try. His car remained stationary and he looked out of the window as though seeing all at once how bad government was ruining human relationships top to bottom throughout the state. He argued with himself about what to do; but, rotten government seemed to mark all possible directions with a sign: "Dead End."

Preaching point: *The need for righteousness in government.*

B Christmas Day; B Easter 6; C Proper 27 (32);
Proper 28 (33) Psalm 98

Chapter 25: New Christmas

It would benefit no one living or dead at Christmas to relate the name of the congregation or the people involved. The situation, although not exactly typical, occurs often enough to be recognized in some form in many congregations.

The task of pastor along with music director was to choose music for Christmas Day worship. They had been through this drill three years already and did not share the same perspective. This year, music director made a pre-emptive strike. He arrived in pastor's study three weeks before Christmas and announced, "At choir practice last night we discussed music for Christmas Day." Pastor, blind-sided, was not able to respond quickly with his usual glibness. "We agreed we like the old carols and do not want any newish songs at Christmas," music director said as he nodded his head devoutly.

"I guess that pretty well settles it?" pastor asked.

"Yes, it does," spoke music director in a reverent tone.

Pastor's sermon planning for Christmas Day was not motivated by sincere dedication to his Lord, as he suspected that music director's behavior was also not inspired by pure religious devotion. This unholy mixture of human nature led to pastor's Christmas Day sermon:

"Our text this morning is Psalm 98, that rousing piece of Israel's liturgy that begins with the command, 'Sing.'" He turned his eyes and voice to the right to address music director and choir with a smile. "We have this command not because our high school's football team won the state championship, not because our troops successfully invaded an enemy country, not because the stock market hit a new high, not because a revolutionary medical treatment wipes out cancer. The command is laid upon us to sing because of God, Yahweh, the Lord Israel, the supreme being, Creator of all, whom we know finally through our Lord Jesus Christ and the Holy Spirit.

"When we hear this psalm we don't respond as did the ancient Hebrews. We don't merely sing about God the Creator, the personal God of Israel. We sing about more. Something new happened after this Psalm was written. Our Lord Jesus Christ was born. So the hymn we sang this morning expresses God's extension into our world in our Lord Jesus: "Joy To The World." When Isaac Watts wrote the hymn in 1719, he was rewriting our text: Psalm 98. He turned it into a Christian, even a Christmas hymn. The tune seems to be borrowed from George Frederick Handel. Together they put something marvelously new into our worship. How impoverished our Christian church would be if Watts had not written that hymn. Can you imagine Christmas worship before people could sing 'Joy To The World?'"

"Or we can ask that same question of the impoverished church before 1738 that would have been robbed of being able to sing 'Hark! The Herald Angels Sing.' "Or the church before 1816 that could not sing 'Angels, From The Realms Of Glory.'" "Or the church before 1849 that could not sing 'It Came Upon A Midnight Clear.'" "Think of the children before 1887 who were not able to sing 'Away In A Manger.'" Or the church before 1818 that could not end its Christmas Eve worship singing 'Silent Night.' And can you imagine one of those *old* churches that would not allow to be sung one of those *new* songs we call classics?"

"Psalm 98, our text, begins with the command to sing to the Lord a new song because God does new things, the newest is the best revealed in Jesus the Christ, born in Bethlehem to the roaring of angels' singing. We are commanded to sing a *new* song, not just our favorites. It is because of God's mercy to us that needs to be told and retold in new ways to new people in new situations — new songs just like new books, new prayers, and new liturgies.

"This is not because we are iconoclasts or dilettantes. It is because of God's goodness. The center of the Christmas event is the always new occasion of God's giving God's very self for the sake of others, so new that we are commanded to sing new songs."

Pastor turned to his right to direct his eyes and voice to the choir. He saw music director bent with his head in his hands. Pastor became silent, aware instantly at how his short message had mercilessly bludgeoned the man. He stood open-mouthed for an embarrassing time, overcome with shame at what he had done on Christmas Day.

No more enjoying his theological quick-step, he turned to the congregation and spoke slowly and much more believably. "Christmas is about Jesus coming to us, us real people, we who are ornery and self-seeking, we who like our own opinions and like those who agree with us. Jesus came in real human life, this daily life we endure, that will not look so good tomorrow when the Christmas tinsel starts coming down. Our only hope is the new life that Jesus offers each of us, not just once, but for our every new day, and for our every new decision. God's new life through Jesus helps us confess our sins and rejoice in God's goodness, even when we are so obviously lacking in our own. Let us sing again this morning the joyous news of God's grace that is described in Psalm 98 and that is always coming to us new in Jesus. Let us sing 'Joy To The World.'"

Preaching point: *God multiplies the good news of Jesus' birth in new human dimensions.*

A Proper 6 (11); Reign of Christ; C Thanksgiving Day Psalm 100

Chapter 26: No-Matter-What

Connie yelled again, "Melody!" She looked up from scrubbing the kitchen floor on her hands and knees. "She was here a minute ago," she said to Daryl. "Melody! Where is she now?"

With a clank, Daryl wedged one more skillet into the large U-Haul cardboard box. He said, "I'll go look." Connie went back to her desperate scrubbing, some of her hair had gotten loose from her ponytail and was swinging beside her cheeks, nearly touching the floor next to her brush. They knew that for their ornery landlord to return their cleaning deposit, they needed to leave the house cleaner than when they moved in.

Daryl had seen Melody on the carpet in her old bedroom — now mostly empty — with a doll and half a dozen fluffy fabric somethings he couldn't identify. He'd left her there not five minutes before. As he walked down the hall, every sound echoed eerily in the near vacant house. He wondered if today's extra troubles was God's punishing him for working on Sunday. That's what his grandmother would say. But the seller urged them to close quickly on their new house. Then their landlord pressured them to vacate by the end of the month so he could get new renters before the worst winter weather. Daryl and Connie agreed, but they'd planned to pay an extra month's rent for the luxury of time, moving themselves across town by the pickup load. The abrupt eviction had created eleven days of laborious chaos — and the worst winter weather crashed into the city anyway. So, early Sunday morning, November 30, they were scrambling to finish cleaning and emptying the house. Four-year-old Melody's being with them topped the pile of moving problems. The friend Melody was going to spend the weekend with got the flu, and Daryl's buddy who'd promised to help with the final work bailed on them at the last minute.

Daryl had been distracted by his list of cleaning tasks, yet he'd thought he was alert to any sight or sound that indicated where Melody was. Not in her room. He rushed to the living room. Not there. Then he heard the toilet flush. "Problem solved," he said as he returned the kitchen to tell Connie that Melody had been found. He was wrapping the spice rack in hand towels when Melody screamed from the bathroom. Both parents dashed down the hall and, when Daryl grabbed the bathroom doorknob, it spun loosely in his hand.

"Honey," he asked through the door, "do you have the doorknob?" They heard Melody sobbing. Daryl and Connie looked at one another in panic. "Melody," Daryl raised his voice, "do you have the doorknob?"

"Yeah," she said through her crying gasps.

"Then, remember how, when the whole thing comes out, that you just slip that long skinny part back into the center where the knob goes?" Then they saw it: water from under the door.

"Oh, crud," Daryl said, "the toilet tank's stuck again, plus it's not draining." Broken doorknobs, malfunctioning toilets, only a few reasons they were buying their own house.

"Sweetie," Connie said to the door, "you need to come put the doorknob back into the door." No answer. "Sweetie, where are you?"

"In the bathtub."

"Honey, first you have to flick the toilet lever, the handle," Daryl said. "Remember? Can you do that? Just like you do after you've used the toilet. Flick the lever down quickly a couple times and then let go of it."

Connie ran back with towels to mop up the water flowing into the hall and after a few minutes the level of water in the bathroom lowered enough for Melody to come to the door. With Daryl's coaching, she pushed the doorknob's shank back into the knob's center. When she was finally out, the parents did their best to calm her and not appear angry, although their rising anxiety over the day's waiting labor was difficult to quash.

They put Melody in her snow suit, because it took too much

time to take it on and off and turned off the furnace that only worked on high or nothing. They were sweating enough that they expected to stay warm the rest of the day.

By four in the afternoon, no other disasters had struck. Their pickup's worn tires had managed two round trips across the ice to their new house while striking neither man or beast. When they stepped out of the old house for the last time, balancing carefully on the crooked steps thick with ice, Daryl and Connie sighed as though they'd defused a bomb. Then Connie remembered, "Evening worship."

"Oh no," Daryl said.

"Oh yes," Connie said. "You promised Pastor Todd."

The congregation was starting an experiment with a Sunday evening worship at five. Pastor Todd had polled members if they wanted such a thing and when they answered "yes," he then asked especially that they attend the first Sunday of the experiment — November 30.

"Gads," Daryl said, slapping his forehead. "I don't think we can make it on time. We're both a mess." He thought this would deter Connie, since she always insisted they attend worship four degrees above neat and clean.

"We'll do it," she said. "We promised Todd."

They didn't make it by five o'clock, but dashed in seventeen minutes late, tired, but rather proud of themselves for keeping their word. They quickly took their place among the forty others as the offering was being received. Melody instantly fell asleep across Connie's lap. They hardly noticed that everyone was solemn. This was supposed to be an evening of praise. Yet those around them looked shocked. The older woman next to them had tears dripping onto her blouse. Connie was just leaning toward her to show concern when Todd stood.

"So, we've come to worship no matter the suffering of the world," Todd said. "We planned to attend tonight, entering the Lord's gates with thanksgiving and his courts with praise. How do we do that in the midst of human pain and tragedy? Is it appropriate? Is it perhaps even blasphemous to do so when so many others suffer?

"Tonight *some* people worship the Lord with gladness and with singing that raises them toward heaven's gates. *We*, however, give thanks to our Lord no matter what. No matter the circumstances, we turn our gratitude to the Lord who is with us in tragedy, who doesn't abandon us when our team loses, our family divorces, our loved ones die, our congregations shrink, or our nation tips toward immorality. We praise our God who sticks with us. That's why the biblical faith summons us to praise our Lord Jesus who held onto us through death and beyond. No matter what we endure, whether minimal discomfort or maximum pain, our God is with us at the beginning, the middle, and beyond life's end. Even if we don't worship with full-throated joy, we can always, nevertheless, affirm that our Lord is good, whose steadfast love endures forever, whose faithfulness is to all generations."

Only near the end of the service did Daryl and Connie learn what the others heard at the beginning of worship: A church van of the neighboring Baptist church returning from a youth event had collided with a bus and burned.

Connie and Daryl sat amidst the others with belated shock. With the rest of the worshipers they turned their spirits toward God in prayer. The irritation that accumulated in their day's moving receded in the distance so far they couldn't even recognize it.

> **Preaching point**: *Thanksgiving that God is with us no matter what.*

C Proper 17 (22) Psalm 112

Chapter 27: Self-Serving

Pastor Moen scooted aside his computer keyboard and grabbed a pencil. What he was going to write needed careful attention to every word, to the point of feeling what he wrote. He resolved to represent Jesus Christ and not to allow his negative feelings to overwhelm God's grace. After a gaze at the ceiling with one last sigh of prayer, he began:

Dear Friends,

I am writing to the congregation to inform you of my resignation. I have not come to this decision quickly or casually, nor am I doing this completely alone. I have prayed and received counsel from my fellow clergy and denominational officials. An explanation is necessary because the size of our congregation limits to about a quarter of our members who know most of what is going on here (including progress and problems) and about half do not know much. The other quarter? As I have said before, I do not know everything.

What I know, *who* I know, is Jesus. That is the crux of the problem here at Trinity Church and why I am resigning. It started six months ago when I was going on vacation and could not find anyone to preach in my absence. I searched among both clergy and laity and was a week away from departing, yet with no one to fill the pulpit. Finally, a member of the congregation said that a friend in another congregation recommended a fellow who had a "great message," which I have come to recognize is his only message. It is known as the "prosperity gospel." Simply put: Everything will go well with believers, especially with money. People in our congregation had not heard of such a thing before because as Christians, our faith centers on Jesus. We believe that Jesus explains life to us, which means that Jesus also interprets the Old Testament — especially noting that the prosperity preacher spoke from the Old Testament.

After I arrived home from vacation, I was overwhelmed by a handful of dear members requesting more of this "gospel," which a critic aptly describes as treating God like the order window of a fast food restaurant or expecting God to slip a winning lottery ticket under your pillow. This eruption of the prosperity gospel among us has revealed some strained relationships within our fellowship and dusted off a few long held grudges — including political differences that stretch from local to national politics.

Since the prosperity preacher spoke from Psalm 112, I would like you to look with me at that psalm from a broader Christian view.

Happy are those who fear the LORD, who greatly delight in his commandments. Their descendants will be mighty in the land; the generation of the upright will be blessed. Wealth and riches are in their houses.

This mention of wealth and riches tumbling to the righteous is not unusual in the Old Testament. The Book of Proverbs abounds in promises of health and wealth to those who are faithful to the LORD. But, the Old Testament books of Ecclesiastes and Job provide a dampening if not the exact opposite view.

Another important part of Psalm 112, however, states: *they are gracious, merciful, and righteous. It is well with those who deal generously and lend, who conduct their affairs with justice.*

Although there are differences in the Old Testament about whether the LORD will automatically bless the faithful, all parts of the Bible summon us — for the LORD's sake — to be concerned for others, not just what we can get for ourselves. That is certainly where Jesus' grace and mercy guide us. Look at his life. He was righteous, but not rich. He did not promise wealth to his followers. In fact, he said they would be persecuted. He went around helping others and pointing them to a life in God's presence, and he did not line his pockets doing so.

This is the liturgical year of Luke's gospel, so I quote a few verses from Luke and ask how much of it squares with the prosperity gospel. Jesus' mother praises God in 1:53 that God has *sent the rich away empty.* Jesus teaches people in 12:33: *Sell your possessions and give to charity; make yourselves purses which do not wear out, an unfailing treasure in heaven, where no thief comes near, nor moth destroys. For where your treasure is, there will your heart be also.* He makes us all gulp when he pronounces: *none of you can become my disciple if you do not give up all your possessions* (14:33). Read the book of Acts (also written by Luke) about the earliest church after Jesus and you will search in vain through the apostles' speeches to hear anyone say, "Follow Jesus and grow rich."

Jesus' message and his life were in perfect parallel. He lived for others and for God's glory. For him, faith meant giving. His entire ministry was to help others. When he prayed for himself, it was so that he would complete his ministry for others. His disciples and earliest followers set out to imitate him. The apostle Paul, for example, worked for a living and at times refused contributions from believers so they would understand that what he gave them was free. He wrote: *for God loves a cheerful giver,* not a cheerful receiver. As Psalm 112 puts it: *They have distributed freely, they have given to the poor.*

Jesus calls us to be faithful and does not promise we will be successful. Pastor Fromm was my first pastor. I grew into adolescence with him and he will always be the image in my mind of a faithful and loving pastor. He drowned at 41 in a Bolivian river where he went to help missionaries. He left a wife and four young children. His faithful Christian life was not one immune from tragedy, but was one of service. I have sat at the bedsides of devoted Christians whose lives were cut short by disease. I have wept with Christian parents whose children were found dead beside drug paraphernalia. I have accompanied police to try to identify a body dragged from a car wreck which might be a parishioner. And in this same line of disasters: *Jesus was crucified.* The tragedy of his cross is the center of our faith. Did he die so we could buy a fancier SUV to drive to our opulent beach house or so we would serve him and trust him no matter what?

Whereas some Christians want to concentrate only on Jesus' empty tomb, a full Christian faith — the kind that has lasted 2,000 years and will last into eternity — embraces both the cross and the resurrection, meaning that both our unearned suffering and Jesus' eternal life infuse our lives now. Not one or the other, but both ... until we meet Jesus in glory.

Christians can mine the Old Testament for texts that promise they will get what they desire; but, they will get only Jesus. The Old Testament leads to him. If they do not like what Jesus lives and teaches, life with God in heaven will be a disappointment too.

As I leave you, I ask you to rejoice with me that I have received a call to help train pastors in the Ukraine. It is not an easy assignment. Dangerous in fact. Yet, I believe this is what I am called to do. I will continue to pray for this congregation. I ask that you continue praying for me that I may faithfully follow my Lord Jesus and, as Psalm 112 says, that *I may rise in the darkness as a light for the upright.*

In Christ,

Pastor Moen

He laid down his pencil slowly and shoved the paper far across his desk. He wished he would never have to look at it again. Yet he knew that to be *faithful, merciful, and righteous*, he must read it carefully and excise anything that would injure others or harm the congregation's ministry after he left.

Preaching point: *The Bible instructs us not in serving ourselves, but in serving God and others.*

A Epiphany 6 (6); B Proper 26 (31) Psalm 119:1-8

Chapter 28: Control

"No," Angie said, pressing her hand on her forehead in exasperation, "I want all the greeting cards beside the big window."

Thirteen-year-old Emma made a quick stop, swung the package away from her body, and turned left.

Angie raised her voice, "The biggest window, the display," she waved her arm and pumped her finger in the direction.

Emma rolled her eyes to her Aunt Heather, turned right, and proceeded with an exaggerated march in the direction her mother pointed.

"I told her to wear working shoes, and she's in flip-flops." No one else was near the cash register except Angie and her sister Heather. Heather had come for a week to help Angie renovate this general store that Angie had purchased with her divorce settlement. The location was intentional, in Angie's term, a wide spot on the road to nowhere.

Angie looked over at Heather who was stocking candy in the checkout lane. Heather quickly looked down, because Angie had seen Emma's gesture toward her aunt. "What?" Angie said.

"Nothing."

"What? What?" Angie persisted, placing her hand on her hip with a thump. "You don't approve of how I parent Emma?"

Heather was 42, Angie's senior by eight years. Although the two hadn't been much in one another's life when they were young, Heather had become Angie's emotional support through the divorce and now this move. She put down the box of candy bars she was emptying and stood. She'd reckoned that the anxiety and labor of setting up the store after it sat vacant for a year was all that Angie could handle at one time. She'd waited, but knew she'd say it sometime. She spread her arms. "It's just that you order her a lot, and about a lot of stuff she could figure out herself."

"Huh," Angie said and waved her aside because a customer was coming to the check stand with a couple of toddlers and an arm load of mustard, mayonnaise, cheese, and lunch meat. The toddlers were vibrating like gerbils around the woman's legs. She placed her load on the counter and with a glance at the two sisters, figured that keeping her children away from the candy that Heather had just rearranged was enough to deal with without getting caught in whatever was going on between the store's new owner and her employee.

After the customer exited, Angie began cleaning the counter again and Heather set a few more Mars Bars in order. Other customers were entering the store, giving them an excuse to bypass the pain of a disagreement. They closed at 6 p.m. and Angie said to Emma, "We're going to stay. Turn over the 'closed' sign on the way out and we'll lock it after you. Go straight home and we'll be there soon."

Emma looked to her aunt with a desperate glance for sympathy and went out.

Angie started counting the till, but again she'd noticed the look between aunt and niece. "You two plotting against me?" She asked with a sideways smile, which meant to Heather: Okay, we can talk about it now.

"Just that you boss her so much."

"She needs direction," Angie said and slapped down a stack of tens.

"Like Wayne gave you?"

Angie threw her hands on her chest. "What? You're comparing me to him?"

"Just to get your attention."

Angie calmed herself and said, "All kids need guidance. That's why I want her to grow up in a small town."

"I know," Heather said. "A whole village. I just think you're taking it too far. You don't give her space to make choices."

"She isn't ready to make many choices."

"You don't give her much chance to learn."

Angie dropped uncounted bills onto the counter. "She's got her whole life ahead and I don't want her making mistakes that will ruin her future."

"She certainly will make mistakes," Heather said, and pressed a hand on her temple, concentrating on how to explain herself. "You were in kindergarten when I was in middle school. You didn't know what my adolescence was like."

"You were long gone when *I* got to middle school," Angie said. "But Mom and Dad said you sailed through school."

"Might I say," Heather responded with a chuckle, "they either intentionally deceived you or maybe they really didn't know." She paused and Angie listened.

"I had as much trouble as anybody else. As I see Emma and listen to her, I don't think my life was much different than hers, in the sense of decisions, I mean. Not many cell phones then. But I remember the group of girls I was in and we were cheating as much as we could, especially in geometry. We worked out a system to communicate across the room. Quite clever, really. I didn't need anybody standing over me shaking a finger and reminding me cheating was wrong. We all knew it was wrong. I needed something inside me, a solid center of myself, and it wasn't going to form just by people ordering me."

"You never told me that when I was a kid," Angie said.

"I wasn't around much. Yet I've been thinking about Emma. I don't know how it occurred for you or how it will happen for her, but for me, I broke free from the pressures around me by my faith. It was vague. I have a few acquaintances who wouldn't call it 'faith.' But it was faith. That included a sense of right and wrong but it wasn't just about right and wrong. It was my whole life. For me, God didn't sweep me off my feet and whisk me to visions and ecstasies. But I was drawn to thinking about God, more and more in what I considered and what I did. It was a day by day thing. Slowly through high school I felt as though I was steadied and supported. Didn't have to remember my lies. Didn't have to worry about getting caught. And I didn't figure it out right away, but I was beginning to understand myself in relation to God and others, and thus I had direction. It was a relief to have something outside of me that was now somehow living in me.

"Funny thing, but later, when I started reading the Bible, what had grown in me seemed to match Psalm 119. It's not as though God surrounded me with prickly commands, but it was God's guiding. As I read that psalm, guidance came from the outside but it landed inside me. It was a kind of control, but it was also protection. It's what I needed to confirm what I'd been growing into for years."

Angie had a blank face. Heather couldn't tell if what she'd said helped or not. After a pause she continued, "That's how it was for me, anyway; and it took some time and mistakes to get there."

Angie started counting the change into piles of quarters, dimes, nickels and pennies. Heather watched her lips moving through the numbers. Angie finished and gave Heather a questioning look. "Think I'm controlling like Wayne?"

"Yeah, some."

Angie slammed the cash register shut, "Then I'll definitely have to think about it."

She grabbed the broad broom and started sweeping the aisles, shaking her head in amazement as she did. Heather followed with the mop, grinning.

Preaching point: *God's gracious, protective control.*

B Proper 27 (32) Psalm 127

Chapter 29: A Good Night's Sleep

Jack bent under his pack and panted deeply. "I calculate that was the day's steepest climb."

Hal stepped up to the small plateau beside him, "I suppose it'd be easier if we did this every day."

"Easier or we'd die," Jack said. "But this is the best view yet."

The two men in their early forties ran their thumbs under their pack straps and gazed over hill after hill of pine and fir trees on the Pacific Crest Trail. Jack unfolded the map and gestured to the northwest. "Looks like the lake's over one of these next turns."

"Well," Hal said, "let's hope it *turns* out all right."

"Oh, no. I'm going to suffer this for a week?"

"I guess some people just aren't very *punny*." Hal smiled wryly.

They were scouting for their church's week long senior high backpack the next month. Their hike would choose each night's campsite and note what precautions or special gear the students would need.

"One thing for sure," Jack said, "I'm going to sleep tonight. Every time we rest I could roll onto my side and plunge into unconsciousness. You too?"

"Mmm," Hal said as he stepped out to take the lead.

Two hours before dusk they arrived at their first camp. At the high altitude the air was starting to chill. Hal pulled off his pack and hurried to gather firewood. As he brought the first load of limbs and brush to the camp, he saw Jack erecting the tent. "That's it? That tiny thing?"

"It works great," Jack said. "Heidi and I've used it for years."

Hal looked stricken.

"What is it?" Jack asked. "You claustrophobic?"

"Mmm," Hal said, "better than weakly *aerobic*. Looks like a fabric sardine can." He dumped the wood and set to kindling the fire.

Although they hugged the heat of the small fire, the two didn't talk much while eating. With a tentative smile, Jack said, "We've got to abandon this little blaze and see if the sleeping bags can do their work."

"Their *smirk*?"

Jack could tell something was wrong, but what was there to do but to crawl into the tent? It was a little late to change plans. "You okay?"

"Yeah. I just have trouble getting to sleep sometimes."

"Oh boy. Now we find out."

"From a *lout*."

After they put out the fire, Jack shrugged, "I'll climb in first." He rustled and rolled for two minutes while Hal waited outside.

"I'm set," Jack called out. "Time for sardine number two."

"The bovine goes to slaughter with a *moo*."

When Hal was finally in his bag and the two were settled in the least uncomfortable positions, Jack said, "How *much* trouble do you have getting to sleep?"

"It's a usual thing," Hal said. "Most of my adult life."

For a while neither spoke. Finally Jack said, "I suppose you've tried medicine or sleep exercises or something." Then he waited, and Hal knew Jack was waiting not just to know what relief he'd sought in getting to sleep but to understand him; because clearly Hal was suffering just to admit his problem. After a long silence he said, "Started in boot camp for Army National Guard."

"I knew you were in the guard."

"So intense. Every minute you're doing what you're told, being yelled at, even when you think you're doing something right. You're in a group just like yourself. You're all defined as knuckleheads — and worse. We'd finally get to bed and we'd be so tired we could hardly speak a couple sentences to commiserate with one another, get some perspective on what's going on. I was so wound up, confused and ashamed at how poorly I was doing everything — I'd never been athletic — that at first I couldn't get to sleep. Soon I began forcing myself to stay awake to have unhindered, I called it 'unattacked,' time to think. Didn't expect it'd become a habit, kind of like an addiction that I couldn't break. And, yes, I've taken those pills and I won't do it again. Left me loopy. So," he said with a sigh, "there you have it. You go ahead and sleep and I'll do my best not to toss and turn much. At least you know."

After a minute Jack said, "I too had an addiction that lost my sleep. Doc called it a 'disorder.'" This surprised Hal as much as he'd surprised Jack. Another silence spread between them until Hal asked, "And?"

"As strange as yours, though not as long. I was addicted to study in grad school. All I thought of was my thesis. I was attempting to do in three years what others did in four. Along with the stipend, I calculated it was all the savings I had. I couldn't get a student loan. That's another story. But I guess not a totally different story. Yet like you, for different reasons, I almost never slept and then soon I couldn't sleep. I was one mixed up person and not nice to be around. Argued with most everyone in the department. Only one person I didn't alienate. A priest. He taught philosophy and I needed some touch with philosophy, a few quotes here and there to show I knew something about life beyond my field of study. This arthritic old man actually befriended me when I had no friends left. I found myself going to him with my problems, finally explaining to him what seemed like a trivial problem: I couldn't sleep.

"For him, it was a matter of faith. First thing he said, 'For he gives sleep to his beloved.' He also realized I had things in my past that were causing me problems. That was a matter of faith for him too. So this one afternoon when I popped in his office, red-eyed and weighing slightly more than a skeleton, he set about to talk seriously with me. He referred me to the Bible, he said, as the source of both good news *and* good advice. He said he had a text that he first prayed whenever he couldn't sleep: 'For he gives sleep to his beloved.' Basically, it was about God's loving him, God always surrounding him. It meant so much to him that it became his habit to recite whenever he lay down to sleep. 'For he gives sleep to his beloved.' I borrowed it from him, and his direction and prayer for me and his Bible verse slowly broke my addiction to studying and allowed me to sleep. 'For he gives sleep to his beloved.' I'm convinced it's helped me these years later finally to serve God instead of just myself. 'For he gives sleep to his beloved.' I cling to that verse. 'For he gives sleep to his beloved.' Kinds of like a spiritual pillow. Know what I mean?"

Hal began to snore.

Preaching point: *God's love offers not just ultimate, but immediate calm and security.*

A Lent 5; B Proper 5 (10); Proper 8 (13); Proper 14 (19) Psalm 130

Chapter 30: Fish And Flowers From The Depths

Jerry said, "Fine"; but he didn't appear fine to Vernon. It was after worship and people were milling in the church entryway. Vernon had sidled up and asked, "How's it going?" which brought the unbelievable answer, "fine." Vernon leaned closer and spoke quietly, "You don't look so fine."

Jerry shook his head and glanced down, "No, I'm not."

Vernon and Jerry had met serving on the church's building and grounds committee and had enjoyed one another during the two Saturdays they'd painted room after room. They had much in common: mid thirties, with young children, and their wives worked together at Springer Tech. Jerry said that he and his wife had been married before, which, as he put it, "does cause strange problems." Two of their children were from Virginia's first marriage. On the men's last Saturday afternoon painting, Jerry had said, "I wish I could go home and be as peaceful as here in church."

Vernon had said, "When the place is empty, of course it's peaceful," and they laughed.

Vernon wished he'd taken Jerry more seriously on that Saturday as they'd cleaned their brushes and tapped the lids onto the paint cans. He turned now to see his wife Karen walking their way, but he caught her eye and with his hand beside his hip motioned her away. "Well, hey," he said, "you free for lunch tomorrow? Let's get together."

On Monday at noon, Jerry was on time to meet Vernon in Blackburn's Café. They got the ordering out of the way quickly because both knew they were going to talk seriously. Vernon waited as Jerry took a deep breath, "It's not good with Ginny and me." He sucked in his lips. "Don't know what we're going to do."

Vernon nodded his head and waited.

"It's like anything and everything sets us off."

"What's pressing the angry buttons?" Vernon asked.

"Hah," Jerry said. "You won't believe it." He paused. "Flowers and fishing."

"You're right," Vernon said and smiled. "Makes no sense to me."

"Yeah, sitting here now it seems foolish. Started with the better weather. Spring's finally here and the high lakes just thawed. So, having no toil awaiting me on the building and grounds committee, I planned to spend Saturday fishing. Waited all winter for it. That's when Ginny hits me with her flowers. She has jumbo flower beds. Says now's the time to work the ground and all the wheelbarrows of manure it takes, you know, and spading. Says she can't do it herself, which is true; but she sneaked up on me. Didn't give me any lead time. I'd spent the last couple evenings laying out my rigging, unwinding the messes of three different sizes of leaders, and even oiled my reels — first time in four years. Then bing! She dumps her assignment on me: flower beds."

The waiter brought their food and Vernon said, "Go ahead and eat. Consider it marriage therapy."

That brought a grin from Jerry. "We sure need healing. Things descended from there. I don't know why. Sitting here, it doesn't seem like something to start a duel over. But the slightest irritation and our anger pops up like the head of a startled deer. Before we know it we're circling closer and closer around an issue, getting more and more tangled — like my tackle box before I cleaned it."

"Did you go fishing or help with the flowers?"

"I helped with the darned flowers, but I picked at her and she picked at me. We just sank deeper and deeper and neither of us could pull out of the cycle. Wasn't a good Saturday, let me tell you. You know, Vern, I'm worried we're circling the drain. Something happens with the kids, or even a problem with the car, and we end up at odds. Can't agree on anything, no matter how trivial."

"I've been praying for you," Vernon said. "Karen too, though

Fragments of Good News

you know she wouldn't say anything to Ginny."

"No, that'd cause more problems. But here's the frightening thing: we've both been through this before with our first spouses. We know it and even mention it sometimes, but we keep being pulled deeper and soon can't even see which way's up."

They'd almost finished their meal when the waiter brought the bill. Jerry said, "Well, that's it. What do you think?"

"I'm pleased you'd tell me," Vernon said, "but I don't have wheelbarrows of advice. Perhaps manure, but not advice," which gave them a chuckle. "I've got an idea where to start, though. You read biographies?"

"Sometimes," Jerry said, "depends."

"You're making me think of a book. Got it in a pile in the car to take to Goodwill. The hymn 'Amazing Grace,' you know the one? This book's the autobiography of the guy who wrote it. I'll give you the book. It's different enough from our world it catches your interest. I don't go for his blaming God for everybody who's killed or injured. I mean, when Jesus healed the crippled woman he didn't say, 'It pleased God that she couldn't stand upright for eighteen years.' He said, 'Satan bound her for eighteen years.' Yet this John Newton fellow crashed into all kinds of difficulties. He endured shipwreck and being held in slavery himself as well as being the captain of a slave ship before the Holy Spirit slipped into his life in a way that helped him live for Christ."

Jerry cocked his head sideways, "Wow."

"Different from your situation, but I've got the sense his experience can translate into your life with God and give you hope and the strength to love when the loving comes hard. And you know why it clicked in my mind to suggest his book?"

"Arguing with his wife?"

"No, because what you said about sinking deeper in your problems. He chose for a title of his autobiography *Out Of The Depths*, which is the first verse in Psalm 130. You and Ginny sure can use some professional help. Karen knows a really good marriage counselor. Just let us know and she'll get you in touch. But I think the book can also help, getting you in touch with God when you're in such a mess. I definitely suggest you memorize the beginning of the honest and desperate prayer of Psalm 130: 'Out of the depths I cry to you, O LORD. Lord, hear my voice!'"

Preaching point: *Desperate prayer.*

A Proper 15 (20); B Easter 2; Proper 7 (12) Psalm 133

Chapter 31: Unity

Pastor Drew was sitting beside Howie when Howie leaped up, pounded his fist in the air and screamed "Yeah!" A couple of the other fellows also yelled their excitement toward the theater's giant screen. There Matt Damon dramatized the South African national rugby team's defeat of New Zealand in the 1995 Rugby World Cup final in South Africa. None in Pastor Drew's young men's group had played rugby; but they all were engrossed in the movie.

Pastor Drew had read John Carlin's book *Playing The Enemy*, about Nelson Mandela's using rugby in South Africa to bring unity to the country. He suggested that the young men's group attend the movie about it: *Invictus*. Most had heard of it, one had already seen it. They'd agreed upon the Saturday matinee. Afterwards they drove to the church for donuts and discussion.

As the fellows clamored into chairs around the table Eric spoke up first, "I think I'll join a rugby club," which brought a roar from everyone. He weighed 105 pounds.

"Let's see your skill," Howie said. "Be a good sport. Throw me a donut."

Eric lobbed Howie a donut, spraying powdered sugar on him as he caught it. "Settles it," Howie said. "You can be the team manager tossing guys a beer as they stumble into the clubhouse."

The fellows slapped and pounded the table as they laughed. Howie raised his hands like a winner. After a few more jokes and comments, they were ready to turn their attention to Pastor Drew. "I wasn't aware of South Africa 25 years ago."

"No class on that in kindergarten?" Howie said, bringing another uproar.

"Yeah, yeah," Drew said, patting down the laughter with his hand, "but I learned from Carlin's book. The world and the

Christian church basically shut down South Africa for its racism: 90% of the population dominated by the other tenth until finally no world athletes attending competition in South Africa or their athletes allowed to compete in other nations. The mills of human history were grinding toward freedom. After Mandela was released from 27 years of imprisonment, in a few years he was president of South Africa." He paused and asked, "What scenes were most memorable for you?"

One young man answered with emotion in his voice, "The prison tour and Damon standing in Mandela's tiny cell. Damon did well in that scene. I just shuddered."

"I was glad the team took the tour there," Wendell said. "And I was pleased we saw their trip to the countryside to teach rugby to the black kids."

"Nothing like we've ever known," Eric said.

"And," Drew said, "all the time Mandela's maintaining the white government workers who'd served in the previous white administration, integrating even his bodyguard with whites and blacks. He's dealing with whites who want to keep their privileges and blacks who want revenge."

The group mumbled agreement. One said, "That Mandela. I'd never thought a person could do what he did. A little like Martin Luther King, Jr."

Drew tipped his head to the side to bring up a different dimension. "Easy to unite people around athletic victories. You see it with the Super Bowl, World Series and NBA championships. You get trophies, speeches, parades and a visit to the White House. We like athletic winners. Brings out the ticker tape. But consider that Hitler set out to use athletics to unite his people with the belief that Germans were the best human beings, the perfect human beings. What differences do you see between him and Mandela?"

"Hitler united people with arrogance and hate," Wendell said. "Mandela with forgiveness and love."

"Pretty basic, isn't it?" Drew said. "But so much easier to get people to fear and hate than to forgive and love. Mandela, this person of the great soul, didn't merely tell others to forgive. I was overwhelmed reading about it, let alone seeing it. He was concerned for the men who held him in prison. He knew his jailors' names and the names of their children. The overpowering strength of goodwill flowed from him."

"I was thinking of Jesus through the whole thing," Howie said. "His kind of loving strength finally sets the world right."

Eric made a broad gesture over the table, grabbing an air microphone and speaking with the voice of a sports announcer, drawing out: "Give me Jesus!"

The fellows all yelled their agreement.

Wendell pointed to Drew as he said, "You can tell that Mandela had done his work of unifying — at least the team — when the field announcer asked what it felt like to 'have 62,000 fans supporting you here in the stadium?' And the captain answered, 'We didn't have 62,000 fans behind us. We had 43 million South Africans.'"

"I'm glad I got to watch the movie with you guys," Drew said. "Every once in a while, even beyond the church, people understand that the deepest kind of unity in human life is generated through forgiveness." He paused, nodded toward them, then spoke with a broad smile. "You guys are about the best group I've ever been around. So," he raised his voice, "Eric, hand me, just *hand* me, a donut please," which Eric did. Then Drew said, "The test of unity is how people get along when they disagree with one another; you know, on opposite sides. So, another donut each and we'll cross the street to the middle school playground and have that basketball game we've been threatening each other with."

"Yeah," they yelled. Drew stepped back as Eric started tossing a donut at each one.

Preaching point: *Unity through the strong forgiveness of love.*

(John Carlin, Playing The Enemy: Nelson Mandela And The Game That Made A Nation.)

B Proper 20 (25) Proverbs 31:10-31

Chapter 32: A Capable Woman, Past And Present

Leon hadn't wanted to perform the funeral for his sister-in-law. He'd been retired from the pastorate for thirteen years. Plus, as he put it, he wasn't emotionally wired to perform a funeral for a dead loved one. Yet his nephews and nieces — as well as his brother — were living loved ones and they as much as begged him to minister to them in their need.

The songs had been sung. Proverbs 31:10-31 was read. Pastor Leon gripped the lectern, coughed, breathed deeply and said:

The Book of Proverbs collects the wisdom of the ancient world and centers it on life among the twelve Hebrew tribes that became Israel and Judah. Proverbs has a lot to say about women, and not much of it flattering. Yet at the end of the book, the last chapter talks about "a capable wife," or, it can be translated, *a woman of strength*. Through this woman's activities, Proverbs records everyday life in a culture far removed from ours, where females were less valuable than males and they certainly didn't vote or even speak up in a town meeting. However, although we must reach across millennia, oceans, and cultures, we can more than appreciate this description of a "woman of strength," we can understand it as we think of how much of it describes Arline.

A woman of strength. It takes strength to love. Love takes effort. A weak person can't love with a self-giving, sacrificing love. A weak person merely surrenders to the will of others. Love, on the other hand, is decidedly work. Love can be the drabbest of labor and involve the deepest of suffering. Lots of people think of love in Hollywood terms — a thrilling first kiss, romantic moonlight nights, fantasies of living happily ever after.

Maybe love is a little of that sometimes; but, when viewed over a lifetime, such things don't occur often.

You can spot love in a woman who cares for her household day by day, enjoying family and friends while working at life's duties. The day-in-day-out life recorded of the woman in Proverbs 31 isn't all a woman does do or can do — then or now. But it pictures the daily living, even the drudgery, in which real love shows itself, no matter the era or culture.

No one makes a person care for family and friends. Only love, though maybe the word isn't used at the time, only love can keep a person going day by day in life's ritual chores, no matter the toll it might take upon one's health or life span.

Think about Arline. Among other things, the word "strong" must come to your minds, or you don't know what strong means. "Energetic" at least. Arline was a person in charge, able to make plans, and carry them out. And people knew it. She had a strong will to go along with a love for life. A capable, knowledgeable, talented person, she was doubly appreciated because she directed her strength for the good of others: her family — first and always her family — but also her friends, her community, her students.

She was enthusiastic and joyful, genteel and downright fun, easy to be around, and worth being around, because her life was centered around Christ and his love for the world. So people loved her in response. She was your beloved wife, sister-in-law, mother, mother-in-law, grandmother. She was your colleague, fellow church member, friend. She was capable of much not just because she took notice of details, but because she lived her faith by caring for others. You'll most remember her for her deep loves and long friendships. You'll think of her at the house, at church, at work, at school, on vacations, and in service organizations, because you there received her love — love, every day common love, and everyday extraordinary love, from God to Arline to you. In her own time and place, she in so many ways duplicated that ancient "woman of strength" in the Bible.

A woman of strength. And so Arline's family agrees with the family in Proverbs 31, verses 28 and 29, "Her children rise up and call her happy," or, as the older translations put it, *blessed*. "Her husband too, and he praises her: 'Many women have done excellently, but you surpass them all.'"

Our Biblical passage concludes: "Charm is deceitful, and beauty is vain, but a woman who fears the LORD is to be praised. Give her a share in the fruit of her hands, and let her works praise her in the city gates."

That's also the last word in the whole book of Proverbs. It won't be the last said about Arline. But for now it's appropriate for all of us to thank God for the gift of Arline, and it's necessary for us to release her and to entrust her to God's eternal love.

Pastor Leon stood silently grasping the lectern. There was nothing else he was prepared to say and nothing more he was able to say. His ten seconds of stillness at the lectern allowed everyone present to silently agree with him and — as Bible certainly intended — to infinitely expand on what the book of Proverbs said …about Arline.

Preaching point: *A biblical ideal observed in modern life.*

A Advent 2 Isaiah 11:1-10

Chapter 33: Less Than A Peaceable Kingdom

Lanny had wanted to work at Peaceable Kingdom since her parents took her there when she was eleven. The street side of the zoo's main building reproduced a giant portion of one of Edward Hick's paintings of "The Peaceable Kingdom." The sign was heaped with round, furry animals like a special welcome for her. The zoo then became the site of her birthday party every year. When she was fifteen, she heard a snooty acquaintance behind her say, "Isn't she a bit old for such things?" Lanny had little difficulty shrugging off attempts to shame her and a month before she graduated from high school, she applied to work at the zoo that had granted her joy and aimed her toward her future profession. She was going to be a veterinarian. After two years as a steady employee, she was promised a summer job as she went off to college.

Three summers later, Lanny was now ashamed of Peaceable Kingdom in a way she'd never imagined. She and her boyfriend had grabbed the first warmth of summer to spend the day at the beach. It was a long drive but they enjoyed every minute of the sun after a cold, wet spring. They drove back in the dark. Lanny jerked to her right and pointed back to a field they passed, "What's that on the right?"

"Didn't look," Mitchell said. He was using his energy to fight off sleep and he was distracted by sunburn on his bald spot that he'd forgotten to slather with sunscreen.

"Just caught a glimpse of it, but looked like a billboard with Peaceable Kingdom's sign."

Next day at work, she found that Peaceable Kingdom had been sold. First thing she said when she arrived home to her parents' house after work: "How can you sell wild animals, and why didn't they tell us instead of waiting a month after the fact?"

"I thought it might be coming," her father said. "Heard a rumor downtown; but didn't want to bother you. Might not've been true."

"Aaah!" she screamed, then jerking her hands into her stomach, she ran to her room. She shook off her green coveralls and threw them at her closet door. When she came to the dinner table her mother was ready to comfort her, "They didn't say anything about your job, did they?"

"No," she said with a surprised look. "I didn't consider that."

"Don't think you've got a worry," her father said. "Altogether you've worked there longer than most anybody."

"They're turning it into a big business."

"Well," her father said, "if it doesn't crank out a profit, it can't continue. Everything's got to make a profit. That's what they pay you with."

"I know. I know," Lanny said, waving her hand in front of her, "but that billboard I saw last night? They're going to line the interstate for a hundred miles in every direction. 'Peaceable Kingdom, Peaceable Kingdom.' Who's going to believe that it's not really just about profit when they plaster the countryside like the sacrilege of Wall Drug signs strung across South Dakota? It's like they're exploiting the animals."

Her father pulled his lips to the side, "Vets advertise now. Nothing new. When I was a kid, no professionals advertised, the just used the yellow pages. Now every kind of dentist and doctor. Other day I heard about an ad for a proctologist —."

"Trevor!" Her mother said.

He laughed and Lanny chuckled despite her rage. "It's like they're somehow abusing the animals. And," she put a hand on her chest, "I'm part of it. That implicates me."

Two weeks later Lanny came home to announce at dinner, "The new company's putting a lot of money into Peaceable Kingdom. Not just the expense of those ugly billboards."

"Great," her mother said. "That otter pond is pretty shabby."

Her father said, "And the lemurs —."

"Not money in that direction," Lanny said. "They're going for an elephant."

Her parents were stunned. After a few seconds her father said, "Where they going to put an elephant? They're fit to burst now."

"Ruby walked through the office and the new manager in conference with 'his deputies' said they'll dig up that new parking lot."

"That dinky spot?" her mother said. "That's hardly large enough for a dozen cars. That's no space for such a beast. Isn't there a law or some kind of regulation about space needed for animals?"

"Don't know," Lanny said. "Haven't had a course in veterinary law yet." She stared into her dinner plate and said, "I'm going to hand in my two week notice tomorrow."

Her father stretched back with a gasp. Her mother leaned forward, "Honey, just six more weeks, then back to college. You need that money."

Lanny shook her head, "Can't do that."

Her father smiled and tried to sound positive. "You can hold on for six weeks out there. I know you can. You're tough."

Lanny put her fork on her plate with a clang, "I'm going to quit. I can't take part in this."

"Honey," her mother said, "vets face things like this the all the time — healing animals but dealing with people. There's nothing perfect. No job —."

"No perfect family," her father said with a laugh.

"Dad!"

"Hush, Trevor," her mother said, but her father had to finish his laughing. Then he said, "Tell you what: you're the one who's working there; but, if you quit, we're the ones who'll be tossing in the extra money you need for your senior year. So, since we're involved in this too, do us this favor: Wait a week. Talk to Mitchell and Ruby about it. Think and pray about it. See if you can adjust to living in this world that isn't perfect. We all have to do it somehow, and it's a matter," he pitched his voice higher, "of how are you going to live in a less than peaceable world?"

Preaching point: *Both the human and the animal worlds portray creation in need of renewal.*

A Baptism of the Lord (1) Isaiah 42:1-9

Chapter 34: The Perfect Candidate

"I don't see why we have to hurry," Shirley said.

"Because," Wendy said, "Greenwald's doing a flyby. He's an important agent and he's only agreed to consider you as a favor. He's giving us a few minutes. He says it's best if right now no one connects him with your campaign. So when we get inside, don't get stopped by a conversation. No eye-contact. Just right through to a back table."

As soon as they entered Denny's Restaurant, Wendy asked to be seated at a back table and told the greeter they had another guest arriving. Shirley did as she was told and followed with her head down as though inspecting the floor. "Don't see why this has to be so hush-hush," she said after they'd been seated.

"It's a major sneak," Wendy said. "As far as the party's concerned, you're going to be the candidate from nowhere, and...." She looked across the dining room to the entrance and jumped up. "It's Greenwald," she said. He spotted her wave and buttoned his blazer as he walked to their booth. Shirley figured he was about 55: both his age and his pounds overweight. She stood as Wendy said, "Shirley, this is Greenwald, who might agree to work as your campaign manager."

"Hi, hi, hi," he said as he shook her hand and squeezed into the booth across from the two smiling women. "Really glad to meet you, Shirley. Wendy's filled me in on a lot. Decided for sure, then, the state's sixth representative district?"

Shirley nodded.

"Wendy says you're a natural and sounds like she's the right chairperson," he smiled at Wendy. He spread his hands toward Shirley, "so tell me, how do you see it?" He looked at Shirley and Wendy was about to answer when the waitress came for their order.

Fragments of Good News

"Back to business," he said as he looked at his watch. "Got to dash up state and be at the capital for the 1:30 debate in the senate. Sure you don't want to run for the senate? I've led four successful campaigns for state senators."

Wendy said, "I agree. Shirley's everything a senator can be."

Shirley said quietly, "Representative."

"Sure?"

"Sure."

"Then, let's hear what we've got to work with."

"I've made notes," Wendy put in. "First, Shirley's absolutely clean. Unimpeachable reputation. One husband, two kids, no dirt."

Shirley leaned back and raised her eyelids, "Good start?"

Greenwald and Wendy laughed. "Just kidding," Wendy said. "But look what our committee — in secret, by the way — has planned. Before Platter knows what hit him, we'll have advertisements plastered around town and buzzing on the radio. Beginning May 1. Testimonials all the way from her first grade teacher to her father-in-law. Platter's reelection folk will be at 'ready' and we'll be at 'go.' When they hear about her, people who haven't voted for decades will be lining up at the courthouse to register. Our citizens will know instantly she's a family and consumer science teacher —"

"What?" Greenwald cut her off. "Never heard of it."

"Home economics," Shirley said, smiling.

Wendy went on, "and a marathoner. She'll leave the opposition in her draft as she speeds by. We've even come up with a jingle for her campaign."

"Let's hear it," Greenwald said.

"It's a secret," Wendy said, pursed her lips and shook her head.

Greenwald smiled at the amateurish approach to campaigning. "All right," he said. "So you're going to catch the Platter people flat-footed. They'll only see your backside as you advance in the distance. Go on."

Wendy chuckled and continued. "All Platter does is tell our

citizens they need to give less and receive more. Anybody who disagrees with him, he turns into a boogeyman and pins a nasty name on them, and —."

"I know all that," Greenwald said. He turned again to Shirley, who was listening to Wendy and tracing her finger in the ring of water on the table from her glass of Diet Pepsi. The two women had been friends since they started as rookie high school teachers fifteen years before. Shirley trusted Wendy's estimation of what she could accomplish by serving under the state's great seal in the House of Representatives. She took a couple breaths as Wendy and Greenwald waited for her. She cleared her throat, then, "Primarily, I plan not to say anything against the personality of my opponent. No name-calling. Just the issues. I don't put others down. I can take people disagreeing with me and not get angry. I've been doing it with students for fifteen years."

Greenwald squinted and tipped his head to the side.

"I want to break the pattern of campaigns in this state … and the pattern of governing. I'll go as far as agreeing with Wendy when she's interviewed as campaign chairperson. She's set to talk about restoring demo-crazy with democracy. I won't say that, but I'll agree with her."

"Pretty good, huh?" Wendy said stifling a chuckle.

Greenwald extended his hand to Shirley to continue.

"I plan to restore civility to politics. I'll treat others in the state house as I have always treated my students."

"We've got a bunch of her old students ready to give testimonials," Wendy said.

Greenwald grimaced and motioned to Shirley to continue.

"I will emphasize that democracy is for everyone and not just struggling to get favors for our family and friends. This is the way our democracy was meant to operate: society working together, protecting the weak and enhancing life for all."

When the women's lunch arrived, Greenwald glanced at his watch again.

Wendy rushed to say, "Shirley will be a shining light, an example, a model for others. She'll bring a new spirit to government. She was born for this."

"I've got to hit the road," Greenwald said as he shifted out of the booth. "Shirley," he said, extending his hand for a shake, "really glad to meet you. And Wendy, I assume I'm to communicate with you if I agree to come aboard on this campaign?"

He made it out of the booth and stood. Wendy also stood and hustled behind him. "Right back," she said to Shirley. She caught up with Greenwald in the parking lot as he unlocked his maroon Mercedes. "What do you think?" she asked with a broad smile. "You can see: no long-winded speeches."

He spoke fast, "Seems you think those boys upstate don't have any more quarters to plunk in the political machine."

"I know it won't be easy," Wendy said, smiling again. "But what do you think about Shirley as a candidate?"

He swung onto the seat with a thump and continued to speak quickly, "I don't think she's got a chance in this world." He closed the door and lowered the window. "But, tomorrow I'll send you an email with a contract for my fees and services."

Preaching point: *God's kind of ruler has no earthly chance to succeed.*

ABC Passion/Palm Sunday; B Proper 19 (24) Isaiah 50:4-9a

Chapter 35: Beyond Comparison

On Wednesday night, eleven-fifteen, Pastor Balken halted outside his front door, lifted his chin and put a deliberate smile on his face. His wife Aileen heard him enter and met him as he took of his coat. "Does the Lutheran pastor need a hug?" She said.

He swung toward her with an even broader smile, "What do you mean?"

"How many church members came?"

His chin and shoulders dropped. "None."

Aileen hugged him. She'd acknowledged it was worth a try: "Bible and Beer" at the local tavern. Outside the church, he'd asked, where's Luther's heritage as appropriate as in a pub, considering his saying that the gospel ran its course as he drank his glass of Wittenberg beer?

"And I only drank one beer," he said. "At least it was a St. Pauli Girl." He drew Aileen near for another hug.

He'd advertised his newest pastoral experiment in the weekly bulletin, monthly newsletter, and local newspaper. "An informal time to talk about the Christian faith." He'd gone prepared with a handful of *Today's Readings*, the coming Sunday's Bible texts printed on the handy scripture sheets so church members who'd join him could at least glance at the coming Sunday's Bible texts. He pulled the stack from his pocket and slapped them onto the kitchen table, pulled the tab from his clergy shirt, and slumped onto a chair.

"Some coffee to sober up?" Aileen asked, giving him a chuckle. She sat next to him, patted his knee, "So tell me. Wild women? Bar fights? Wild women?"

"Hah," Pastor Balken said. "The closest table to me was a married couple discussing their divorce — rather amiably, I will say — and how to distribute their debts." He shook his head. "Basically others steered clear when they saw my collar. A couple Catholics, who don't know their local priest, said, 'Hi Father.'"

"Well, you are a father," Aileen said with another pat.

He grinned. "Just bothers me that people clamored to see Jesus when he entered Jerusalem, not to mention his impact on all western civilization, yet the church has spun down to mediocrity until agnosticism is the default spiritual position."

"What did you do besides drink German beer?"

"After a while I heard two at the bar debating the physical assets and skills of Russel Wilson and Tom Brady." He paused. "They're football players."

"Oh," she said.

"So I said a prayer and took a stool next to them. They welcomed me and asked my opinion about the two football stars. I figured the safest was to say Wilson was better. That got me in. Nice fellas. Seems they spend a lot of time at the bar in front of the TV. They asked me why I chose Wilson. I admitted it was because of glances at the *Seattle Times* sports section.

"That's when I thought I'd move toward things spiritual. So okay, I didn't spend much time comparing football players. I didn't tell them I never watch football. I said that on Sundays I was in worship and I spent my time comparing people like Martin Luther with the apostle Paul. They listened politely enough to let me go on. I quickly stated that Paul on a road from Jerusalem to Damascus had his religious turnaround from Judaism to Jesus and fifteen centuries later in Germany, Luther was released from a frightening legalism into a free and joyful faith.

"They nodded their heads a little and looked up to the TV a few times. 'It's about Jesus Christ,' I said. 'He started it. Easter'll be here in a week or so. That's when it began, with his resurrection.' I pulled out the scripture pages and gave them each one. I pointed to the Isaiah text. After Jesus' resurrection, the New Testament church made their comparisons too. Hundreds of years before Christ, Isaiah talked about what it's like to be God's person with a special and overwhelming message of God's loving activity.

After Jesus' followers experienced his resurrection, they looked at this Isaiah passage and saw how much it was like Jesus' ministry. The similarities were so startling that God was obviously linking those ancient words with Jesus' life, death and resurrection."

He took a deep breath and let it out slowly. Aileen waited. He puffed out his cheeks. She asked, "And...?"

"They made their excuses and left."

"Think you'll see them in worship Sunday?"

"Don't expect them. If I want to see them again, I suppose I'll have to go to the pub with all those bar fights and wild women."

"Going to mention this in worship on Palm Sunday?"

Pastor Balken rubbed his knuckles on his cheek. "Don't know right now; but I was sure thinking about it on the way home. I seemed to come from an alien world; and, when I felt such anxiety just mentioning a few things about the faith, how does that compare with the opposition to Isaiah's ministry, not to mention Jesus's? I wouldn't call my evening — and remember, it's just the first time — I wouldn't call it a failure. Yet my gratitude for Isaiah and Jesus has grown hugely. Compared to the weight of their difficult ministries and their suffering, I experienced about an ounce and a half."

Preaching point: *Isaiah's life and message predicted Jesus' suffering in dogged obedience to God.*

ABC Good Friday Isaiah 52:13-58:12

Chapter 36: Bearing Our Infirmities

On Tuesday morning while Jeanie Graft was on her knees reaching deep into a shelf, shuffling small boxes of number eight two-inch screws to the right and returning the number six two-inch screws to the left, she heard, "Hey Jeanie."

The voice came from the end of the aisle and she hadn't quite identified it before she was able to manipulate her head out of the shelf and toward the sound. She watched Mr. Corey, her high school biology teacher advancing with his huge smile. She slid on her knees back from the shelf and used a hand to help her stand, "Hi, Mr. Corey," she said. She waited for him to speak next, knowing he would. He was a great talker.

"Good to see you," he said. "Didn't know you were back in town."

"Yeah," she answered with a forced smile. "Been working for Dad for a couple months."

"You were in…"

"Portland," she answered.

"And how long you say you've been back in the hardware store?"

"Six weeks. Feels like two months." She gave a sideways grin.

"Haven't seen you in worship."

Ordinarily Jeanie wouldn't appreciate such an observation, but she'd known Mr. Corey all through high school. Two years ago in her senior year, she was in his last advanced biology class before he retired. "No," she said, and didn't quite tell the truth, "working in the store."

"You're looking swell," Mr. Corey said. He tipped up his voice. "Hope you're glad to be home."

"Not every day," she said as she dipped her head and attempted a laugh.

Mr. Corey stood silently a moment, looking serious. "You still drink that perfumed coffee you spilled on the dissected frog?"

That brought a genuine smile from her. "Yeah, a definite addiction, twice a day."

"How about coffee together sometime?"

Jeanie was pleased to agree. She hadn't taken many steps toward melting into the town again. Other than her family and a few in Graft's Hardware, she'd only met up with one high school friend.

On Thursday at Tim's Coffees, as soon as they sat at their table, Mr. Corey leaned over his cup and asked, "Why you home?"

Jeanie came expecting this. It's the relationship they'd always had. She wagged her head slowly, "Nothing, just nothing worked."

"Nothing?" He bent further over his coffee. Jeanie rearranged herself in her chair, closing her eyes, then taking a deep breath. After a moment or two Mr. Corey said, "Big city life?"

"No," she said, too loud for the coffee shop. People near her turned. She lowered her head and her voice, "that's the thing. Not just in the big city. Everywhere."

"I'm not following," he said with spread hands.

"I'll give you an example. You know my oldest brother, Darrell, he teaches in the middle school."

"Not well. Never had him in class."

"I come home and one of the first things he tells me is how many of the middle school teachers are divorcing and marrying spouses of other middle school teachers and the bunch that's switching around and not even marrying. Any different in the high school?"

He made a waffling gesture with his hand. "Could be."

"And that's the world. Not the protected little place I grew up in and learned about in school and church. The internet glows with stories of pedophiles and payoffs. Our national leaders act like fifth graders on the playground. Calling each other names and sounding like 'My dad can beat up your dad.' And my fellow citizens seem to love that kind of stuff. You're going to have to forgive me, but I just don't see much integrity left in individuals or groups. Everyone's in it for themselves and no concern for anyone else." She bit her lower lip with a sigh.

Mr. Corey spoke slowly, almost solemnly, "You've earned another A. This time in recognizing reality." He paused, then, "You talk to your folks about this?"

"Not a word."

"How about Darrell?"

"I've hinted at it, but he comes out with 'cynic' and I just leave it."

Mr. Corey stirred in two teaspoons of sugar and Jeanie took courage in his obvious acceptance of her. "I've thought about it a lot. And, no, you haven't seen me at church."

He nodded and clucked his tongue, "I can tell you're angry; and this …this is what I think: You're angry because you're disillusioned, like you've been lied to about life and you don't find anything you can trust. You're not the first with the affliction."

"Close enough. There's a bunch more. But that's enough, way more than enough."

Mr. Corey took a sip of coffee and so did Jeanie and they sat quietly hunched over their cups. Mr. Corey maintained his bright look and the sound in his voice, "Tell you what: You working on Sunday?"

"Late afternoon to closing."

"Would you come to worship with Marie and me? And," he raised his hand to prevent her from refusing, "and we'll take you to a pre-worship event that might help you some."

"What?"

"Something that happens every Sunday. Has happened every Sunday for longer than I know. What do you say?"

His inviting smile won her agreement. On Sunday, Mr. Corey and his wife Marie picked her up at her parent's house at 10:15. Marie was in the back seat. "Here," Mr. Corey patted the passenger's seat. "Sit up here with me."

"We've got plenty of time to get to church," she said.

"First," Mr. Corey said, "we're going somewhere else."

Mr. Corey drove to the Lifecare Center and parked across the street half a block away. "Right here 10:30 most every Sunday morning, worship begins, worship of the one we say 'has borne our infirmities and carried our diseases.'"

In a few minutes a twenty-year-old four-wheel-drive Ford pickup drew up and parked in front of the Lifecare main door. A stooped, gray-haired man stepped out and limped inside.

"What?" Jeanie asked.

"Doc Fuerney. You probably never went to him. He's been retired fifteen years at least, but he's been coming to this spot every Sunday morning before worship as long as we've been in town. We know because one Sunday we had to drive this route when our street flooded. Saw him years ago. We've never talked about it, though others know."

The three sat facing the Lifecare door. It opened and a wheelchair came out with a thin, white-haired lady crunched sideways. She was waving her limp wrists and talking incessantly, showing the lack of half her teeth. Doc Fuerney pushed her wheelchair.

"Beth Summers," Mr. Corey said. "She's been this way from birth. Cerebral palsy. Affected both her body and mind. You might never have noticed her. He wheels her into the back of worship."

"I've seen her," Jeanie said.

"She's there every Sunday Doc's in town."

They watched Doc Fuerney lift Beth from her chair into his pickup then put her wheelchair in the back. None of the three spoke.

"He'll take her into worship through the alley and then return her here after worship. I'm sure he'll do it until one of them dies," Mr. Corey said. "Whenever Marie or I think life's been tough on us or the world's swirling down the drain because love and integrity have fled the earth, we drive here to begin worship."

Marie leaned over from the back seat, "We're willing to pick you up any Sunday and drive by here if you'd like."

Jeanie didn't say anything; but, she was swallowing hard when she nodded her head.

Preaching point: *God's Spirit is recognized in selfless service.*

A Proper 13 (18) Isaiah 55:1-5

Chapter 37: A (Really) Free Lunch

Other kids circled around, a few in a shoving game, some chattering and giggling; but Monica looked over the crowd until she spied the two who looked her way. She was sure she had their attention. "Come on. We have plenty." She held up two sack lunches. The girl appeared to be about nine and the boy eight. They were both skinny with black, fly-away hair. The girl gently restrained the boy from moving forward. Monica raised her arm to point behind her at the banner roped over the park gate:

> SUMMER LUNCH PROGRAM
> FIRST UNITED METHODIST CHURCH
> The Church In The Heart Of The City
> With A Heart For The City

The children were old enough to read; yet, they remained a dozen feet outside the orb of the other kids. Again, Monica, on tip toes, spoke over the group to the two. "A lunch for each of you."

When they didn't come closer, Monica stepped beyond the serving center and wove her way through the crowd like going through a turnstile. She watched the two. The little boy nudged the girl to go forward to the lunches. The little girl held him back. Monica didn't know what was going on, but when she was eight feet from them, she got down on a knee, as she would to pet a new dog, and said, "We have a lunch for each of you."

The little girl turned around and led the boy away. The boy was looking back. Monica stayed where she was and spoke after them, "We'll be here all summer. Back tomorrow. We've got enough for everybody."

Monica stayed on her knee until Ralph came. He looked down, "You need help?"

"Yes," she said, and, as he lifted her, she moaned a little. "Arthritis, gets worse every year."

"Mine too." Ralph pointed to the two children as they left. "Those kids didn't get lunches."

"Don't know why. I tried. We'll wait."

"It's your decision," Ralph said. "In fact, it's your baby."

"Thanks," Monica said. It was her baby. She'd read about summer lunch programs in other churches and cities. She convinced her church's retired group: "*Retired* Christians are not retired *Christians*." She pushed the idea at the church council. She and a handful of others presented their project in two stages to the city council that finally granted permission to work out the details with the parks department. The congregation pitched in for months to raise money. Now on her creaky knees she moved back to the picnic table and helped the others pack up for the day.

The next noon, the Methodists were back to string up the banner and set up the lunches and drinks. Dozens of neighborhood children occupied swings and other playground equipment or just jostled one another where yesterday's line up for the lunches was. Monica noticed a police car park across from the lunch center. Good, she thought. The city council kept their word to encourage and protect our mission.

Most lunches had been distributed — and the scooping of ice cream begun — when Monica spotted the two children from the day before. They walked across the park's poorly mown grass with a woman. She appeared tired, about 40, and had an inquisitive look on her face. They stopped ten yards away and the woman bent to talk with the children. The little girl pointed to Monica and still the three stayed distant. Monica saw the police officer approach the three. He said something to the girl, nodded, and smiled to the woman. Monica left the food center and, as she came up to them, the officer walked back to his cruiser.

"Everything okay?" Monica asked.

"Okay," the woman said. She shooed the children toward the lunch center and they ran by Monica.

"Sure?"

"Yeah," she said and chuckled. "They're my neighbor's kids. I sit them three days a week and yesterday was the first time I let them come alone to the park."

Monica glanced back to the two children as they received their lunches.

"Francine came home and told me about the lunches but she was scared. She heard about a man in a park who gave children candy and warned them they must become radical... ah... Muslims or something. With everything on TV, she didn't know what to do."

"Oh," Monica said. "Well, we're going to be here all summer. We'll mostly be the same people. That should make it less frightening for the kids."

The woman nodded. "I was pretty sure this would be okay, but I told Francine I'd talk with the police and come with them today and check it out."

Monica laughed, "Police! Not what I expected, but that's fine. I suppose the kids told you about our sign and that we're Methodists and that set your mind at rest."

"No," the woman said, "because you didn't wag your finger and tell them what they must do, but you got down on your knee."

Preaching point: *When God offers us a gift, it is truly good for us — and for others.*

C Proper 17 (22) Jeremiah 2:4-13

Chapter 38: The Old Egyptian

On a clear morning in the first oasis east of Tahpanhes, the old Egyptian gathered the group of children. He waved away three sheep and spread his rug in the shade of a palm tree, careful to miss the sheep manure. Each child or two also brought a small rug to sit on. "Your clan rescued me in the desert and I'll earn my keep as your teacher." He spoke while getting comfortable on his rug. "That's what you need to know about me and why you're here today." As their parents had instructed them, the thirteen children sat looking attentively at the oldest man they'd ever seen. Once seated, he scooted himself nearer to the oasis's spring whose water was trickling into a trough. He spoke Hebrew with a decided Egyptian accent. The children, having heard both Hebrews and Egyptians all their lives, understood him well. They often translated the Egyptians' language for their older relatives. "I'll be here with your tribe to tell you what you need to know to live well. You already can herd sheep, cook meals, and pack, unpack, and pitch your tents. I'll tell you day by day about life itself, life with one another and with God." No child moved.

"First, you need to know that your people haven't always been here in Egypt." The old Egyptian spoke in a quiet growl, "Of course, some of your relatives were in Egypt 1,500 years ago. But your immediate families only arrived two generations ago, fleeing from Judah which is northeast of here, a three weeks walk for you children."

Each child peered at the old man. They were as intrigued by the shaggy appearance of the ancient human heap in front of them as by the words that rumbled from his mouth. At the end of the day they must return to their family tents and repeat what he told them and they'd be punished if they couldn't give a good accounting of the old teacher's stories.

"Your great-grandparents arrived here when I was a child. They'd abandoned their homeland, hopeless that they could live peacefully, being occupied by the Babylonians who kept conquering them. You know what that means?" he said, pointing to the largest boy, perhaps ten or eleven years old. The boy was startled and answered, "Uhh."

"It means the Babylonian armies had thrashed the armies of your nation Judah and its allies. It means your great-grandparents were a beaten people. That's who you are: You remain in Egypt as a defeated people. Did you know that?" he asked, pointing to a little girl. No matter what she knew, she had the presence of mind to nod yes and look confident.

He coughed heavily, turning his head down and away from the children. "Because I don't know how long I'll be worth your tribe's providing for me, it's important to tell you about two men your great-grandparents dragged around with them. They brought a prophet along with his helper: Jeremiah and Baruch. The two didn't want to join your great-grandparents escaping from Judah, but once here they continued to serve your one God, the Lord Yahweh.

"Although you live on the edge of Egypt with its array of gods, this one God whom you Hebrews worship always summons you — points to you personally, no matter what group you're sitting in — to be faithful to his way of life, meaning treating others justly and kindly, as Yahweh does with you. And if you don't first live justly and kindly with others, you won't live with Yahweh. That was Jeremiah's message and his entire life. He started serving Yahweh when he was your age." He pointed to a boy on his rug. "And he served until he was as old as I am." Two children covered their mouths as they giggled.

The old Egyptian paused as a small swirl of wind sent a sprinkling of sand onto his rug. He looked at the newly deposited sand and said, "Jeremiah talked about a kind of life that doesn't blow away with the sand. He told your people — I heard him — he told them about being faithful to Yahweh-God. You're supposed to love Yahweh's kind of mercy, which means caring for the most vulnerable and needy people and not trying to get every good thing just for yourself. When you live Yahweh's life, it becomes satisfying to care for others. His life becomes who you are."

He took a deep breath, wagging his head slowly side to side. The children wondered if he'd be able to keep speaking. "Jeremiah proclaimed that Yahweh's people must know what's worthwhile in life, what will last, what this living we do every day is all about. Our human lives won't last long. I know that as I see the rope of my life burning ever closer to the end.

"He constantly taught how useless idols are. You've bumped into them in the villages and tents of others, those little statues you'd think were dolls to play with. People paint then, clothe them, bow to them, kiss them, and pretend to feed them. You've seen that?" He pointed to the back of the group. The boy must have been listening carefully, for he answered, "Yes, sir. Father says they think that's worship."

"And I'm here to tell you, show you if I can, where that kind of worship leads. I've seen it, watched it here in Egypt and Jeremiah convinced me — even if he wasn't always able to teach your ancestors — that your one God, not a group or a family of gods, deserves our complete attention, constant worship, and the devotion of our lives. There's no comparison between those worthless idols and your God Yahweh."

He turned to the spring beside him. "Yahweh and the life he offers is like this cool, flowing water. You look forward to coming to this oasis for the water don't you?" They all nodded. "Then think of it this way. Yahweh offers a life to his people like this water. And those who turn away from Yahweh are like those trying to store water in cracked cisterns. They're as pitiful as those who'd direct this clear spring into a channel that just empties into the sand." The children looked appalled. "Don't want that to happen, do you?"

"No," they all spoke together, shaking their heads.

While the old Egyptian had taught, the shadow of the tree had moved so that now he squinted and tipped his head to the side in order stay out of the sun without moving his whole body. He seemed to use all his strength to conclude, "I don't want you children to become worthless and wasteful with an idolatrous life. To begin life within your one God, obey Yahweh as you do your parents and trust his love for you as much as you trust your parents' love. You'll learn more about life for Yahweh, but that's a beginning." Without another word, he swished a hand back and forth to send them away.

When the children were gone, he took a long time struggling to his feet. He shuffled toward his host's tent, dragging his rug, and listening to the bleating of the sheep. He seemed almost like Jeremiah, wondering how long these ex-patriot Judeans would keep carrying around someone whose only value was to tell them about Yahweh.

Preaching point: *Will a new generation listen to Jeremiah's message?*

B Lent 5; ABC Reformation Day Jeremiah 31:31-34

Chapter 39: Remember Their Sin No More

Colin realized he was on his back. Straps held his body tightly and he was being bounced. A siren vibrated all around him. It felt like it took an hour, but he was finally able to open one eye to a slit and see an emergency medical technician, who bit his lip nervously. The few seconds of consciousness was all he needed to determine he was in an ambulance. The last thing Colin recalled was stepping into the crosswalk toward his office building as he did every morning by 7:55. But now with a mere twilight ability to think he didn't aim his concentration upon the immediate past. With a mere scrap of his mind to work with, only one thing from the past mattered and that one thing vaulted him toward the future.

Fear of death propelled his limited thinking toward having to face God. His childhood pastor often spoke of the horror of facing God in the judgment. He scattered warnings of mortal sins throughout his sermons as children throw sand at the waves. Colin had heard all the standard — even the best — Christian reasons to act morally and not to sin. That's why, since he was seventeen, he'd been haunted by the thought of facing God. He'd sinned, knew he'd sinned. It was an embarrassing out-of-his-character sin and no matter how he'd attempted to approach God on tip-toes to admit the sin and explain the circumstances, he was never satisfied he'd thoroughly confessed the harm he feared his sin might cause to others. Worse, he was never certain God forgave him.

Throughout his life, this one sin and his dread of facing God in judgment occupied Colin's dreams. Always in the dream God waited somewhere to condemn him, and this nightmare — God didn't always just wait, but inched toward Colin with heaven's final calculation of eternal condemnation.

Fragments of Good News

It was Colin's private sin. No one knew, never his childhood friends nor his wife who often woke him as his screams shook the dust off the bedroom light fixtures. No matter his weeping, shaking, or sweating, he couldn't tell her the content of the dreams or what he knew to be the source.

In a dream, God approached as a gelatinous tornado sweeping the ground like an atomic powered vacuum cleaner sucking ever closer to his feet. God charged him as a warrior swinging a sword the size of a building, the ugly sword shouting and announcing his sin as it spun over the warrior's head. One dream started quietly in a green, rolling field only to see locusts rise and devour it in an instant and then form into a person walking toward him buzzing with red eyes glowing like stop lights.

He was disturbed for weeks by the dream of his high school English teacher who was his favorite teacher and his friend beyond those years. He'd see Mr. Schultz at the black board chalking the day's writing assignment. His perfect handwriting crafting: "300 words. Use three infinitives. What is your greatest sin?"

After dreams of his parents' shaming him at a family reunion, or a dozen shepherds beating him with their staffs, or a church rolling downhill to crush him, the dream of a mere glowering judge slamming his gavel on the bench with the sound of a car crash was almost a relief.

He heard the EMT say something and felt his touch, but he couldn't respond. His limping brain was circling his entire existence around the only reality worth considering: meeting God and having to fully confess. The ambulance stopped abruptly. With one more bounce Colin was there, a double there. He was there rolling into the emergency room and also there in God's presence. His breathing became erratic.

A woman's voice said, "What was his pulse when you picked him up?"

The EMT mumbled. Colin asked himself, did I say that?

He felt his consciousness expanding like the inside of a balloon until it filled the whole emergency room. Every movement around him, although he remained immobile, was somehow his movement, and every sound, although he was silent, became his own… or was it?

The woman's voice, also seeming to go through him, asked, "Didn't you write down anything?"

Along with the EMT he could only float another mumble.

The woman's statement reverberated through him, "If you didn't write it, just tell me and I'll scratch it in here."

The lights on the ceiling became a dozen dazzling suns shining in Colin's eyes. He was as speechless as the EMT being questioned, while God seemed to stride toward him dressed in white and carrying a clipboard.

Colin concentrated on this shining, smiling God when the woman again spoke, "We must know the patient's complete initial condition."

His life was speeding up and slowing down at the same time as the EMT's trembling voice again became his own, "I made a terrible mistake."

"We've got to have some accounting," Colin and the woman said, at which instant all life united in Colin's mind. The white-shining, clip-boarded God stepped closer to lay a hand on Colin's forehead. Colin attempted to confess; but the EMT's frantic statement became God's words to Colin, "I don't even remember it."

Preaching point: *God not only forgives our sins, but also forgets them.*

C Proper 10 (15) Amos 7:7-17
B Proper 10 (15) Amos 7:7-15

Chapter 40: Lonely Prophet

"Not again!" Hamul said as he looked down from the unfinished roof of the lambing shelter. "You just got back from Israel a week ago, and you barely got out alive!"

Amos didn't make an excuse, merely stated the LORD's sending him again from Judah to Israel.

"Some partnership," Hamul said. "I do the work. You scramble off north delivering unwanted messages from the LORD. Can't you wait until after lambing season?"

Amos tried to explain. "I have to do what the LORD showed me."

Hamul shouted down, "Why don't you just predict earthquakes or divine where shepherds can find wandering sheep?"

"The Lord showed me," he said. "The LORD was standing beside a wall built with a plumb line, with a plumb line in his hand. And the LORD said to me, 'Amos, what do you see?' And I said, 'A plumb line.' Then the Lord said, 'See, I am setting a plumb line in the midst of my people Israel; I will never again pass them by.'"

"Amos, that was me up here with the plumb line," Hamul said. "I wondered why you were dawdling beside the watering trough, your eyes looking like a crazed ram."

Even Amos's wife chided him, "Traveling to Israel every few months to sell sheep is one thing. Showing up every other week to scold a foreign kingdom is batty. They think they're rich because the LORD has blessed them. In their opulent wealth, you're not going to convince them they've abandoned the LORD."

Nonetheless, Amos trekked north as though lugging a terrible burden. He barely noticed Jerusalem when he passed it, just thought "Why do I have to explain myself? Elisha had his group of prophets. Why do I have to do this alone? It's not my choice. It's the LORD's doing. I didn't train for this. It's strange enough and frightening enough that my partner and wife question me. No matter what, *I saw the LORD* with that plumb line."

Still feeling alone when he arrived at Bethel, he immediately stepped up to the gathering of elders at the city gate. They recognized him and shuffled away. He began to report the LORD's dispute with their kingdom. He repeated that because the LORD had rescued Israel in the Exodus and because Israel had been exclusively his people, the LORD would punish them for their iniquities. He delivered his message that their demise was as good as done. "Fallen, no more to rise, is maiden Israel." He pointed to the nation's iniquity: "You trample on the needy, and bring to ruin the poor of the land, saying, 'When will the new moon festival be over so that we may sell grain again; and the sabbath rest, so that we may offer wheat for sale again? We'll make the ephah measure small and the shekel weight great, and practice deceit with false balances, buying poor people for silver and the needy for a pair of sandals, and selling only the sweepings of the wheat.'"

The first to confront him from the crowd was Amaziah, the king's priest. The crowd scattered as Amaziah approached. One could hardly call him the LORD's priest. His religion merely confirmed the king's every decision about national interest. Amos glimpsed him descending the street through the city gate and noticed he almost tripped on his flowing finery. His lackeys followed. Priests as well as the royal household had benefited greatly by the nation's systematic oppression of the poor and dispossessed.

He watched Amaziah approach and knew that the priest's report to King Jeroboam was public: "Amos has conspired against you in the very center of the house of Israel; the land isn't able to bear all his words. For thus Amos has said, 'Jeroboam shall die by the sword, and Israel must go into exile away from his land.'"

Amaziah halted and stood before Amos with his hands on

his hips. "O seer, go, flee away to the land of Judah," he said, gesturing south. "Earn your living there, and prophesy there; but never again prophesy at Bethel, for it's the king's sanctuary, and it's a temple of the kingdom."

The handful of elders stood to the side whispering to one another. Some sneered and others egged on Amaziah, "You tell him!"

Amos eyed the crowd and caught no sign of interest in the message he brought from the LORD.

No one, friend or foe, seemed to take Amos seriously about his task for the LORD. The message from the LORD was important, not the prophet. He interrupted Amaziah, "I'm no prophet, nor a prophet's son." He realized he was asserting himself as well as delivering the LORD's message, but he couldn't stop himself. He raised his voice, "I'm a herdsman, and a dresser of sycamore trees. The LORD took me from following the flock, and said to me, 'Go, prophesy to my people Israel.'"

Amaziah listened with a self-satisfied expression. Amos became enraged. He squared on Amaziah and pointed. "Now therefore hear the word of the LORD. You say, 'Don't prophesy against Israel, and don't preach against the house of Isaac.' Therefore thus says the LORD: 'Your wife shall become a prostitute in the city, and your sons and your daughters shall fall by the sword, and your land shall be parceled out by line; you yourself shall die in an unclean land, and Israel shall surely go into exile away from its land.'"

Amaziah's face showed a ripple of anger, but he didn't move or speak. Amos turned slowly, almost solemnly, to walk away, wondering if he'd be struck in the back and killed. He'd successfully borne the LORD's word. Yet how he wished he had a group of fellow prophets to confirm or modify his message. As he made his way back to Judah, he considered again Hamul's and his wife's questioning his calling. All of Israel questioned his calling. He questioned himself. The lonely prophet asked, "That last bit I said about Amaziah's doom. He didn't kill me when he had the crowd to do it, but I predicted a horrible fate for him and his family. LORD," he prayed, "Was that your word or just my frustration?"

Preaching point: *The loneliness and necessity of being the LORD's prophet.*

A Proper 26 (31) Micah 3:5-12

Chapter 41: No Matter What, Yahweh's Word

Even in the dawn's slight glow from the east, Micah recognized Shelem running up the steep path from Jerusalem. He ran the way a camel would run if a camel were a man — arms flailing and feet flapping like paddles. Micah could tell Shelem was yelling to him. His noise and gestures summoned Micah to wait and so he did, taking the moment to gaze upon dark Jerusalem. It looked the same this morning as when he first came from Moresheth years ago. Glorious Jerusalem was nearly overwhelming to a village boy — Yahweh's capital city, the faithless, sinful city.

Shelem came where Micah usually prayed — on the road leading west toward Moresheth. He scampered up the last few steps. "Samaria's finally fallen," he gasped as he threw his arms in a circle. "Completely destroyed."

"I know," Micah said. "I heard late last night." Micah's prophetic imagination saw the ruined city, Assyrian soldiers murdering those who fled and enslaving those who didn't. The news the night before was like a boulder flattening him. Yet stone-faced he said, "Jerusalem will be next."

Shelem was bent, breathing in great heaves; but, he reeled backward in a start as though Micah had struck him in the face. "You going to keep saying that," he forced through ragged breathing, "even as Samaria's bleeding remnant wanders into the gates? Moans and wailing. Little ones weeping." He stood straighter and spoke as though he'd rehearsed his request: "The city's in panic. They need you to speak a prophet's comforting, strengthening message."

Micah pictured Samaria's destruction, cruelty unleashed and savagery reaping the city like a harvest. With his prophetic empathy, he was nauseated. Yet he spoke with a steady voice, "I have nothing to say except what Yahweh spoke. Jerusalem as well as Samaria is corrupt from the top down. Not just the businesses and royalty, but the priests and prophets. They trick people out of their land and homes and rattle coins for a good decision in court. That's what people think prophets are for now: Offer him a couple pieces of silver, let him close him eyes, lean back and out comes a fortune-telling word from Yahweh: "Peace, prosperity. Now pay me."

Shelem shook his head, "We need hope. Thousands of Assyrians will come clipping off village by village, just as they did up north, and finally they'll lay siege here and no one has withstood them. Refugees pour in like drowned gnats poured off wine. Terrible to see and smells bad too. Come to the north gate and meet them with Yahweh's word."

In his prophet's imagination, Micah gazed upon it all — the suffering, the needy, the hopeless. He perceived the pain and fear, shrieking women and children, trembling old people helped by younger, all of them ragged, some collapsing.

He said, "Amos and Hosea told Samaria the same things I tell Judah. Yahweh wants justice: fair balances and mercy for the poor. The accumulation of luxuries shouldn't be people's number one goal."

"Think about it again," Shelem pleaded. "Consider that the temple precincts are filled like an overflowing basket every sabbath and festival. No space left for another person. These people are religious and they do listen to the prophets. That Isaiah. He bothers them some, but he says nothing will hurt Jerusalem. It exists under Yahweh's special protection. If we just trust him. People like Isaiah. He's homegrown. You're always going to be hampered as an out-of-towner. But come back. Ease up some. You can help in this tragedy. Maybe then people will take your message seriously."

He looked over Shelem to Jerusalem. He said, "As for me, I am filled with power, with the spirit of Yahweh, and with justice and might, to declare to Jacob his transgression and to Israel his sin. That's who I am and what I'm here for. That's what Yahweh says."

"All right," Shelem said, "you can stay here and bring nothing but trouble to yourself and everyone else. You could moderate your message, which you won't do. You can head for Moresheth and criticize Jerusalem there and it won't bother people so much. But please, as you speak for God-Yahweh, consider this real human need. I know what I've got to do for Yahweh. I need to bring relief and succor to the wounded. A couple prophets, a handful of priests, and palace officials are gathering blankets and arranging food and shelter for Samaria's refugees. I'm going to pitch in."

Micah looked again at Jerusalem as the morning's light increased. He said to Shelem. "Thank you, friend. I'll think about it."

Shelem started away. Micah watched him pick his way awkwardly down the trail. He was the best friend Micah had. Maybe he was Jerusalem's best friend also. Micah stood and gazed long at Jerusalem. No matter how long he gazed, he still beheld a pile of stones in a heap of brambles.

> **Preaching point**: *A true prophet must maintain the message received from Yahweh even if it is vastly unpopular and contradicts other prophets.*

A Lent 1 Matthew 4:1-11

Chapter 42: Thorough Temptation Of The Thoroughly Human

Now it's like a distant dream, those early days when Jesus first stepped into the wilderness. Maybe only three weeks? Feels like three years. He's lost count. At first, the hunger and thirst attacked only his body. His thinking remained as certain as the flow of the Jordan. But that was the beginning. How could starvation do this? He hadn't realized the way weeks without food consumed both flesh and reason.

His diminished senses have slowly failed until life for him is a fog of pain spreading around and through him. He struggles ever onward, barely conscious. He might not even be moving. How long can he keep this up? Again he hears a loud mumbling, maybe a banging, and then again, "If you are the son of God."

He's been hearing things like this lately, though he can't recall how long ago it began. Time has stretched and collapsed, slipped sideways and wobbled like his unsure steps. No matter the effort to clear his mind, his reckoning seems as constrained as his ability to move — twisted, tortured. He didn't expect it would be this difficult.

He tries to concentrate as a locust leaps high before him and lands on a rock within his reach. He decides to leave it for John the Baptist. He clearly, almost clearly, recalls John the Baptist. The water. The sky opening. A bird upon him like a spirit. "Son," that overwhelming word shaking the sky. To him. Wasn't it? Upon the edge of consciousness he tries to drag his thinking into his command, as he staggers amid the dry Judean landscape: thirty shades of brown, twenty grit of sand, vicious bushes ready to ambush him in a blink with a handful of stabs. Alone, day after day. Where did he go yesterday? Where is he heading today? Must be wandering again, mind or body, like ancient Israel in the wilderness? Are they with him again?

He remembers his father and mother telling him of his birth and how they'd whisked him to Egypt's freedom. That's his deepest memory, like the foundation of his very self, recalled many times across a lifetime... and these last few days. But now the pain has distorted even that memory until all he can make of it is God's bringing Israel from Egypt.

What was that? Something to the side. Noise. Sounded like a voice. But out here? Why can't he see them? Why can't he see anything now? Has he been struck blind? Thought it was about noon, noon under the sun's punishment. Now total darkness, midday yet as though the earth is covered by a basket. Maybe someone really is near him, although he can't grasp a feather's weight of neighboring life. Why can he only hear and... of course, feel such pain? A noise — is that outside of him or inside?

"If you are the Son of God. If you are the Son of God." The taunting keeps pounding into him. Where's it from? Not from heaven. From heaven he was positive he'd heard "My Son." It was spoken to him, Jesus, who's now out in the middle of Judea's nowhere.

He'd been firm in his intention not to compromise with any temptation to be less than God's person, like God's very son. Nothing could flick past his awareness that would pull him away from complete devotion to God. He wouldn't presume upon his heavenly Father to yank him out of this trial, no special privileges. He just hadn't realized it would take this long and cause this kind of suffering. Can he maintain his faith here in this forsaken wilderness, spinning dizzily so close to death? Is he deranged still to trust that he's special?

He'd grown up believing he was tight with God. Leaning into anything that would serve God and others. But others now seem like a problem as great as Satan — mocking him. Where's it coming from, here in the wilderness? Even if people laugh at his suffering, they're still the ones he's here to serve, and heal, and forgive.

His breathing is ragged, his mouth... not just dry. It tastes like wine mixed with gall. "If you are the Son of God," pummeling him, like the echo of a hammer on nails. His life has dwindled to this place and this act of obedience. And, it wasn't his decision in the first place. Only his to follow the path he felt was laid out for him, whether Israel had followed it or not, whether for forty years or forty days.

It's a matter of faith, whether in this uninhabited wilderness, or especially with this clamor. Clamor? Wilderness clamor? About trusting God. Is he imagining this? Can he trust his senses? Can he trust God? All this confusion. Has everything gone wrong? What could have happened? Isn't this what he's supposed to do? Isn't this the direction he's to walk for God? Isn't God going to lead him even in this valley?

Yet abruptly, the ordeal ends. Suddenly God's help hasn't arrived this time. His body and mind sag. Is it really ending? How can it be complete if he's only just started? How can death tumble down like God's displeasure, like the sound of a great curtain ripping?

He's had little to say during all these days; but now he's able to open his eyes. He sees a mob, an execution squad, dying thieves beside him, his mother not far away, a couple of his students, and within him a scream bursts forth, "My God, my God, why have you forsaken me?" His temptations have been long and difficult; but, he has endured it for God's sake and for the sake of all those gathered around him and for all those through the centuries who will follow. "Then Jesus cried again with a loud voice and breathed his last."

Preaching point: *Jesus' life — a series of tests /trials /temptations (Luke 22:28).*

A Epiphany 4 (4); A All Saints Matthew 5:1-12

Chapter 43: Pup

Because Pup had a thin face and a receding chin, he always looked weak, especially so when he stood, as now, with his mouth open waiting for Yannai. The villagers noticed his habit of latching onto the young man Yannai and so they nicknamed him "Pup," because he followed like one. Younger children played on the edges of the square but Pup had never been welcome to play with them. For him, it was the grudging companionship of Yannai or nothing.

A wheat merchant brushed him aside, ordering his slaves where to place their baskets. Other merchants brought dried fish, some had pottery, laying it out on a carpet, and one arranged tanned leather on the ground. Pup stepped out of their way and then pushed rocks around with his foot while he searched right and left for Yannai.

He was eleven and had come to live with his mother's sister six years ago, but in this Galilean village he'd always be a stranger because people knew about his parents. His aunt didn't say much about him to others, just that when his father tired of beating his wife he'd joined a handful of revolutionaries in Trachonitis, dying as they tried to rob a supply caravan bound for Rome's legions. Pup's only memory of his father was his furrowed forehead. His most vivid memory of his mother was her stare. No matter what she was doing, she seemed to look above or beyond it with unfocused eyes.

In the late morning, his aunt finally agreed that he'd finished his chores, so he stood now on the edge of the market and waited. He didn't know why he did this every day, never asked himself why. It's what he did each forenoon at the market, although hardly anyone spoke to him there or he to them. But he listened. His little free time from the women's household chores was filled with listening. He heard about the caravan that just arrived by Lake Galilee, about a ship that was beached in a storm at Sidon, about how one merchant was hiding from the tax collector, and how an agitator against the Romans was now in chains rowing a trireme. Listening fit him like an old sandal. The more interested, the wider he opened his mouth.

He licked his lips that were dry from his open-mouthed breathing and strained to spot Yannai through the merchants' bustling in the square. He stepped from one foot to the other and almost had to dance to stay out of everyone's way. Then Pup spied him. Yannai was on the other side of the square and departing the village. Pup rushed to catch up, bending low and elbowing through a tight group, dashing to Yannai. He ran to him and tugged his sleeve twice before Yannai turned around. Pup was always tugging on Yannai's sleeve. Yannai had thick black eyebrows and he squinted as though irritated when he talked with Pup. He finally turned and spoke as though he didn't remember that Pup followed him every day. "Oh, hi."

"What we doing today, Yannai?"

"*We*? I'm going to Cana to see a friend." He turned as though he didn't expect Pup to follow.

"I'll go with you," Pup said too eagerly.

With nothing more expressed, Yannai continued out of the village, Pup following. As they walked over the first low hill Pup said, "Heard about Jesus?"

Yannai answered over his shoulder, "Who hasn't?"

"In the market everyone said he's setting up to speak right over there," he pointed down a trail to the right where groups of travelers were heading. "Everybody says he's speaking outdoors now."

Yannai spoke again over his shoulder, "*We're* outdoors. *Any*body can talk outdoors."

Pup drew nearly beside him, "They say he's been teaching in the synagogues, but now he's doing open-air speaking. Look," he said and gestured toward groups who'd followed the two of them from the village and then turned off the trail, clearly aiming to attend Jesus' outdoor event.

"Let's go listen," Pup said, shocking Yannai. The boy had never made a suggestion of what they should do. Yannai turned almost toward Pup, "I'm going to Cana today," and continued walking. Within a few steps, he realized that Pup wasn't following. He turned around in surprise, "What you doing?"

Pup was anxiously gazing toward clumps of people gathering on the trail toward Jesus.

"I want to hear Jesus. Word in the market is that people are flooding to see him from all over and we're just half an hour away. He talks about the kingdom of heaven. Maybe he's the Messiah who'll kick out the Romans."

The young man struck with one foot toward Cana, but held his body toward Pup like a question, "You coming?"

Pup looked uncertain, but he didn't follow. Yannai's eyebrows came down over his eyes as he said, "All right. We'll give a little time, but I need to make it to Cana and back today." And for the first time in three years, Yannai walked a direction he hadn't chosen while Pup followed him close behind and babbled about what he'd heard of Jesus' teaching and preaching and curing all kinds of illnesses. "Everybody was chattering about him in the market. A bunch of the merchants are packing up early to go hear him."

Within an hour, the two had spotted Jesus. He led a huge crowd up a slope, then stopped near the top to speak. Pup said, almost bouncing, "We got here at the beginning." Yannai replied with a snort.

People shuffled closer after Jesus sat. In a clear voice that projected over the crowd, he began, "Blessed are the poor in spirit, for theirs is the kingdom of heaven. Blessed are those who mourn, for they will be comforted. Blessed are the meek, for they will inherit the earth. Blessed are those who hunger and thirst for righteousness, for they will be filled. Blessed are the merciful, for they will receive mercy. Blessed are the pure in heart, for they will see God. Blessed are the peacemakers, for they will be called children of God. Blessed are those who are persecuted for righteousness' sake, for theirs is the kingdom of heaven. Blessed are you when people revile you and persecute you and utter all kinds of evil against you falsely on my account. Rejoice and be glad, for your reward is great in heaven, for in the same way they persecuted the prophets who were before you."

Pup leaned forward as he listened. Yannai tugged on his sleeve. "Come on. We've heard enough. Sound like a Messiah who's going to free us? Such rot!" He turned to go but realized that Pup wasn't following. He was listening intently to Jesus. His mouth was wide open.

Preaching point: *Jesus draws people to him.*

A Proper 6 (11) Matthew 9:35-10:8

Chapter 44: Called And Freed To Serve

The new Stephen ministers sat in the front row smiling, nervous about the vows they would take and anxious about the service that awaited them as Christian caregivers. The pastor, white hair hanging in his eyes and leaning on a cane, read the gospel of Matthew and nodded his first sentence to them: "After months of training, our first class of Stephen ministers awaits its commissioning. Why all the hubbub? Why don't they sneak off and do what they're trained to do? Stephen ministers are bound by confidentiality and that's almost like secrecy. But before that, we need to ask: Why train the laity at all for Christian ministry? The congregation already has two pastors.

"One reason, not often considered, is to free them to exercise their Christian gifts, gifts they didn't always know they had. The laity is what I call the 'real Christians' because they aren't paid to serve Christ. I can say that because you pay me. But the laity, the real Christians, are often blocked from genuine Christian service because of tradition.

"Now, we live within the Christian tradition. Everything the church does is guided by the past. The disruptive aspect of 'tradition' as I view it this morning, is the conviction that only pastors are supposed to do 'real' religious work. Where do such ideas come from — extreme reverence, superstition? Whatever, it's a tradition that creeps into the church generation by generation like mice into the garage every winter.

"Maybe no one in this congregation has the slightest thought that these new Stephen ministers are somehow spiritually inferior in caregiving to a pastor with seven, eight years of college. If you hold such a doubt, however, I want to share an event that happened long enough ago and far enough away to be safe to tell. In a Presbyterian church. Some of you know I served Presbyterian congregations for the first twenty years of my ministry.

"There are all manner of Presbyterian denominations, but always a clerk of session, somewhat like our secretary of the church council but with more clout, in charge of all records. Every *T* crossed, and every *I* dotted. Every record of baptisms, weddings, funerals, congregational, and session meetings signed, while maintaining the congregation's decency and order. The oldest joke in Presbyterian circles is that in a conflict between decency and order, decency disappears first.

"This clerk of session, we'll call him 'Bradford,' believed that the pastor was supposed to perform all important religious functions in the congregation. I know that sounds medieval, but such things can occur in almost any church. When Jesus spoke of sending more 'laborers into his harvest,' it's interpreted as meaning more seminary-trained pastors. Bradford would regularly read the prayer for the beginning and end of the session meeting; but, by the force of his personality that was the laity's closest touch to purely religious ministry — other than singing in the choir, teaching church school, caring for the building, and raising money, of course.

"Bradford considered himself progressive in that he didn't object, as some Presbyterian churches do, to the use of musical instruments in worship. However, in his odd way he made sure that the congregation used the oldest hymnal, out of print for forty years, although they'd become a handful of beaten rags, constantly mended. If the subject of encouraging the ministry of the laity came up, his response was, 'Why, soon they'd be wanting to baptize and serve the Lord's Supper like some of those Baptists.' As I said, there are all kinds of Presbyterians.

"As contrary as Bradford seemed to be, the new pastor, we'll call him 'Pastor Ansel,' straight from seminary, realized that the man was truly dedicated to Christ's church. Wherever he believed that the laity could do something for the church, he did: pulling weeds, cleaning toilets, patching the roof. He leaned his shoulder into everything he considered allowable and also gave a bundle of his income. Pastor Ansel, although disagreeing with his clerk on the ministry of the laity, came to know the man's devotion to Christ and was genuinely fond of him. He assumed that Bradford had simply made a wrong turn in his thinking way back in his life and had continued where that road led him.

"Pastor Ansel had served the congregation for three years when he was found in his office one Tuesday morning, slumped on his desk, barely breathing. After two days in the hospital, the diagnosis was a stroke and the prognosis wasn't good. Bradford did his clerk's duty, telephoning to the nearest Presbyterian congregation for their pastor to minister to Pastor Ansel. We'll call him 'Pastor Carlson.' Pastor Carlson had already visited him and reported that Pastor Ansel's condition had improved and he appeared well on the way to recovery.

"The news encouraged Bradford to call at the hospital in order to complete a clerkly detail. The Presbytery was meeting within the week where all records of congregations were read and reviewed. These records must be signed by the clerk and the pastor; yet, the clerk had only just typed up the minutes of the last session meetings, thus needing the pastor's signature. The Presbytery's pack of clerks that met to read minutes had never dinged him for mistakes or omissions. Because Pastor Ansel was recovering, Bradford felt it allowable to visit and have him sign the eight pound minutes book.

"He entered the hospital room to find a middle school girl fussing with the pastor's many tubes. He was stunned. What was she doing? For a moment he stood at the foot of the pastor's bed holding the giant book to his chest. Then the little girl turned and he saw her badge, 'L. Kelly, R.N.' She seemed a little shaky. In fact, it was her first week on the floor without a supervisor. Just then the pastor said something to her and she turned to him and he appeared to shrug. The room then sounded like a dozen church bells ringing for all the clanging that broke loose. Bradford stepped closer. He could see the pastor's tense face, and Nurse Kelly's tenser face.

"Pastor Ansel grabbed her hand and said, 'Pray for me.' Her eyebrows shot up like a broken window shade and she froze.

David O. Bales

'Pray for me,' he choked out. She swished her hair back and forth for an answer and turned to Bradford. 'I... I... I can't.' Bradford stepped forward and Pastor Ansel saw him, reached, and grabbed his wrist like Jacob wrestling with the angel. Nurse Kelly fled for help and there was Bradford, clutched by the person whom he believed should do all the religious things... like praying for the dying.

"Bradford took three seconds to obey the summons from Pastor Ansel and the Holy Spirit. 'Almighty God,' he prayed, 'Creator above all, holy, exalted...' Pastor Ansel squeezed his wrist harder. He looked into the pastor's eyes, gulped, and said, 'Lord Jesus, come here now. To your servant now. Upon pastor I pray, in his desperate need. You are his Lord, and his only hope in life and death. Touch him. Heal him. Restore him. He's your servant, grant him mercy. Mercy, Lord.'

"Nurse Kelly dashed in with half the hospital staff clattering behind her and Bradford was hustled out. He stood outside the room, back to the wall, eyes shut for three hours and prayed... and prayed... and prayed.

"Have you heard of the Christian writer C.S. Lewis? Wrote a couple dozen wonderful books, many for people who didn't believe or who'd like to believe. The movie *Shadowlands* was about him and his wife Joy. He was a professor in England and she was a US citizen visiting in the UK and working with him. She became ill and was dying of cancer. Suddenly the UK government, without giving reasons, refused to renew her resident permit. As an act of friendship, Lewis married her in her hospital room, allowing her and her two sons to remain in England at least until she died.

"Then, of all the tricky things God does, she recovered. The two of them, now married, fell in love. Well, Pastor Ansel also recovered from the edge of death. He walked with a limp after that, but mentally he returned to at least 90% of his former faculties. And Bradford? He had found by the Holy Spirit's piercing him that Christ had given him the gift of compassion and care for others in prayer.

"Within a few years the Presbytery trained and commissioned

Bradford as a minister to pastors. Who knew better the inner workings of the church? Who else had more concern for pastors? What he didn't know about those Christians who served as pastors he learned every day by listening to them, every one of them, calling on each of them regularly and praying with them. And soon pastor Ansel's congregation set about to train the laity to express Christian care for others. As far as I know, they still are."

The pastor turned again to those in the front row waiting to be commissioned as Stephen ministers and said, "Traditions come and go. Some good, some harmful. You now take your place in the tradition of Jesus who gifts you, calls you and frees you to have compassion on those who are harassed and helpless. Please come forward for your commissioning."

> **Preaching point**: *God's people called, equipped, and freed to serve Christ.*

A Proper 12 (17) Matthew 13:31-33, 44-52

Chapter 45: Mustard Seed Yard

"It's in the agreement," Marlin said to Gilbert. "It's standard."

"I didn't understand when I signed it," Gilbert said. "Can't you just let me, as a friend, I mean?"

"It's not between you and me," Marlin said. "It's the way properties are brokered. The company has operated like this long before I got here. If you show up at the house when I bring prospective buyers, what're they supposed to think: You're pressuring them — or you don't trust me?"

Marlin and Gilbert had been friends in Kiwanis for decades. Now Marlin's real estate company had listed Gilbert and Louise's house; yet, Gilbert arrived at Marlin's office asking to be present when it was shown.

Gilbert rubbed his hand on the arm of his chair, then stood to leave. Marlin said, "I'm really sorry."

Gilbert walked to the door and turned. "Just the backyard? That's all I'm talking about. Let me tell them about moving the dirt and making the terraces. That's what's important."

"Dirt and rocks?" Marlin said with a questioning frown. "Like I said, Gilbert, it's not personal. It's usual."

Gilbert stood at the office door, brushed his hand over his chin and spoke with a sorrowful tone, "Once," he said, holding up an index finger with a hopeful look. He could see Marlin was softening. He continued, "Let me show that first customer the backyard. I'd be telling you at the same time and you could pass it on to others. I won't go in the house. Won't be watching them gawk or mock the place." He leaned toward Marlin. "Just once."

"For crying out loud," Marlin said. "*You* should've been a salesman. Okay, one time, and don't tell anybody about this — especially any of the bosses."

"No problem. Got it. Thanks Marlin," and for a moment

Marlin thought Gilbert was going to cry. Until now, the process of listing his house had seemed businesslike. Gilbert and Louise had moved to assisted living six months before. Their house just came on the market, a choice house on a big lot in a select area. That's all the background Marlin knew. Another associate had handled the signing and posted the website details. It would attract a crowd of prospective buyers. If Gilbert's being present once at a showing ruined a sale, others would stand in line to view the merchandise.

Three mornings later Marlin arrived late with clients. Gilbert was waiting street side. Marlin hustled over to him by the curb and spoke quickly, "I'll introduce you to the clients — they're a nice young couple, met them yesterday — and we'll do the backyard first." He slapped a hand on Gilbert's shoulder, "I assured them you're not a kook and you're not here to influence them in any way."

Gilbert met Carlton and Wyna Cotton in the driveway and the four walked around the house to the backyard. Gilbert was all smiles, as though about to lead a grand tour. Carlton and Wyna hung back. Marlin hoped that Gilbert hadn't put them off already and, although he wanted to sell the house, he didn't want the morning to become a bad experience for Gilbert. By their expressions he considered that the couple might not really be interested in the house. This could be just for practice or entertainment. It wouldn't be the first time he'd dealt with such customers.

The backyard held three walled terraces, ground close trees, multicolored flowers in both stripes and bunches and a water feature trickling down one side. "I call this the 'Mustard Seed Yard,'" Gilbert said, spreading his arms. "When we moved here, this backyard was a hillside so steep you couldn't walk up it. Had a zig zag trail in order to get to the top. Quarter acre of hillside."

Marlin took a step back so he could watch how Carlton and Wyna responded.

"My wife has always been an artist," Gilbert said, "mostly oils, and she'd been crippled with polio when she was a kid.

When we moved here 42 years ago, we'd been married six years and the doctors confirmed we couldn't have children." Gilbert's expression registered Carlton and Wyna's response of "what have we gotten into?"

Gilbert waved his hand as though trying to regain their attention. "That's when, over about six months, Louise transitioned into a fulltime, commercial artist, right here at home. Don't know if you've been around artists," Gilbert said, directing his statement to Carlton and Wyna. They timidly shook their heads.

"This backyard grew from her perfecting her craft."

Carlton and Wyna listened, but Marlin saw that they were only being polite and they wanted it over quickly. So did Marlin.

"So, the backyard came into being when I'd tell her it was time for us to do something else, like eat," he laughed, "or go to the store, or go to bed. She'd say, 'Just a couple more strokes,' or something about feathering a cloud, puckering a nose, or pluming a tree, which could last anywhere from two minutes to two hours. For the first few months I was bothered by having to wait. Know what I mean?" To which Wyna peeped a "Yes."

"That's when I lit on the idea of doing something with the time. I built it myself. Kept a shovel and wheelbarrow here and I'd just step out and place another rock or move a few more shovels full." He smiled as though his smile would help them understand.

"That's the only time I worked on this project," he said, waving up the hill, "just while I was waiting for Louise."

The three almost gasped as gazed up the slope and considered how he conveyed half a mountainside into huge terraces by hand.

"I want whoever buys our house to know: just a bit at a time. For a long time. Freed Louise to develop her talent, do what she was good at and what she loved. Brought her joy and joy to others. She still teaches oil painting one morning a week where we live. But this hillside was an investment of small moments." He gave an exaggerated nod of the head, as though he'd thoroughly clarified everything that needed to be explained. But he was clearly not communicating what he felt was most important. "Just by a few minutes waiting," he said, restating his meaning.

Marlin hadn't known what the clients might think of Gilbert, but they appeared anything but enthusiastic. He couldn't tell if Carlton and Wyna looked foolish or embarrassed. Mostly they looked like spanked puppies. Gilbert slumped in disappointment. He cast his head toward the hill and back twice, trying to find something else to mention that could convey the hillside's great significance. He mumbled goodbye and trudged away like a teacher who'd failed his students.

As Marlin showed Carlton and Wyna through the house, he decided that in the afternoon he'd drive to Gilbert and Louise's apartment to explain about Carlton and Wyna. He'd seen them when they arrived to his office that morning, twenty minutes late. He could tell they were angry with one another and only toned down their argument slightly as they entered. Carlton had turned away from Wyna to speak to Marlin. "Sorry we're late," he said with a grimace. "I have a wife who's always slow to get ready."

Preaching point: *The small starts of God's grace.*

A Proper 19 (24) Matthew 18:21-35

Chapter 46: If You Don't Forgive

Monday at lunch Phil made sure to sit by the factory's new hire, Milo. He knew what it was like to be new to a job or group and Milo was pleased for the company. Five minutes into their lunch break, their mutual unbelief popped up in their conversation.

"Sunday after Sunday," Phil said, "and the whole family every Wednesday night. Droning hymns and having to sit quiet for the preacher," he laughed and rasped his voice: "Oh, he of sour face and asphalt speech." Phil had told this story so often the intonation was down pat. "No matter the preacher's theme he always warned us against drinking, smoking, dancing, playing cards, and going to movies. If we disregarded his threats we'd end up joyless and bitter." He slapped the table with a smile, completing his comedy routine.

"I caught it from the Catholic side," Milo responded, but without a smile. "Catholic school. All forty kids in a classroom and a nun dominating with an iron hand and a wooden ruler. I grew up there in a school so small we couldn't even have sports teams. Just playground scrimmage between kids, some of them four years apart in age. I'll never, ever forgive my parents for sending me to that prison, nor will I forgive the nuns for being the jailors."

On Tuesday at lunch Milo sought out Phil's group, sat, and immediately said, "'Devote yourself to God,' the nuns told us adolescent boys, when all we could think about was devoting ourselves to some of the older girls. We did better than a lot of boys who became priests. They devoted themselves to little boys." Phil and the other men at the table laughed and started talking about their high school crushes.

At Wednesday's lunch Milo took up the conversation, "You know the Catholics don't allow birth control. Stuff the village with hungry little mouths and who's going to feed them all? Ever wonder about that?" No, Phil hadn't wondered about that. He mentioned, however, that the advertisements on television about starving children bothered him something awful.

"It's power, you know," Milo said. "Religion is people wanting power over you, get you to do what they want for their sake. I compare it to wives pushing their husbands around, twisting them with whines and complaints. Definitely not healthy."

By Thursday lunch break Phil was trying to turn the conversation to recent NFL rules changes, but Milo said, "The politicians and the priests are in the same game. They're going to get something from you and everything they say and do, no matter how plausible, is for their benefit — you know, like money!"

On Friday Phil didn't go to the lunchroom. He ate at his work station, half the time with his fist bunched under his chin. For the rest of the day whenever he needed to check another section, he found a route away from Milo.

The factory had to work Saturday to catch up on an order. It meant time and a half and most workers liked it. Phil's group was standing in the lunchroom talking about sports and families. Sid was the tallest and opposite Phil. He looked over Phil's shoulder, ducked down slightly and left as Phil turned to see Milo entering. Milo joined the group.

Pablo said, "We're really moving on our line. I think we'll be done before three. Foreman says that if we do, we can punch out and go home."

"Not ours," Stu said. "No way he'd let us go. Says section eight's further behind than everyone. Stuff's piling up. Don't even have space for more pallets."

"Bosses are a lot like priests and pastors," Milo said. "Ever notice that? They enjoy telling you what to do. You can figure it out if you think about it. Maybe not when you're younger, but when you grow up. All that humbug about knowing what's best for you. Bosses, priests, and pastors, all the same. It's power."

The subject changed to Sunday's NFL games. Each had his

favorite. "Packers and *Bears*," Juan almost jumped when he announced his preference. "That's my team. I grew up in Chicago. When they're on TV, I put on my blue jersey, plant myself in my favorite chair and shout the windows out of the house."

One by one the six workers mentioned their favorite teams and what they were going to do when the games started on Sunday 11 AM. Phil was last and said, softly, although loud enough for all to hear, "I'm going to go to church."

Preaching point: *Forgiving others is the center of church life and is for our sake as well as for those we forgive.*

ABC New Year; A Reign of Christ Proper 29 (34) Matthew 25:31-46

Chapter 47: The Other Wise Man

For 125 years Christians have heard, in some form, Henry Van Dyke's "The Other Wise Man." Here follows a condensation, slightly rewritten for our time. May it bless and inspire you as it has thousands before you.

* * *

You know the story of the Three Wise Men of the East and how they traveled from afar to offer their gifts at the manger-cradle in Bethlehem. But have you heard of Artaban, the other wise man who also saw the star in its rising and set out to follow it, yet did not arrive with his brethren in the presence of the child Jesus? I would tell the tale as I have heard fragments of it in the hall of dreams, in the palace of the heart of man.

I

In the days when Augustus Caesar was master of many kings and Herod reigned in Jerusalem, Artaban lived in the city of Ecbatana, among the masses of Persia. He wore a robe of pure white wool, thrown over a tunic of silk and a white, pointed cap with long lapels at the sides. A winged circle of gold rested on his breast. It was the dress of the priesthood of the Magi, called the fire-worshipers, the worshipers of the God of purity. Along with his fellow priests of Zoroaster he studied the stars as well as the Hebrew scriptures. Those Magi believed they had found a prophecy in the Hebrew scriptures that would lead them to the Jews' promised Messiah. It was the ancient word of Balaam the son of Beor who announced: "A star shall come out of Jacob, and a scepter shall rise out of Israel."

Artaban explained to his father that he and his three Magi companions — Caspar, Melchior, and Balthazar — had searched the ancient tablets of the Chaldeans and computed the time of the stars. They decided that the star announcing the Messiah's birth would occur this year. "We have studied the sky, and in the spring of the year we saw two of the greatest planets draw near together, in the sign of the Fish, which is the house of the Hebrews. We also saw a new star. Now again the two great planets are meeting. This night is their conjunction. My three brothers are watching by the Temple of the Seven Spheres at Bosippa in Babylonia, and I am watching here. If the star shines again, they will wait ten days for me at the temple, and then we will set out together for Jerusalem to see and worship the promised one who shall be born King of Israel."

To prepare for the journey Artaban had sold all his possessions and purchased three jewels — a sapphire, a ruby, and a pearl — to carry as a tribute to the king. He placed the jewels in the tight band of cloth next to his body, then later that night climbed to his roof to watch the stars, as he knew his three friends also searched the sky 450 miles away.

As Artaban watched, a steel-blue spark was born out of the darkness beneath, rounding itself with purple splendors to a crimson sphere, and spiring upward through rays of saffron and orange into a point of white radiance. Tiny and infinitely remote, yet perfect in every part, it pulsated in the enormous vault as if the three jewels hidden in the Magian's clothes had mingled and been transformed into a living heart of light.

He bowed his head. He covered his brow with his hands.

"It is the sign," he said. "The king is coming, and I will go to meet him."

II

He set out on his strongest horse Vasda. Artaban must ride wisely and well if he would keep the appointed hour with the other Magi; for the route was 450 miles and 50 was near the limit of what Vasda could cover in a day. Ten days. His fellow Magians would wait until midnight of the tenth day, and, if he did not appear, they would leave without him on the caravan to Judea.

On the evening of the tenth day Artaban approached the shattered walls of Babylon. Vasda was almost spent and Artaban would gladly have turned into the city he was nearing to find rest and refreshment for himself and for her. Yet it was still three hours journey to the Temple of the Seven Spheres and he must reach the place by midnight if he would find his comrades waiting with supplies to carry them to Judea.

A grove of date-palms made an island of gloom in the pale yellow sea. As she passed into the shadow, Vasda slackened her pace and began to pick her way more carefully. Near the farther end of the darkness she gave a quick breath of anxiety and stood stock-still, quivering in every muscle before a dark object in the shadow of the last palm-tree.

Artaban dismounted. The dim starlight revealed the form of a man lying across the road. His humble dress and the outline of his haggard face showed that he was probably one of the Hebrews who, having been exiled here by the Babylonian armies 500 years before, still dwelt in great numbers around the city. His skin, dry and yellow as parchment bore the mark of the deadly fever which ravaged marshlands in autumn. The chill of death was in his lean hand, and, as Artaban released it, the arm fell back inertly upon the motionless breast.

But as he turned away, a long, faint, ghostly sigh came from the man's lips and his boney fingers gripped the hem of the Magian's robe and held him fast. Artaban's heart leaped to his throat, not with fear but with a dumb resentment of this blind delay. How could he stay here in the darkness to minister to a dying stranger? What claim had this unknown fragment of human life upon his compassion or his service? If he lingered but an hour, he could hardly reach Borsippa at the appointed time. His companions would go without him.

But if he went now, the man would surely die. "God of truth and purity," he prayed, "direct me in the holy path, the way of wisdom which You only know."

He turned back to the sick man. Loosening the grasp of his hand, he carried him to a little mound at the foot of the palm-tree. He brought water from the canal and mixed it with healing herbs which Magians always carried. Slowly, hour by hour, he labored to revive the old man.

Finally, the man's eyes opened and he asked, "Who are you and why have you sought me here to bring back my life?"

"I am Artaban the Magician, of the city of Ecbatana, and I am going to Jerusalem in search of the one who is to be born King of the Jews, a great prince and deliverer of all men. I must not delay longer, for the caravan that has waited for me may depart without me. Here is all I have left of my bread and wine, and a portion of the healing herbs. Now I must go."

The Jew raised his trembling hand solemnly to the heavens and blessed Artaban, then said, "But not Jerusalem. The Messiah must not be sought there. Our prophets say Bethlehem is the place."

It was already long past midnight. Artaban rode in haste, and Vasda, restored by the brief rest, ran eagerly through the silent plain and swam the channels of the river. At the first beams of dawn they drew near the mound of Nimrod and the Temple of the Seven Spheres, yet with no sign of his friends.

At the edge of the terrace he saw a little cairn of broken bricks, and under them a piece of papyrus. He caught it up and read: "We have waited past the midnight and can delay no longer. We go to find the king. Follow us across the desert."

Artaban sat down on the ground and covered his head in despar. "How can I cross the desert," he said, "with no food and with a spent horse? I must return to Babylon, sell my sapphire, and buy a train of camels and provisions for the journey."

III

There was a silence in the Hall of Dreams where I was listening to the story of the Other Wise Man. Through this silence I saw, but very dimly, his figure passing over the dreary desert, high upon the back of his camel, rocking steadily onward like a ship over the waves.

Through his journeying I followed Artaban moving steadily onward, until he arrived at Bethlehem. It was the third day after the three wise men had come and had found Mary and Joseph with the young child Jesus and had laid their gifts of gold and frankincense and myrrh at his feet.

Then the other wise man drew near, weary, but full of hope, bearing his ruby and his pearl to offer to the king. Yet the streets of the village seem deserted and Artaban wondered whether the men had gone to the hill pastures to bring down the sheep. From the open door of a cottage, he heard the sound of a woman's voice singing softly. He entered and found a young mother hushing her baby to rest. She told him of the strangers from the far east who had appeared in the village three days before and how they said that a star had guided them to the place where Joseph of Nazareth was lodging with his wife and her new born child and how they had paid reverence to the child and given him rich gifts.

"But the travelers disappeared again," she continued, "as suddenly as they had come. We were afraid at the strangeness of their visit. The man of Nazareth took the child and his mother and fled that same night secretly, and it was whispered they were going to Egypt. Since then a spell has been upon the village; something evil hangs over it. They say Roman soldiers are coming to force a new tax from us, and the men have driven the flocks and herds far back among the hills and hidden themselves to escape it."

Artaban listened to her gentle, timid speech and the child in her arms looked up in his face and smiled, stretching out his rosy hands to grasp the winged circle of gold on his breast. His heart warmed to the touch. "Why might not this child have been the promised prince?" he asked within himself, as he touched its soft cheek. "Kings have been born before this in lowlier houses."

The young mother laid the baby in its cradle and rose to minister to the needs of the strange guest. She set food before him, the plain fare of peasants, willingly offered. Suddenly the noise of wild confusion rose in the streets, a shrieking and wailing of women's voices, a clangor of brazen trumpets, a clashing of swords and a desperate cry: "The soldiers! Herod's soldiers are killing our children."

The mother's face grew white. She clasped her child to her bosom and crouched motionless in the darkest corner of the room, covering him with the folds of her robe lest he should wake and cry.

Artaban went quickly and stood in the doorway of the house. His broad shoulders filled the portal from side to side and the peak of his white cap all but touched the lintel.

Soldiers hurried down the street with bloody hands and dripping swords. At the sight of the stranger in his imposing dress, they hesitated with surprise. The captain of the band approached the threshold to thrust him aside. But Artaban did not stir.

"I am all alone in this place," he said, "and am waiting to give this jewel to the prudent captain who will leave me in peace."

He showed the ruby, glistening in the hollow of his hand like a great drop of blood. The pupils of the captain's eyes expanded with desire, and the hard lines of greed wrinkled around his lips. He stretched out his hand and took the ruby.

"March on!" he cried to his men. "There is no child here."

Artaban reentered the cottage and prayed: "God of truth, forgive my sin! I have lied to save the life of a child. And two of my gifts are gone. I have spent for man what was meant for God."

But the voice of the young woman, weeping for joy in the shadow behind him said gently, "Because you have saved the life of my little one, may the Lord bless you and keep you. The Lord make His face shine on you and be gracious to you. The Lord lift up His countenance on you and give you peace."

IV

Again, there was a silence in the hall of dreams, deeper and more mysterious than the first interval and I understood that the years of Artaban were flowing very swiftly under the stillness.

I saw him moving among the throngs of men in populous Egypt, seeking everywhere for traces of the household that had come from Bethlehem. I saw him again in an obscure house of Alexandria, taking counsel with a Hebrew rabbi. The venerable man, bending over the rolls of parchment on which the prophecies of Israel were written, read aloud the pathetic words which foretold the sufferings of the promised Messiah — despised, rejected, a man of sorrows and acquainted with grief.

"And remember, my son," he said, fixing his eyes on Artaban's face, "the king whom you seek is not to be found in a palace nor among the rich and powerful. The light for which the world is waiting is a new light, glory that shall rise out of patient and triumphant suffering. And the kingdom which is to be established forever is a new kingdom, the royalty of unconquerable love. Those who seek him will do well to look among the poor and the lowly, the sorrowful and the oppressed."

So I saw the other wise man again and again, traveling from place to place, and searching among the people of the dispersion. He passed through countries where famine lay heavy on the land and the poor were crying for bread. He visited the oppressed and the afflicted in the gloom of subterranean prisons and the crowded wretchedness of slave-markets and the weary toil of galley-ships. In all this populous and intricate world of anguish, though he found none to worship, he found many to help. He fed the hungry, and clothed the naked, and healed the sick, and comforted the captive; and his years passed more swiftly than the weaver's shuttle that flashes back and forth through the loom while the web grows and the pattern is completed.

Then, at last, while I was thinking of his final gem, the pearl, I heard the end of the story of the other wise man.

V

Thirty-and-three years of Artaban's life had passed away. Worn, weary, and ready to die, but still looking for the king, he had come for the last time to Jerusalem. He had often visited the holy city before, but now it seemed as if he must make one more effort, and something whispered in his heart that, at last, he might succeed.

It was the season of passover. The city was thronged with strangers. On this day, a singular agitation was visible in the multitude. The sky was veiled with portentous gloom. Currents of excitement seemed to flash through the crowd.

Artaban joined a group of people from his own country, Parthian Jews who had come up to Jerusalem to keep the passover, and he inquired of them the cause of the tumult and where they were going.

"We are going," they answered, "to the place called Golgotha, outside the city walls, where there is to be an execution. Two famous robbers are to be crucified, and with them another, called Jesus of Nazareth, a man who has done many wonderful works among the people, so that they love him greatly. Though the priests and elders have said that he must die, because he gave himself out to be the Son of God. Pilate has sent him to the cross because he said that he was the 'King of the Jews.'"

How strangely these familiar words fell onto the tired heart of Artaban. The King of the Jews. These words had led him for a lifetime over land and sea. Could it be the same who had been born in Bethlehem 33 years ago, at whose birth the star had appeared in the heavens, and of whose coming the prophets had spoken?

He said within himself: "The ways of God are stranger than the thoughts of men, and it may be that I shall find the king at last in the hands of his enemies and shall come in time to offer my pearl for his ransom before he dies."

So the old man followed the multitude with slow and painful steps. Just beyond the entrance of the guardhouse a troop of Macedonian soldiers came down the street, dragging a young girl with torn dress and disheveled hair. She broke suddenly from her tormentors' hands and threw herself at his feet clasping him around the knees. She had seen his white hat and the winged circle on his breast.

"Have pity on me," she cried, "and save me. I also am a daughter of the true religion which is taught by the Magi. My father was a merchant of Parthia, but he is dead, and I am seized for his debts to be sold as a slave."

Artaban trembled.

It was the old conflict in his soul, which had come to him in the palm-grove of Babylon and in the cottage at Bethlehem — the conflict between the expectation of faith and impulse of love. Twice the gift which he had consecrated to the worship of religion had been drawn to the service of humanity. This was the third trial, the final and irrevocable choice.

Was it his great opportunity, or his last temptation?

He took the pearl from his garment. Never had it seemed so luminous, so radiant, so full of tender, living luster. He laid it in the slave's hand.

"This is your ransom, daughter. It is the last of my treasures which I kept for the king."

While he spoke, the sky darkened, and shuddering tremors ran through the earth heaving convulsively like the breast of one who struggles with mighty grief.

The walls of the houses rocked to and fro. Stones were loosened and crashed into the street. The soldiers took the pearl and fled in terror, reeling like drunken men. But Artaban and the girl whom he had ransomed crouched helpless beside the wall of the governor's palace.

What had he to fear? What had he to hope? The quest was over, and it had failed. But, even in that thought, accepted and embraced, there was peace. He knew that all was well, because he had done the best that he could. He had been true to the light that had been given to him. He knew that even if he could live his earthly life over, it could not be otherwise than it had been.

One lingering pulsation of the earthquake quivered through the ground. A heavy tile, shaken from the roof, fell and struck the old man on his temple. He lay breathless and pale, with his gray head resting on the young girl's shoulder and blood trickling from the wound. As she bent over him, fearing that he was dead, there came a voice through the twilight, very small and still, like music sounding from a distance, in which the notes are clear but the words are lost. The girl turned to see if someone had spoken from the window above them, but she saw no one.

The old man's lips began to move, as if in answer, and she heard him say in the Parthian tongue:

"Not so, my Lord! When was it that I saw you hungry and gave you food, or thirsty and gave you something to drink? And when was it that I saw you a stranger and welcomed you, or saw you naked and gave you clothing? And when was it that I saw you sick or in prison and visited you? Three-and-thirty years have I looked for you; but I have never seen your face nor ministered to you, my king."

He ceased, and the sweet voice came again. And again the girl heard it, very faint and far away. But now it seemed as though she understood the words:

"Truly I tell you, just as you did it to one of the least of these who are members of my family, you did it to me."

A calm radiance of wonder and joy lighted the pale face of Artaban like the first ray of dawn on a snowy mountain-peak. A long breath of relief exhaled gently from his lips.

His journey was ended. His treasures were accepted. The other wise man had found the king.

Preaching point: *Does anyone really need guidance in understanding this story?*

B Proper 9 (14) Mark 6:1-13

Chapter 48: Serving Light

Rebecca struggled down the hall, her ancient suitcase screeching on the floor. Her father had said, "Take the big old one. Who knows what can happen to it." The humid Belize weather made it feel twice as heavy. She'd slept little in the past two days, partly for the nightmare delays of three airports ending in the two hour bus ride and partly for having put off packing until the last minute and needing to shop at midnight for a week's supplies. Rebecca said, "I'm doing this for Jesus," but it didn't make her suitcase any lighter.

The driver who'd picked up her along with two other arriving volunteers at the airport had carried her luggage to outside the dorm. Then someone yelled that there was a problem at the bus. "Sorry," he said, as he put down her suitcase. "Your room, let me see," he rummaged his pocket for a paper, "is number twelve here at the end of the hall. Be to the cafeteria at noon. We'll all be getting together there."

Rebecca pushed and pulled her suitcase like she was herding it. The suitcase together with her backpack weighed half as much as she did. Her high school youth leader had told her the mission trip would strengthen her faith. So far it felt like a two-day survival course and she wished it had strengthened her arms. She thrashed against the suitcase, lugging and shoving it, looking at the doors for numbers. Her eyes were still dazzled from the Belize sun and not adjusted to the dim interior. Some numbers were clearly painted, others scraped off. She decided that, since she could read eleven on the next to the last, the last must be twelve. She'd gotten the door open a crack and was pushing the suitcase ahead of her when the door swung in quickly and a head poked around with an expectant look, which immediately changed when it saw Rebecca. "Oh," the girl said. "When that suitcase poked into the room, I thought for sure you were Cassie."

Behind her came a girl's voice: "Not Cassie?"

"Nope, not yet" she said over her shoulder, and then to Rebecca, "I'm Bernice. Call me Neecy. Come on in. We were expecting a girl we roomed with last year." She smiled and helped scoot Rebecca's luggage into the room. The room was small and had two bunk beds. Atop one a girl waved to her, "Hi. I'm Ellen." She closed her Bible and hopped down. "Neecy and I are from Mississippi. Where you from?"

"Michigan," Rebecca said.

"Well," Ellen said, "we're all from 'M' states." They chuckled.

The girls quickly exchanged other information about their lives and churches. They were all high school seniors, one Baptist, one Methodist, one Quaker. They were going to spend their spring break repairing and painting buildings for a Belize orphanage.

"There's not much storage space," Neecy said, as she helped Rebecca empty her suitcase. "We found that out last year. This your first time?"

"Yeah," Rebecca said.

"I guessed it by how heavy your luggage is," Ellen said and they all laughed, Ellen and Neecy more than Rebecca.

Ellen looked at her watch, "It's already 11:45. We've been waiting for Cassie. You'll like her."

"The driver told me there was one more bus to arrive," Rebecca said.

"We have to be at the cafeteria at noon," Ellen said, "where before lunch they'll tell us our assigned groups. The 'groups' mean which truck we'll crawl in at seven in the morning to undergo an hour and a half drive to the orphanage. Did you know how far we have to bounce each day in the back of a truck?"

"I don't think the web site stated an hour and a half," Rebecca said, "but it did say it was a slight ordeal, part of which I think I've already endured."

"Lots of kids bring too much," Ellen said, "but last year Cassie won the prize. She's a legend."

Neecy said, "She's really smart and really nice. She took our razzing well last year. She told us she came so she could include a service project on her college applications. It's a good sign she's coming back."

Rebecca finished unpacking and stuffed her suitcase under the bed. The door opened and another teenaged girl stepped in, "Hi guys," she said, holding out her arms. Ellen and Neecy squealed as they leaped to her and hugged her. "Great to see you two," she said.

"This is Rebecca," Neecy said, as she held her arm out to Rebecca, "our other roomy for a week." They said hello to one another. "Which one's my bed?" Cassie asked. Ellen pointed to the bunk below hers. Cassie tossed her backpack on it and said, "Driver said we have to be to the cafeteria at noon. Better get ready."

"Ok," Ellen said, "let's get the rest of your luggage."

"This is it," Cassie said, pointing to her backpack.

Neecy and Ellen opened their mouths and it was a couple of seconds before Ellen chuckled, "What do you mean 'this is it?' Come on, let's get your stuff."

"Don't have anything but what I'm carrying."

"Are you crazy?" Neecy said. "You can't spend a week with just what you've got in the backpack."

"Sure I can," Cassie said as she looked around at Ellen, Neecy, and Rebecca. "If I need anything, I can borrow from you guys."

"Us?" Ellen and Neecy said in unison. They looked at Cassie in astonishment and then at Rebecca as if she could answer their unspoken question of what was wrong with Cassie. Rebecca stepped back, leaned against the bunk bed, and waved her hand in front of her, gesturing that she wasn't involved in what was going on between the three.

"Last year you guys told me I had four times more than I needed and you could loan me anything. So, our youth leader said Jesus instructed his missionaries not to take anything extra and they'd be provided for." She paused as she gazed at Ellen and Neecy's gasping faces. "A lot of things have happened to me this year, good things with following Jesus. I couldn't wait to tell you. I've left a lot of things behind for Jesus. I knew you'd be happy for me."

Ellen and Neecy looked sideways to Rebecca as if awaiting her opinion. Cassie smiled at her too. Rebecca nodded, "That's great. I'm pleased for you. I'm not sure that's exactly what Jesus meant, but I can tell this is going to be a great week serving him."

Preaching point: *Sometimes serving Jesus is more important than how we prepare to serve him.*

B Resurrection Sunday Mark 16:1-8

Chapter 49: Failures For Jesus

His first day in the eastern synagogue was ending badly. "Jesus' traveling with women isn't the most important," his disciple Thaddaeus said. "I'm surprised you're stuck on this." The men, sitting around the tiny synagogue, gave no indication that his statement made any difference to them. Always before Thaddaeus found unbelief in Jesus' resurrection to be the greatest impediment to faith. Not in this village far to the east of Judea.

An older man rose slowly. "It's not proper," he spoke with his hands lifting his back, "even in the countryside for women to be with men they aren't married to. You told us Jesus traveled with men and women who weren't married to each other. This is a scandal. We can't accept a person who doesn't practice basic propriety."

Thaddaeus was about to respond, but another man stood up, younger, yet with bushy, old-man eyebrows, "And we've heard Jesus resisted sacred things, from the sabbath to the temple. While he was still tramping around Galilee we received word of his sacrilege. This was at least a year before news of his crucifixion reached us. We're two weeks walk from Judea, but we're observant and for every festival some of our men journey to Jerusalem. A couple of them were near the temple when Jesus tossed out the animals and money changers." He paused, cradled his chin in his hand, "I'm not pleased with animals being sold in the temple. Many others must have agreed; because the chief priests left him free for a few days. But, his practice with women wasn't proper."

Thaddaeus was stymied. Somehow his message about Jesus' resurrection had meandered into a side stream about Jesus' relationship with women. The men in the synagogue were friendly, hospitable to another Jew, and eager to hear news from beyond their small Jewish outpost. For now, he thanked them for receiving him and exited their gathering before he stirred up trouble.

After an evening of prayer he returned the next day to take a different tack. As he arrived at the assembly building, a number of women stood outside, obviously having accompanied their husbands. Thaddaeus wondered what conversations might have transpired between husbands and wives the evening before.

A few men spoke pleasantly to him as he entered their small gathering room. They led him to the front, expecting him again to speak. "Friends, thank you for receiving me today," He said. "I'm glad you've come and I appreciate you brought your wives." A young man let out a chuckle, but quickly stifled it.

"I've prayed about how I should fill in what you know about Jesus. I believe you're hanging precariously onto a small branch because you missed the tree's trunk. I respectfully must state that you're wrong about Jesus. I'm not sure how fully you know Jesus' earthly ministry; but, strange as it might sound, we were all wrong about him during his life.

"You've heard of his healings and casting out demons. I told you he multiplied food for the hungry and calmed the sea for us imperiled with him in the boat. True, he resisted strict sabbath restrictions, but always for human good as a way of glorifying God. Yet for all his graciousness to us, our religious officials deemed him possessed and his family believed he was out of his mind. Now, this is what I think you also need to learn: We, his closest disciples, never fully understood him either. He'd tell us he was going to be betrayed, suffer, and be resurrected and we never caught on. We wanted him to be the grand earthly savior who'd free us from the Romans and set us on top of the world's government. That's the kind of kingdom we wanted God to inaugurate on earth.

"Jesus never went along with that. No matter what we wanted, he continued to care for the weak and despised or forgotten — children, the deaf, the blind, the leper, the poorest, — and even the rich. Even Gentiles. Even women. All because his love was beyond anything that had ever walked the earth. Yes, he befriended women, forgave them, cured them and they loved him and followed with us. They couldn't help following him. No one could who felt the compassion of his heart. It wasn't a matter anymore of sex, rank, or race. He included everyone.

"However," Thaddaeus sighed deeply, "I'm here to report more than our being drawn to Jesus by his love and concern. I've come because no matter how much he cared about us, put up with us, even mediated our squabbles; in the end, as throughout his ministry, we failed him. When we could've stood up for him, we fled.

"And you know what? Those women who followed with us, who took care of him when we didn't, those women first at the tomb, failed Jesus also. At Jesus' empty tomb the angel commanded them to tell us he'd been raised from the dead. Those women, who had a dozen more reasons to be grateful to Jesus for how he elevated them to the level of true children of God, fled in terror and didn't say anything to anyone.

"We all failed him. Having been loved greatly, we failed to respond to God's goodness." His voice became softer, "Yet God raised Jesus from the dead to forgive us and to start the world over in a different way." He placed both hands on his chest. "I recognize your concern about women in the old world before Jesus. But in Jesus' resurrection, God started life over—men and women, old and young, Jew and Gentile. We all fail God, but in Jesus, God loves us, forgives us, and accepts us anyway. That's the center of Jesus' resurrection, and I pray that you'll join in this faith and share in God's wonderful new life."

The men asked a few questions. Some exited the gathering. Some stayed to pray. When Thaddaeus finally left the assembly, he noticed that the women seemed particularly eager to join their husbands and to hear what they had to say about Jesus.

> **Preaching point**: *No matter our reasons to be grateful, we fail God; yet, in Jesus' resurrection God loves and forgives us, welcoming us into a new realm of existence that disregards earthly distinctions of sex, rank, or race.*

ABC Nativity of the Lord I Luke 2:1-14

Chapter 50: A View From The Very Top

The angel, for the only time since creation, had spoken his piece. He'd practiced it throughout eternity and delivered it surrounded by the glorious solemnity that accompanies a heavenly being: "Do not be afraid; for see — I am bringing you good news of great joy for all the people: to you is born this day in the city of David a Savior, who is the Messiah, the Lord. This will be a sign for you: you will find a child wrapped in bands of cloth and lying in a manger."

Then it was over, his individual task completed. The angel gazed across time with the realization he'd never perform another singular assignment. He melted back into the mass of angels and joined to praise God and promise peace on earth.

Yet... yet, the experience had affected him as he hadn't anticipated: from heaven to earth, from eternity to time, from hiddenness to visibility. He'd participated in one of those rare angelic events, a lone angel. Michael or Gabriel, yes, they were dispatched alone and a handful of others here and there, but this angel was one of the few graced to step out of the ranks, distinct from God's heavenly troops, to touch the human realm. In a human's blink, the further weight of the event surged into his awareness after he'd observed firsthand the confusing and misled antics of humans and his part in correcting it.

His thinking, in the space of a lightning strike, flashed in two directions: joy for what was now planted on the earth with Jesus' birth in Bethlehem and wonder at his role in the event. In that instant he not only sensed God's eternal love embracing the planet, he also followed Jesus' life and ministry, his death and resurrection. He knew the end from the beginning and the beginning from the end. Such is the privilege of spiritual beings, which is satisfying beyond anything earthly, along with the

Fragments of Good News

gratification of seeing humans nearly scared out of their hair when an angel approaches them.

Yet... yet, he was distracted by this nearer, inside-out experience of human life. His preliminary instruction had only covered elementary information about relations between angels and humans. Basically, he was God's spokesman which, if God chose, God could brush aside and take the place of the emissary. When you're God, you get to do things like that. An angel is just a spiritual delegate delivering God's message and activating God's work on earth.

No matter his knowing of Jesus' ultimate victory, what disturbed him was the future for his fellow angels. He was overwhelmed and consumed in his task for God and Jesus. That's why he couldn't help but deplore what would become of angels.

Before he'd been designated to report the good news of the Messiah to the world, he'd been informed, along with all of heaven's angels, not only what was to come of Jesus, but what would become of God's angels. For all he'd tried to erase it from his memory, the terrible news had struck him and all of heaven's angels like the pealing of doom.

"Jesus must increase," the archangel said, "and we all must decrease." Sounded spot on. That summarized any angel's task: God's ambassador. But the archangel continued, "After Jesus' resurrection, his believers will often concentrate upon you instead of upon him," at which heaven shook with angelic grumbling. He continued, "They'll say you have wings and feathers," which brought a gasp sweeping through heaven like the explosion of a thousand volcanoes. "From being God's 'holy ones,' they'll turn you into trinkets like pagans worship, cute little idols tacked on refrigerators, posted in gardens, and dangling from rear-view mirrors. You'll even be downgraded by official translations of the Bible. Instead of noting that you're God's troops, the translators will call you 'hosts,' as though everyone knows what that is. They'll expect you're all inviting them to lunch. They'll treat you like a carryout person at the grocery store, a parking attendant, or a magic wand. They'll even refer to other humans, especially babies, as 'such an angel.'"

The angels were used to abiding what other religions thought of them, confusing them with stars, moon, sun, or underling gods. At least such perversions were somewhat exalted. But when the angels heard what Jesus' believers were going to do to them, they leaped into a thundering grumble that shook heaven for an aeon…, or a second in human calculation.

"But, think about it," the archangel continued, attempting to mollify God's spiritual army. "If people trivialize God, won't they trivialize you?" At which a saddening silence struck the ranks. "No matter what people think of you, your task on earth will be to serve God invisibly, which is exactly what Jesus will do visibly. And people? Many will sentence Jesus forever to a manger, as they will demote him from Lord to teacher or reduce him from Savior to martyr."

What more was there to say… or to do? The angels will continue steadfastly delivering God's messages and glorifying God until creation rattles. They will remain faithful, as will their Lord Jesus, until his resurrection finally flips human life right side up, recreates the totality of existence, and releases angels to perform forever their intended and most joyful function: Praising God in the highest.

> **Preaching point**: *Christmas is centered completely on Jesus, not angels.*

C Epiphany 6 (6) Luke 6:17-26

Chapter 51: A Messianic Message?

Shemaiah plodded toward his village, grateful to be home in Judea but shaking his head in disappointment. *The elders entrusted me and what can I report? A week's trek for nothing.* He walked along mumbling and didn't notice the lone spider strand floating across the road. In the late evening sun, it undulated slowly as it drifted toward the village. It was dozens of times thinner than a fishing line and that many times more irritating. As it swept into his mouth, he angrily brushed his hand across it. He spit and kicked the dust in anger. He continued spitting as he walked, the spider's bitter invasion seeming to hang in his mouth. Such a little thing shouldn't bother him so much; but it was about the Galilean and a wasted week.

His synagogue had deputized him to chase down the Galilean wonder worker and bring a suggestion of what the synagogue should do: support him or, more probably, condemn him. The decision was crucial, because the village's response could bring down the wrath of the Romans. Ostensibly, Shemaiah must determine if Jesus was teaching within the area fenced around the Jewish Torah by the elders. But his real task was to find out if he claimed to be a Messiah, and opinions differed on what a Messiah would be like.

Shemaiah's assignment hadn't seemed difficult. For months news had sifted into Judea about the Galilean who was preaching, healing and casting out demons. Others had done similar things, but never for long. They were exposed as frauds or they gathered an army for a failed revolt against the Roman occupiers. Much about Jesus sounded different. Word was that when Jesus met with faith, miracles happened. His hometown had given up on him, but that just showed he was strong enough to go against the grain of Galilean bumpkins. He might be what old Israel waited and prayed for.

Shemaiah had spent three days reaching Galilee and following the trail of Jesus' activity village by village. By his fourth day, he'd hit upon a crowd tracking Jesus. He circulated in the dusty multitude and questioned anyone who knew of him.

One man told him, "My brother-in-law met a blind man given sight by Jesus." A woman spoke up, "In our neighboring village they say he cast out a demon." Many in the crowd were bringing sick and disabled people for healing. Most everyone mentioned the word "Messiah," whether in whisper, wish, or ridicule. A few admitted they were seeking to prove Jesus an ordinary Galilean lunatic. After all, if he couldn't get along with his neighbors, could he be genuine?

Shemaiah stayed near these folks as the crowd met and merged with the horde already surrounding Jesus. They were on a level field, adequate for thousands to cram together.

He couldn't penetrate to the front, but word was drifting back that Jesus was right then healing people and casting out demons. Shemaiah was doing his best to seem inconspicuous and move closer, but everyone was crowding forward, even some foreigners. Jesus' apprentices surrounded him, muscling back the most frantic. By mid-afternoon, Shemaiah had shouldered and elbowed his way close enough to clearly identify the man that everyone was mobbing. He was only fifteen or twenty people away from Jesus. A few women were weeping and some men were angrily shoving others, but all were pressing forward and trying to touch Jesus. Shemaiah concentrated on not being emotionally carried away. He was here to evaluate, not join. He was near enough to Jesus that it seemed some people were cured and others were freed of their demons. He couldn't be certain. These so-called healed individuals would need to survive a few days to demonstrate they were whole again.

Then, almost suddenly, Jesus switched from ministering to the suffering individuals. He began to teach. If he were to claim to be Messiah and rouse people against Rome, now was the time. With such a fury surrounding him, this was possible.

Fragments of Good News

The crowd quieted slowly, family and village groups hushed themselves and over their heads Jesus began to speak. He started strangely enough, "Blessed are you who are poor, for yours is the kingdom of God. Blessed are you who are hungry now, for you will be filled. Blessed are you who weep now, for you will laugh. Blessed are you when people hate you, and when they exclude you, revile you, and defame you on account of the Son of Man. Rejoice in that day and leap for joy, for surely your reward is great in heaven; for that is what their ancestors did to the prophets." This could be a shifty way to state a messianic agenda. No matter how bad things are under the Romans, they will be reversed by the Messiah's forces: taking back our independence, cancelling taxes, reviving Israel's rightful place at the top of the world, all nations flowing to Jerusalem with offerings.

Shemaiah crested the last hillock to his village. He fussed about the news he was delivering to Judea. This problem had crashed into Shemaiah's perception when Jesus continued teaching: "But woe to you who are rich, for you have received your consolation. Woe to you who are full now, for you will be hungry. Woe to you who are laughing now, for you will mourn and weep. Woe to you when all speak well of you, for that is what their ancestors did to the false prophets."

Jesus had gathered people with miracles only to grind them into the ground with his teaching. He wouldn't keep drawing crowds with such a line. He needed to declare them God's greatest people, God's select, better than anyone else. He should claim that God was going to make our nation magnificent again and promise that rain will fall on our crops only, our sheep will all have twins, our clan will always be the village leaders, our wheat will yield fifty-fold, our children will all marry into rich families.

Shemaiah trudged toward his house, knowing that tomorrow in the synagogue, he must report that a man with such a negative message definitely wasn't the Messiah. He's a dry well, a wind that brings no rain. But the synagogue need take no action. Jesus' message will get him killed soon enough. After a while, for every one person attracted to him, twenty will shun him. His twisted message will leave listeners with just a bitter taste in the mouth.

Preaching point: *Jesus' teaching is not thoroughly attractive or immediately understandable.*

C Proper 13 (18) Luke 12:13-21

Chapter 52: The Way Jesus Would Have Told It

"I wish you'd seen Jesus' face when he said that," the disciple Thaddaeus stated. "Seeing his expression would explain better than I can. It was over in a few heartbeats. The man in the crowd had piped up, 'Teacher' — sounding like, 'if you're so smart, tell my brother to divide the family inheritance with me.'"

Thaddaeus nodded to the family of four he was teaching about the resurrected Jesus and smiled as though what he'd explained about Jesus and the greedy heir was perfectly clear to them. This family was the only one in the whole village with any interest in Jesus. They sat comfortably on the ground: father, mother, and two young boys. The parents glanced at each other; but, whether they understood Thaddaeus, they smiled to him and he continued.

"Jesus sized up the fellow in a blink," Thaddaeus said. "He could do that. Spooky when you saw it. He instantly pegged the man as greedy, refused to give a decision between two greedy heirs, and went on to show why in his parable. You could say that basically Jesus nailed the fellow's sandal to a plank and left him spinning in a circle." The father smiled. The mother looked puzzled.

Thaddaeus continued, "Jesus was telling the parable to a particular man. The parable just popped from him at the moment. Jesus didn't carry the story around in his bag waiting to pull it out and slap it on someone. He'd never spoken that parable before nor did he again, even though he often repeated himself. People have memorized his two long sermons and you can hear between the two how he said things differently. He even taught his prayer with variations. He didn't mind changing. With the Syrophoenician woman, he changed his mind right in front of everyone. I told you about that didn't I?"

The boys squirreled around behind their parents' backs and pinched one another. The mother and father nodded to Thaddaeus and waited for him to tell more about Jesus' encounter with the greedy heir.

"Well, if you'd seen Jesus' face," Thaddaeus said again, and shook his head in wonder. "We'd been with him long enough to watch it happen — his responses to others that matched what they really needed. Jesus trained us to do the same things. He said, 'A disciple isn't above the teacher, but everyone who's fully qualified will be like the teacher.' That's why I'm confident he'd have told this story differently to a specific man I lived near all my life. His name was Benaiah. Jesus would have included Benaiah in the parable — and if he didn't, I will.

"Benaiah owned properties all over our region. Started rich, stayed rich. About the most fortunate life one could imagine because he was rich, and he and his wife Yael loved one another. Everyone knew of their love, talked about it, joked about it. Imagine that: a man and woman betrothed at birth by two rich families, yet they married and loved one another." The man and woman Thaddaeus was teaching glanced to one another.

"This year, again Benaiah's land produced record crops: bushels of wheat and barley beyond carrying. Orchards dripping with olives and dates. Merchants lining up at his door bidding on this season's harvest. Since his crops increased every year, his first thought was to dig and plaster more granary cisterns. Hire a better crew than the last incompetent bunch. Build more barns — solid and water shedding. Make them larger than needed this year, because surely the crops will continue to increase.

"One evening at dusk Benaiah and Yael stood in their yard gazing over their property in the sunset. They were thoroughly satisfied with their lives and didn't have a second thought about plans to increase their wealth. He turned to her suddenly and said, 'After the harvest, how about we throw a grand party?'

"'Yes,' Yael said brightly, 'like after the twins were born. I'll have the steward start the list of those to invite and another list for what the servants need to get started on.' She turned happily and dashed off to the house, humming.

"Jesus would have told the story that, after the two fell into pleasant slumber that night, a dream assaulted Benaiah. He dreamed God spoke to him, 'You fool! This very night Yael will be demanded of you. And the things you have prepared, what will they do for you when she is dead?'

"And Benaiah, as I picture the parable Jesus would have told, would surely respond, 'God, Yael is more valuable than all this land can produce. Please let Yael live. If someone has to die, let me die, but let Yael live.'"

Thaddaeus squinted his eyes slightly and bent toward the family that was listening to him on the ground. "As I said, I knew Benaiah and that's the way he would have answered. I grant you that's not the parable Jesus told, but *if* he spoke it to someone like Benaiah, he might have told it with Benaiah saying: 'Let me die instead of Yael,' — an idea Jesus thoroughly understood."

The husband and wife sat unusually still in front of Thaddaeus, the two boys heard their father gasp and looked up, surprised by tears on their mother's face.

Preaching point: *The relative value of wealth.*

C Lent 4 Luke 15:1-3, 11b-32

Chapter 53: Second Cutting

When Rod answered the phone, his mother was talking and her voice blasted him, "— elp in the hay."

"Mom," he raised his voice into the phone.

She hadn't heard him and talked over him, "...broke the contract and your dad's been trying to do everything himself."

After a couple tries Rod was able to shout his way into her nearly deaf ear and get her to start over. Rod's parents had retired from farming five years before and leased their hay fields to neighbors. The neighbors, the Swansons, in the middle of haying season, broke the contract and moved somewhere Rod couldn't understand.

"Matthew's trying to do it himself and he's too old. Equipment keeps breaking down. You and William need to come help. Please come right now. Be here tomorrow morning."

Rod tried to explain it was "just impossible," but she couldn't hear him. He hung up the phone, knowing she hadn't heard his 'goodbye.' It took some first class begging with his boss and extra promises to Flo about a later and better weekend trip, but Rod was in the pickup before light the next morning for a two hour drive to his parent's farm.

He arrived half an hour before Billie, whom he greeted coldly. Their father was all joy, nearly jumping as he said, "Good to have both the boys back, isn't it Arleen?"

She answered, "I will, Matthew. I will. Soon as I make the coffee."

Rod stepped back to gaze at his nuclear family: an irresponsible brother, a mother who couldn't hear, and a father who repeated, "We'll work this out somehow." He thought, how can I physically survive this? I don't even jog anymore.

"The second cutting was down and windrowed and they

just left," Matthew said. "The alfalfa is ready to bale. After two days, I started nosing around. Where were the Swansons? They'd skedaddled. Not a word to anybody. When I met the guys for coffee at Pancake Flats, everybody guessed they were running away from debt."

Matthew had managed to bring their ancient baler back to life — constant problems with the knotter — but his hay picker had broken down years before he retired and he said it was "beyond the reach of mechanic or magician." And there lay the bales, begging to be gathered into the barn. So your mom says "call the boys." Awful glad you came. Let's get at it."

Next to the barn, the old man asked who wanted the privilege of spinning the John Deere's fly wheel. Rod stepped over. His father said, "Remember how to open the petcock and then close it when one cylinder starts?" How could Rod forget? After a strenuous and slightly frightening minute, the old Model B began its 'pop, pop, pop.' Their farming equipment had always been a month away from the wrecking yard. When their father retired he sold the few pieces that still worked, but he couldn't part with the John Deere. "We can fix it and fix it and it will run for a hundred years." That was one of his favorite sayings. Another was, always with outstretched arms, "Someday this will all be yours," a promise the brothers neither requested nor appreciated. Matthew climbed painfully onto the tractor's seat and pointed forward like a general ordering the charge.

The brothers hopped on the back of the flatbed trailer to ride to the field. They'd done the same all their youth, taking turns to drive the tractor from the time they were twelve. Rod was 42 and Billie was 40, but to Rod riding on the trailer was the same as thirty years before. Every year aimed to the alfalfa harvest. "The Washington Farmer" calendar on their kitchen wall might as well have had its months start with the spring fertilizing, then the regular irrigating which led Matthew to say, how "those beautiful little sprouts started greening the field." Then every year before they knew it, the boys and their father were snaking through the field with tractor and trailer retrieving hundreds of dark green, very heavy bales of alfalfa.

With a clank of the hitch the tractor and trailer lurched toward the field. The task was so simple that a new hired hand learned it in five minutes — or quit and went home: driving through the bales and tossing them onto the trailer, lacing them row by row, alternating bales like bricks to hold them against the occasional jerking of the clutch. Three crops a season. Rod knew that he and Billie both hoped that by the third cutting this year their father would have arranged for custom cutters. Rod didn't, however, say this to Billie. The brothers sat silently next to one another.

In fifteen minutes, they'd bounced to the far end of the west field and Matthew turned to start the picking. Rod dreaded what awaited them. Their long sleeves and straw hats offered the slightest of comfort. These bales would surely maim both brothers.

The tractor stopped squarely between two rows of bales. The old man looked back at his sons, his face no longer tanned as it had been in their youth, but his same ridiculous hat flopped so low he had to tip his head back to see higher than the end of the tractor. "Here we go, boys," he said with that goofy smile that was half a gasp. "Gotta' make hay while the sun shines." Another of his favorite sayings.

Rod hopped off to his side of the trailer and Billie to the other. With the trailer empty they were visible to one another and in unison, they sank a hook into a bale and dragged it to the trailer, grunting to lift. The tractor tugged through the waiting bales, stopping for the next two. Rod was exhausted after the first row of twelve and was glad it was a short trailer. By the second row the boys were lifting over waist high and Rod expected that Billie was as tired as he was. They'd both been strong boys. Life on the farm guaranteed that. Rod had played on the school teams. Billie was the fastest boy in high school. His junior year in gym class he set a school record running the 400 meters in gym shoes, not track spikes. Yet he never joined a team. The closest Billie got to organized athletics, Rod thought, was one of many short-lived jobs in a sporting goods store.

Fragments of Good News

The tractor stopped for the fourth layer. Rod wondered if his father would consider driving to the barn with only three layers instead of the four they'd done when they were younger. He walked behind the trailer to see if Billie agreed that three layers were high enough. Billie was at the front of the trailer and Rod watched him snap the bale up, balance it against the third layer, and toss it onto the top, almost like shooting a two handset shot in basketball. All right, Rod thought, I guess we go four layers.

Even with leather gloves, by the third trailer load Rod felt blisters on his uncallused hands. By the fifth load, blisters on each hand had burst, lubricating the inside of his gloves with watery blood. His allergies were kicking in and his resolve to breathe through his nose had ended in the first five minutes. He could see that Billie also was breathing through his mouth and both their tongues hung out. He wondered how much longer they could continue. He began to worry about his middle-aged heart.

The more he labored, the more he recalled how often he'd had to make up for Billie in the past. He thought of his mother's saying, "William will be better this time. He promises." Unfortunately, she'd said that at least three times. Billie's early alcoholism had robbed Rod of a good deal of his childhood and it had left Billie, finally sober at 35, having lost his edge on thinking, slow even balancing his checkbook, unable to remember the phone numbers of his children who lived with his ex-wife. Soon Rod's past anger began to drive him as he lifted each bale. When they finally finished this horrible work, he was going to inform Billie how much extra labor his irresponsibility had cost him over the years and how many things he'd missed because he was doing the work of two.

He was jerked back to the present because the trailer didn't stop. It drew away from Rod and Billie and, hooks in their bales, they stood looking at one another. The trailer didn't stop. They gazed stupidly at it and by fifteen yards realized something was wrong. They couldn't spot their father's head and the tractor began to turn slightly to the left side. "Dad," Billie yelled, and they both ran as fast as their worn out legs could move. The trailer had swerved toward Rod's side. It hit a bale which clipped his leg and knocked him down. He'd just gotten up when he saw Billie's head appear over the hitch as he leaned forward to pull his dad up. He struggled to reach over him and disengage the clutch.

Arleen and the brothers weren't allowed to stay with Matthew in the emergency room. The small hospital was jammed, so they sat two hours in a hallway as medical personnel shuffled past without a look. Rod didn't realize it, but he was constantly rubbing one shoulder, arm and wrist and then the other.

Billie said, "Pretty sore?"

Rod grit his teeth and said, "Just tired. I don't know if I can keep this up."

"When you're tired, you need to be extra careful. Halt."

Rod stared blankly at him.

"'Halt' is what we learned in recovery. Stands for 'Hungry, Angry, Lonely, Tired.' When you're any of those, you need to guard against abusing alcohol, but also of causing an accident."

Arleen shouted to the brothers, "What's going on with Matthew?" Billie stood directly in front of her to state loudly that no one had told them anything. Then he had to move for a cart with food trays to pass.

Billie watched it pass and, when he sat down, leaned to Rod, "When I was out of recovery and trying desperately to stay sober, I worked in a hospital for a year. Mostly mopped floors, disposed of the worst kind of messes, and passed food trays. The stinkiest jobs pay the least. I barely earned enough for a small apartment. Lots of times when I rounded up the trays after the patients ate, or didn't eat, I picked from the trays."

Rod looked at him with wonder. Billie never told him about his wrestling with alcoholism and he'd never asked. For all the times the police phoned about Billie and for all the times the family visited him in recovery, Rod remained obedient to his parents' command not to say anything negative about it to Billie. Thus year by year he said less and less, until in the last decade he'd hardly spoken to Billie.

"We'll call it sunstroke for now," the doctor said when

they allowed the three into Matthew's room. "Not a scientific diagnosis. Certainly dehydration."

Matthew spoke weakly to the doctor, "We had to make hay while the sun shined."

The doctor continued facing the family, "We're giving him IVs and he's responding. He seems a fairly healthy seventy-year-old. We'll run more tests in the morning."

As the doctor left he held the door for the chaplain to enter. "Nurse said you'd like a prayer here," she said.

Billie shouted to Arleen that this was the chaplain and she'd come to offer prayer.

"Yes. Good, good," Arleen shouted back. "Matthew needs prayer!"

After talking with the family for a few minutes, Chaplain Woodly stepped beside the bed and gently took Matthew's hand. "Matthew, I'm the hospital chaplain and I'm going to pray for you." Matthew tipped his head on the pillow and gave his goofy, gasping smile. Arleen was on the other side of his bed and held his other hand. The chaplain said, "Let's pray together," and reached out to Rod. He hesitated only slightly to take her hand while Arleen grabbed Billie's hand. Arleen glanced at one and then the other of her sons. Then, as though working in tandem on the hay trailer, each looked at his father, and, knowing that their mother wouldn't hear if they refused, they grabbed the other's blistered, bloody hand in prayer over their father.

Preaching point: *Hope for broken relationships.*

A Thanksgiving; C Proper 23 (28) Luke 17:11-19

Chapter 54: Aunt June's Thanksgiving

Whenever the three Bracken children had friends to their house, they warned them about their stepfather. Never contradict him. Never cross him. Vince, whose name they never called him to his face, was never wrong.

Gigi, Mimi, and Dan, 13, 11, and 10 years, had learned how to stay out of their stepfather's way. Vince stomped into the house with his big boots and swung his arms as he gave orders. The children must say, "Yes, sir," and do what he said.

Gigi, who was the only child to remember their real father, complained to their mother about Vince's arbitrary decisions for everything from the kind of clothes the children wore to their choices of food. Mother only said, "You need a father. He provides well for us."

Vince got his way everywhere, since he owned his business and ran it as tight financially as any general ran an army. His only sibling was June. He called her the religious one. She was the only person who didn't do what Vince ordered, maybe she never had. The Bracken children loved their Aunt June, even though they only saw her twice a year. They loved her because she hugged them and called them silly words that rhymed with their names. At Independence Day and Thanksgiving, Aunt June Selberg and her family gathered with the Brackens. The families took turns hosting one another for these holidays.

The Selbergs had been to the Brackens' on Independence Day in Longview. The Brackens were set to go to Willamina for Thanksgiving. Since the two families were only together twice a year, Thanksgiving was also when the families exchanged Christmas presents for one another — all wrapped and set to wait for another month's opening. Gigi, Mimi, and Dan got to choose presents for their four cousins. Shopping to give their cousins gifts was almost as exciting as receiving gifts.

This was sixty years ago and the highways weren't like today, few freeways, lots of two lane roads. Almost nobody had televisions, and many didn't have telephones or even radios. So the distance traveled between the two families from Longview, Washington, where the Brackens lived to Willamina, Oregon, to the Selbergs — over 120 miles — was a slower and a more difficult drive than today. Especially in late November along the Coastal Range, rain could dump by the truck loads.

When the Brackens woke on Thanksgiving Day, water was sweeping trash cans and basket balls down their street. Mother had just taken her specialty pumpkin pies from the oven when Vince squinted out the window and said, "I don't know. Looks pretty bad." They turned on the radio to get the forecast. It predicted the same rain and possible flooding continuing for another day and a half. Vince stomped around the house for 45 minutes looking out window by window.

At 9:00 Vince announced, "It isn't safe to travel. I'll phone June." Mother said, "Can't we wait and see if it lets up?"

"It might let up here," he spoke loudly, "but we have no idea what it's like farther south. I'm phoning June."

The children were in tears; but, they knew they couldn't change Vince's mind. They listened to his phone call.

"Nope. Can't make it. Not safe. No, I'm not going to phone again. Long distance costs seventeen cents. Yeah. Sorry. Say hello to everyone from us too."

The day was ruined except the kids knew they'd have plenty of pumpkin pie. That was slight compensation. The children retired to their rooms. Mimi tried to get the three of them into a board game, but they were all grumpy and soon were arguing. Vince decided Dan was most to blame so he stationed him by the front window to stand at attention until relieved. Vince and Mother sat in the living room listening to the radio. Dan was certain he'd been forgotten. Seemed he'd stood there for hours. It was, however, exactly 11:52 when he yelled, "They're *here*! They're *here*!"

"What in the world?" Vince said.

Dan ran to his sisters' bedroom. "They're *here*! They came *here*!"

The Brackens all met at the front window to see the Selberg's piling out of their station wagon, each person with packages, pots, bowls, and baskets. Aunt June and her husband were the last to enter. She walked to Vince, smiled and said "Hi, little brother. We thought we'd come to you."

Decades come and go. Family members move away or die. But holidays become defined by what happened before on those holidays. For the Bracken children, once grown, their three families and descendants always celebrated Thanksgiving together. When they gathered at the table all members, whether with wine, water or cider joined the toast, "To Aunt June."

Preaching point: *Gratitude is fueled by memory.*

B Epiphany 2 (2) John 1:43-51

Chapter 55: Further Visions To Follow

Philip searched in and around Cana, but he didn't know it well. He dashed down street and alley asking everyone if they'd seen Nathanael. The third person directed him to the rabbi's tree — the village's area for prayer and contemplation by the rabbis.

Philip knew he should be quiet, but from a stone's throw away he yelled, "Nathanael. Nathanael," as he rushed to him. Under the fig tree, Nathanael seemed to be in a trance, for Philip had to shake him to get him to look up. Nathanael's eyes slowly focused on Philip who stood gasping. "We've found him. We've found him and he found me and enlisted me as his follower."

Nathanael's eyes struggled against the sunlight, "What are you doing here Philip?"

"You've got to come. We've found him about whom Moses in the law and also the prophets wrote - Jesus, son of Joseph from Nazareth."

"'We?'" he said.

"Andrew and Peter, fishermen with me in Bethsaida. They too were John the Baptist's students. We're sure Jesus is the Lord's promised prophet."

"He's a teacher and he found you? Where's your sense, Philip?" He rubbed his shoulders against the tree to wake his body, "Teachers don't choose their students. And 'Nazareth', you said? Can anything good come out of Nazareth?"

"You'll understand. You've got to come see for yourself. He and his students are on the road from Nazareth. If we head south we'll meet them. We've got to start now," Philip pulled him to his feet.

"All right," Nathanael yanked Philip's grip off his tunic. "Let me get my sandals." Philip followed him, doing his best not to push him to his house then onto the road south.

David O. Bales

On their way, Philip couldn't restrain his enthusiasm, "I've never been more sure of anything. Never." He walked along nodding in agreement to each positive thing he said about Jesus. "From your life with God and your understanding of the scriptures, you'll see — I know you will — Jesus' place in God's new world."

Nathanael seldom spoke. He didn't have much chance, because Philip talked all the way, prodding him to rush so they'd meet Jesus before sundown.

Nathanael's meeting with Jesus was more than Philip could have prayed for. At first sight, Jesus praised Nathanael as the genuine innocent Israelite and told him that he'd seen him under the fig tree before Philip found him. Then Jesus uttered the promise that overwhelmed Philip as much as Nathanael, "You will see heaven opened and the angels of God ascending and descending upon the Son of Man." Jesus seemed to be all that Nathanael had waited for and prayed about and also much that he had prayed to.

That sealed the deal for both Philip and Nathanael. As often as they could, they left their homes and families to go with Jesus and his students, to learn from him, and to spread his message. Whenever people rejected their message, Philip reassured Nathanael, "You'll see. Further visions to follow." And everything that Jesus did, though not exactly what the two expected, confirmed that he was God's special person: healing people, casting out demons, reinterpreting scripture, feeding the hungry, forgiving sinners, resisting the proud.

When Peter, James, and John hinted about a wonderful experience with Jesus on a hilltop, Philip said to Nathanael, "Further visions to follow." Even though the opposition to Jesus increased after he reached Jerusalem, Jesus' followers shared their conviction of Jesus' special place in God's plans for Israel and for the whole world. Philip added his constant declaration, "Further visions to follow."

Yet, Jesus was apprehended in Gethsemane's garden and Jesus' students fled. When Philip and Nathanael heard of Jesus' arrest, they tried to devise a way to help him. They didn't know how short the time was. And all of Jesus' followers had deflected his teaching that he was to suffer. Consequently, they were unprepared for his crucifixion.

They were stunned by Judas's betrayal and immobilized by Jesus' death. His remaining eleven students gathered in the home that had welcomed him for Passover. Philip and Nathanael joined them. No one even suggested what to do next. None of them had been able to aid Jesus during his trial, and thus Jesus' death struck his chosen eleven twice as hard. Nathanael was so defeated that he just sat or laid on the floor. When he walked he acted as if he wasn't sure the ground would support his steps. He didn't eat, barely drank, and occasionally mumbled a prayer of lament.

Philip was undone also. He, however, dealt with his grief by repeating what had happened, reciting the order of Jesus' last days in Jerusalem and then becoming nearly hysterical when he recalled how not one of them stood by Jesus. Nathanael, wearied of Philip's prattling, finally said with a sneer, "Further visions to follow?" That silenced Philip.

On Sunday morning Nathanael woke to Philip's dragging him off the floor, laughing and crying at the same time. "He's alive. He's alive." He pulled Nathanael to his feet. "Jesus is alive."

"What?" Nathanael said.

"Jesus has risen from the dead," Philip said, nearly crushing Nathanael in a hug, at which Peter and Andrew tumbled into the room laughing and shouting that Jesus was alive. He'd appeared to Peter. Nathanael shook his head to clear his thinking as the news sunk in. Others of Jesus' students crowded into the room shouting about Jesus' resurrection and praising God. Nathanael remained dumbfounded. Philip leaped in front of him, throwing his head side to side laughing. He raised his arm high and pointed down at Nathanael, "Hah!" he shouted as he laughed. "Hah! Further visions to follow! Further visions to follow!"

Preaching point: *The good news of Jesus' resurrection is always more than anyone expects... or deserves.*

ABC Holy/Maundy Thursday John 13:1-17, 31b-35

Chapter 56: Lord, Where Are You Going?
Domine Quo Vadis?

Within two hundred years after Christ, the message of his resurrection spread throughout the Mediterranean world. Also, legends grew about Christ and his disciples. As time went on, the legends included wilder fantasies. Christians had to decide which stories to believe. This caused confusion especially for children, as was experienced one morning in a fish market in early fourth century Rome.

Eleven-year-old Claudia smelled her parents' pickled fish market four shops away. She ran into their market and brushed the elbow of an old man throwing dice on a table with another old man. "Watch it!" he said and scowled at her. The other man laughed, "It's all right, Claudia, he just lost three denarii."

She rushed around the counter to her mother. "Mother," she said excitedly; but her mother held her hand toward her and frowned, "Wait until I give this woman her fish." The woman dumped the fish into her basket and left with a wave to Claudia. Her mother turned to Claudia, who was breathing hard from having run. She'd been to Sylvia's home to help prepare their courtyard for the Thursday night worship before Resurrection Sunday. She knew she had to wait for her mother to rinse her hands in the basin, dry them on the towel, and turn to her, which she did. Claudia was finally able to blurt out, "While we were sweeping, Sylvia told me what the Apostle Peter did here in Rome."

Her mother rolled her eyes, "Oh, really?"

"Yes, all kinds of things I'd never heard in the Christian gathering. The apostle solved crimes, made a dog speak, brought a dead fish back to life, and — of all wonders — by prayer he made a flying magician fall from the sky."

"Hmm," her mother said. She stared down at Claudia's eager face, her mind swirling with how to explain that not all stories floating around about Christ and the apostles were true. "I've heard those stories also," she said, drying the counter with her cloth. She bought more time to think by pushing aside a wooden crate. Another customer came and she quickly sold her twenty sardines. The two old dice players at the table by the door yelled at one another about whether it had been a three or a four. She motioned to a stool and Claudia sat.

"Every Lord's Day we listen to the gospels read, and we hear stories of his apostles and what they taught and wrote." Claudia nodded and brushed from her eyes the hair that still dangled in her face after her dash from Sylvia's house.

"But for whatever reason, people keep adding to those stories. Maybe they get bored with what they already know or maybe they don't even believe in Christ and want to make Christianity seem silly; but most things they make up are flatly contrary to what we know about our faith."

Claudia listened intently with her mouth open. "Close your mouth," her mother said, "before you catch a fish fly." She shut it with a pop and knew her mother would get around to telling her what she wanted to know.

"About those stories of Peter in Rome," her mother said. "I've heard them. Usually I laugh at them. But even though I think somebody made it up just for entertainment, there's one episode that, even if it didn't happen, makes us think about Christ's truth."

A die flew onto the floor and the players blamed each other, as they did every day. Her mother raised her voice to them, "The die is cast," but the two looked confused. She said, "You don't know the history of your own empire." They gave her no account. She sat down opposite Claudia. "The only part that strikes me as likely in those Peter stories," she said, "is where Peter's in danger and friends convince him to leave Rome to escape being murdered. He gets out of the city and meets the Lord Christ who's entering. Peter asks, 'Lord, where are you going?' Christ answers, 'I go to

Rome to be crucified.' And Peter says, 'Lord, are you going to be crucified again?' To which Christ answers, 'Yes, Peter, I shall be crucified again.' Peter understands that he himself must return to Rome and be crucified for his faith and then Christ ascends again to heaven.

"Peter, like us, is part of Christ' very body on earth. So when Peter was crucified, we could say that Christ, in Peter's martyrdom, was crucified again. I also think that if Peter wouldn't return to Rome and be crucified, Christ would have gone to Rome and been crucified again for him — as he would again for each of us."

Claudia's eyes were wide and she said, "But, but —."

"Just someone's idea of what could have happened, knowing what Christ and Peter were like. But a powerful one. Christ did surprisingly sacrificial things for us. He surprised us with the way he died for us, but he also surprised his disciples on that last Thursday, serving them by washing their feet. Those strange stories about Peter in Rome are surprising; but, if one's going to create an extra story about Christ, it should surprise us again with how he served us with his life and death."

That seemed to satisfy Claudia. She nodded and was about to thank her mother when, instead, she reached quickly to the floor to pick up the die before either old man could blame the other for dropping it.

Preaching point: *Christ in surprising ways sacrificed himself for his followers.*

*(**Domine Quo Vadis?** is Latin for Peter's question to Jesus in John 13:36 and occurs in the non-canonical Acts Of Peter, chapter 35.)*

C Trinity Sunday John 16:12-15

Chapter 57: The Spirit's Guidance

Nola's grandfather died in World War II, yet her world history class in high school had barely advanced to World War I before the end of the school year, as had her elementary school history class six years before. So Nola anticipated that her university's History of Western Civilization course would inform her about World War II. It did.

The lecturer for "World War Two: Precursors" was Dr. Freedman. His few sentences hit the lecture hall like a bomb. "'Germany first! Make Germany great again!' That was Hitler's message, in his own rambling compound German words, of course. He didn't hesitate to break treaties unilaterally and he laced his racism into constant communications through the newest propaganda medium, which at the time was radio. Over and over he and his henchmen repeated their outlandish lies, twisting every fact and advertising the Fuehrer's supposed genius while they encouraged and appealed to the lowest nature of humans: greed and fear of 'those non-Germans... the Jews.'

"Germany's Christians went along with Hitler, not just the Protestants. The Roman Catholics didn't do well either. All the Nazis had to do was to quote the gospel according to Matthew where at Jesus' trial in Jerusalem a handful of Jews said, 'His blood be on us and on our children.' If that wasn't enough justification, the Nazis could pull out the Apostle Paul's instructions to the church at Rome, 'Let every person be subject to the governing authorities; for there is no authority except from God, and those authorities that exist have been instituted by God. Therefore, whoever resists authority resists what God has appointed, and those who resist will incur judgment.' Besides, who dares disagree that your country is greatest? That was enough to spark and fuel World War II in Europe."

Within these three minutes, the lecture hall became alive with mumbles and whispers, then with grumbling and shouts. Dr. Freedman continued: "And…, and, to see what that kind of political leadership creates, tomorrow instead of your discussion groups, all Western Civ students will attend and tour the Holocaust Museum Traveling Exhibition. Buses will pick you up at the student union. Religious groups in the city are paying your transportation. Be outside the student union at ten tomorrow morning. Attendance will be taken by your discussion group leaders not only when boarding here, but when you reboard at the exhibition. This will make sure that, after you see what happened in Germany, you won't be able to decide right there to flee the university and never learn factual history again. One function of a university is to teach you how to reason with genuine facts, not merely how to react to propaganda or to follow the newest Pied Piper. If you don't know about the Pied Piper, look it up on Wikipedia. Even more radical, you could go to the library and find it in a *book*. Class is dismissed early. I strongly suggest you use this extra time to read your assigned chapter 17: 'The Tragic Decade of Global Conflict.'" He repeated: "Tomorrow, ten AM at the student union. Your discussion group leader will take roll," and left the lecture hall.

Nola stayed seated while students around her stood, some chattering with smiles, some frowning with curses. A few, as did Nola, remained silent. She assumed that what Dr. Freedman said about Hitler was correct; and by now students recognized his interposing over-the top, left-wing jabs about modern politics into any historical era he lectured upon. What struck her like a rifle stock smashing her foot was his assertion that German Christians were for Hitler. She'd never heard that. After a few deep breaths she jotted down the scriptures Dr. Freedman mentioned and walked straight to the chapel to find Chaplain Wendy. Her door was open.

Nola was glad that the two already had a relationship. She knew many students who said they were Christians but never joined a campus Christian group or even attended worship. The

Fragments of Good News

fact that dozens of her fellow World Civ students weren't at this moment piling up outside the chaplain's door confirmed Nola's minority status. She sat and quickly told Wendy why she'd come, summarizing what Dr. Freedman said about the German Christians and the biblical reasons they obeyed Hitler. "Is that true?" she asked.

Wendy took a quick breath and curled her hair behind her ears. Nola had seen her do that just before she preached. "Freedman gave a similar lecture last year. This sounds a little more radical, as far as his allusions to contemporary politics. But what he said about the German Christians is true. The majority obeyed Hitler, no matter what they believed as they did so. Hitler even appointed the Protestant church's bishop. The Nazis also hijacked Christian songs and plugged in Nazi ideology. Wasn't a good time or place to be Christian."

Nola's face showed her pain. "Those Bible texts. Did the Bible really mean that?"

"In a slight degree," Wendy said with a lower voice. "They meant something like that in the past for some people. Certainly not to everyone, everywhere. Here's the thing: there's more in the Bible to think with than those two scriptures. And those texts aren't necessarily to be taken as prediction or law. Lots of things in the Bible were meant for a past age or a definite place. We trust that Jesus' Spirit has led us beyond them. Anti-Semitism? What people don't think about is that Jesus and Paul and all the first Christians were Jews." She laughed and Nola, recognizing the irony of Christians hating Jews, began to laugh also. "Pretty dumb," she said.

"Since biblical times," Wendy continued, "the Spirit has led us to denounce slavery, which the Old Testament and New Testament supported. We don't execute witches. We've abandoned racism as an artifact of ancient societies. We don't believe in the subjection of women, which the entire ancient world held to. They'd never give women the vote, let alone allow them to be pastors. And except for a few remote primitive tribes, no one believes in the divine right of kings, which our 'western civilization' held to for quite a while."

Nola leaned forward, "You said Dr. Freedman gave a lecture like this last year. Did he continue in the next lectures to say more? I mean, there must be more."

"He did. The Holocaust Exhibition wasn't here then so I don't know what he'll say this year, but I expect he'll also mention Christian resistance to Hitler. Freedman's a shocker, certainly gets your attention. My experience is that, if you demonstrate a genuine grasp of history and don't just spout an opinion, he'll listen to you. I've never had a problem with him."

Nola gave a relieved smile.

Wendy said, "You want to read about the Christians in Germany who felt led by the Spirit to interpret those verses differently and defy Nazism?"

"A little, maybe. I've got a real load this semester."

"I understand, believe me. But here," she pulled a volume from the bookshelf behind her. "This is a biography of Dietrich Bonhoeffer. He's become famous for having resisted Hitler and was executed by him. This deals with the whole movement of the confessing Christians to the end of World War II. If you're like me, when I first learned of Bonhoeffer and found a biography of him, I couldn't put it down. There you are, right in the middle of Nazi Germany and it's like reading a horror novel. Only it's true." She handed Nola the book. "Have it back in two weeks?"

"Absolutely," Nola said and rose to leave.

"And tell me what Freedman lectures about in the days after you attend the traveling exhibition. I'll want to know what you think of the whole experience. And Nola, the Spirit still leads us in new ways. Hold to that tomorrow, because you're in for a jolt. I'll be praying for you."

Preaching point: *Jesus' Spirit guides Christians into further truth.*

B Reign of Christ (34) John 18:33-37

Chapter 58: Pilate's Point Of View

It's the spring smell in the wind and the fully rounded moon. Does it to me year after year. I regret and rehearse what I should've done. I should've smacked him with the haft of my sword, or ordered the soldiers to crack his kneecaps. But I was distracted by all the hubbub, and I was surprised. I was startled out of sleep by the guard, and I'd rushed to pull on my armor to arrive fully official for examining a prisoner. I immediately bumped into my wife Procla, who was stumbling around in the dark again.

Yet no matter the passing decades, I remember the details. Seemed I'd been asleep only an hour after I'd received the last reports of the patrols, and the patrols were late to headquarters because they'd been monitoring some incipient mob. The Jews' temple police, as usual, had been snarling all day about our men needing to stay clear from the religious rigmarole that goes on in there. The tribune could've received the late reports, but at that time of year — Jerusalem swelling with an extra half million people — I wasn't about to trust that recently stationed, snobby, status seeking tribune.

The Jews insisted I come outside. Of course, they just *couldn't* enter the headquarters where I was warm. Oh no. Couldn't let our Roman dust *de*file them. If they were *dee*filed, they couldn't eat their super-holy meal. So out I go, then in I come with this…, hmm …, individual. I just wasn't mentally prepared. Thought it was a normal incident: An idiot dragged in to receive my judgment, which usually was quick. But here's the fellow, split lip, torn ear, bleeding nose mashed to the side of his face. He strikes the pose of a king who's been captured in battle and ready to endure public execution in a manner that is, to the end, an example to his beaten army. I'd seen a couple like that before, just not so close. His blood was dripping on the floor and splattering my boots.

So, all right, I was unnerved. I gave a last glance around to make sure what was going on. Then, figuring I'd get into the sham interrogation with the very tip of the spear, I asked him how he pled. "Are you the King of the Jews?" Pretty simple. If he answers, "Yes," off he goes to a cross. If he answers, "No," as I expect, I'll rough him up some more and run him out of Jerusalem, teaching him and other screwballs a lesson in Roman justice tinged with mercy.

But he's going to debate with me. He answers, "Do you ask this on your own, or did others tell you about me?"

I've got this Galilean in my hand. I whisper a command and he's immediately on his way to a slow death. But my thinking was disheveled. Procla sends me this desperate written message. I stand there feeling like a fool reading it and, basically, I was tricked into this conversation with a prisoner. I should've sent him right back to those priestly wild bulls lusting for violence upon him. I didn't mind the idea of violence. Comes in handy sometimes. But what can I do? I can't let him get one up on me. Everything in me screams forget it. Fling him away or just kill him, but don't get caught in anything approaching a genuine interrogation. I look in his eyes. He thinks he's going to stare me down. His swollen left eye blinking faster than his right, but he won't turn his gaze off me. I reply, "I am not a Jew, am I? Your own nation and the chief priests have handed you over to me. What have you done?"

I'm stuck, caught in this verbal dance. He goes on, "My kingdom is not from this world. If my kingdom were from this world, my followers would be fighting to keep me from being handed over to the Jews. But as it is, my kingdom is not from here."

So, fine. I could care less about fantasies of world domination, but I can't let him sneak out of this verbal tit for tat. He's completely beaten, abandoned by all his followers. Why does he pretend? But if he's going to keep it up, I'll dislodge a confession from his smart bleeding mouth and get him off my door step. I call him on it: "So you are a king?" It seemed this time he couldn't wiggle out without a plain "yes" or "no." But he slips through that noose and answers, "You say that I am a king. For this I was born, and for this I came into the world, to testify to the truth. Everyone who belongs to the truth listens to my voice."

As I ponder it these decades later, I add him to my memory's pile of unsolved problems. But none bothers me quite as much. The full moon of every spring....

Considering everything, I've done all right. I'm satisfied living out my life here, not exactly in exile. So I drag a foot and need this cane to prop me up? Adequate house, enough honor from the village, money. I've no power, of course, but I didn't seem to have much power over that one Jew either. And I've never gotten over him: His bloody stare and his absolute certainty—almost nonchalance. I still see him. I hear his voice. Most of all I remember my first impression: A king captured and on his way to execution, who by his every word and gesture demonstrates his royal status to the end."

Preaching point: *Recognizing Jesus as king.*

A Pentecost John 20:19-23
ABC Easter 2 John 20:19-31

Chapter 59: Claustrophobia

Until today, no stranger had walked into Pastor Rahlf's office and said, "Tell me about your sermon last Sunday."

All Pastor Rahlfs could respond was, "Ah, I'm Monty Rahlf." He held out his hand, "And you?"

"Lake," he said. Name's Ray Lake. Everybody calls me Lake." He was about forty. His face was drawn and his words strained. His handshake was weak and shaky.

"Have a seat," Monty said.

Lake sat, folded his hands in his lap and looked down. Monty sat opposite him. Lake didn't speak. After half a minute Monty said, "You came about last Sunday's sermon?"

Lake looked up, "Yeah, the title was on the marquee."

Monty felt a ping of guilt. He had no qualms about the sermon title for his congregation, but he'd debated whether to publicize it to the community.

"You saw the title on the marquee," Monty nodded, encouraging Lake to say more.

"Uh huh," he said with a little cringe. "When I was driving by."

"It troubled you?"

Lake relaxed a little, "Not at the time."

"What can I tell you?" Monty said, "More importantly, why do you want to know?"

"It said, 'Faith is Claustrophobic.' I've never heard of such a thing and I...."

Monty leaned forward and spoke quietly, "I see this bothers you. I'd like to understand what's going on and what does last week's sermon have to do with it."

Lake sighed and shook his head to clear his thinking, "Okay.

Fragments of Good News

I'm from Idaho. Took two days' drive to get here. You know the Ramsey house?"

"Everybody does. Charming old place, sitting on that hill with all the trees around."

"That was my great uncle's."

"Oh."

"I'd heard his name, but never met him. I've never met any relatives. Dad and Mom are dead. A month ago, I got a letter that my Great Uncle Ellis Ramsey died. I was his only relative. The house and grounds are mine — free and clear — and some money.

"When I could arrange it, I came, and on my way into town I saw your sermon title, 'Faith is Claustrophobic.' Catchy. It didn't mean anything to me until after the attorney left me at the house and I went prowling around."

Lake swallowed hard, "I wasn't there ten minutes until I wandered into this little room, turned on the light and shut the door after me and the doorknob came off in my hand. I looked at this antique knob and it didn't even have a set screw in it. The shaft was still sticking out toward me, but nothing to turn it with."

Lake breathed deeply, "This room was absolutely empty — no windows — and no matter how hard I tried, I couldn't turn that shaft without some kind of tool."

"Scary," Monty said.

"Man, I panicked. I kind of ran in circles and pounded the walls a few minutes. Took a while just to get my breathing back."

"How'd you get out?"

"I tried to budge the door. Couldn't spring the pins from the hinges with my fingernails. Then I started using my keys to scratch a hole to get my hand through the door and turn the knob from the other side.

"I started to get bothered by claustrophobia. I thought about the *Star Wars* scene in the gigantic trash compactor and felt the walls squeezing in on me. So I scratched harder, but it also tired me out sooner. I'd sleep and then scratch again, alternating my hands." He held out his hands. They were red and bruised. "It sounded like a cat trying to get out of a shoe box.

"After a day I was getting thirsty. Thinking about water made me imagine I was in a doomed submarine with water gushing in. It was terrible." He held his feet on his toes and rapidly raised and lowered his heels, shaking the floor.

"I remembered your sermon title. I was angry about it and fascinated at the same time. I was sweating my way through the door with tiny scratches and making God all kinds of promises. Two and a half days," he sighed, "before," he pulled out his key chain and showed two bent keys, "I got a hole large enough to reach my hand through and turn that blessed knob from the other side." He huffed up his shoulders and blew out, experiencing the release again.

For the first time Lake had a faint smile, "So, I've told you. You tell me what in the world faith has to do with claustrophobia."

Monty was glad to be able to laugh, although nervously. "I'll put it as briefly as I can; but, don't tell the congregation I can summarize a sermon in a couple sentences. They'll opt for the short version."

"Sure," Lake said and grinned.

"I talked about Jesus on the night of his resurrection, meeting his disciples who were huddling behind locked doors for fear. My point was that Jesus is alive and his message must get out—like from Jesus' tomb and from the disciples' locked room—, and the tremendous fear we humans have of being locked in is slightly comparable in degree to the divine compulsion to get out the good news of Jesus' resurrection. I've experienced both claustrophobia and God's love and they're both tremendously strong things. God's love is stronger. And God's Spirit wants to get out of us to others."

"You've been claustrophobic," Lake said.

"Still am. While you were telling about your accidental imprisonment, believe me, this room was getting smaller."

"No kidding!" Lake said.

"Yeah," Monty said.

Lake hadn't noticed the perspiration covering Monty's

forehead.

Monty, stood, breathed deeply, and looked out the window, "You hungry?"

"I think I'll be hungry for another couple days," Lake said.

"You want lunch? We can catch a bite and I can explain more about the Christian faith. And I can show you a little of the town."

"Fine," Lake said.

"And," Monty said, "how about we choose a restaurant with a large seating area?"

Preaching point: *The powerful drive to spread faith in Jesus.*

C Easter 3 John 21:1-19

Chapter 60: Second Chance

Jeffry and his family had worshiped twice in Pastor Phil's congregation and, as Jeffry did when his family moved to a new town, he now met to chat with the pastor. Over the first half cup of coffee he told Pastor Phil about himself, his family, job and why they'd moved to this remote mountain village. Then he was knocked back in his chair when he'd asked Pastor Phil what brought him to this congregation.

"I committed adultery." Because Pastor Phil had explained it many times over the past fifteen years, he could state it almost flatly. To Jeffry's surprised look he continued, "It's in the Bible you know; and I'm not exactly recommending it."

After a moment Jeffry closed his gaping mouth yet found nothing to say. Such an admission doesn't usually pop up with a new acquaintance, let alone with a pastor. Finally, he was able to push out, "Really. I did wonder why a PhD would be here, especially after last Sunday's sermon when you seemed to sling quotes by memory from a Roman Catholic saint, a Methodist missionary and a Presbyterian theologian."

"Different, I know; but, it's not just a matter of what I've done. It's who I am: an adulterer." He paused and looked down at his coffee cup. "I don't mean to shock you. Sometimes the truth is hard to hear. Believe me, it's still hard for me to say."

"That's why you're here, in this tiny congregation."

"And why I'm wearing this chafing clergy collar."

"You tell everybody this?"

"Anyone who needs to know. It's information I silently drop into my confession on Sundays when we acknowledge our sins in 'thought, word, and deed.' I'm forgiven by God; but, even if everyone I've injured forgave me — and they didn't — the consequences still go darting into the world, crashing into innocent and guilty alike."

The two sat silently, Jeffry looking as though he wished he could quickly get out of the conversation.

"If it would help you, I could tell you more of what led me here."

"Well," Jeffry said slowly, "If you want to."

"Not a matter of my wanting to. I said if it would help you."

"Hadn't thought about it that way." Jeffry was leaning back, his chin tucked down. After a deep breath he said, "Yes. I think it would be helpful."

Phil rearranged himself on his chair. "The PhD is an indication of my former drive. From the moment I entered seminary, I wanted to be the best — well, best preacher and theologian, if not pastor. Marjory was in agreement. We wanted the biggest congregation, not just the best salary but with the greatest influence in town. I'm not saying that was always most important. But it was always there, pushing its nose into every pastoral activity.

"We did okay in the success area. Paid off our student loans even while having our babies. Again, success wasn't on the front edge of the brain every moment, but safely tucked in the mind's back pocket. It mostly came out in our wanting more things. In search for more, I got my real estate license and showed houses once a week. That's how we found the house we bought on the river. It was just what Marjory wanted. The kids grew up there and had just moved away.

"But as the years went by, the ministry proved not to be what most satisfied me. I took more joy in selling a house than I did in teaching people about the grace of Christ. If I'd been wiser, or if I'd joined my fellow clergy to strengthen and encourage one another in the ministry, I might have dodged Satan's bullet. As it was, I kept showing houses and met a gorgeous younger woman, newly divorced, new to the town. Lonely.... You can fill in the rest."

Jeffry leaned forward, "How did you find the time?"

"You don't need to know that."

"You're right," Jeffry said, chastened. "Go on."

"Our relationship progressed until we planned to escape together. She was a travel agent. She deposited some of our moneys into banks we could access outside the US. Through her travel contacts, she received a job offer in the Dominican Republic and was assured I could get on with the same hospitality company when we arrived there. She'd even purchased the airline tickets. 'Going to start a new life'" we said.

"That's when the hurricane approached. My mind was somewhere else by then, the Dominican Republic. I was oblivious to the developing catastrophe. Drove home through the wind to snatch my final things and noticed a lot of activity on the other side of the houses on our street. I went through our house and looked toward the river. Marjory and the neighbors were over the lip of the bank, sandbagging in the rain and wind. Here I was, peeking out the window, while they struggled to save the neighborhood. Marjory's hat had blown away, hair plastered on her head. She strained with a shovel filling a sandbag. It was a terrible scene, but I hesitated only a moment. Grabbed my stuff and left."

Jeffry grumbled and shook his head.

Phil cleared his throat, rubbed his hand over his forehead and continued. "Drove as fast as I could. I'd driven around that corner half a thousand times, yet here's a tree blown down. In my guilty state of mind, even in the last split second, I felt it was God's judgment attacking the front of the car. Spun me sideways and into the rail on the other side of the road. Bruised me a bit and sprung the doors open. I was defenseless to the sideways rain. I got out and hobbled against the wind into a clump of trees whose tops had blown off. Got in the lee and was there most of a day. Cell phone coverage was destroyed. Nearly died of hypothermia. My brain was still working, however, at least my conscience. It was eating me up.

"In a nutshell I admitted to myself that the adulterous relationship was wrong, also that our marriage had basically been over for years. Both proved to be true. When I confessed to Marjory, she got an attorney the next day. She died six years ago and as far as I know she'd never forgiven me. Our two kids are kinder to me as the years go by. But before I told Marjory, actually the very first thing I did after I was rescued, I phoned our executive presbyter and confessed.

"I was immediately out of the house and out of the marriage and put on administrative leave by the presbytery. But I'd intentionally contacted the presbytery first and confessed. Their administrative commission soon set about heavy duty wrestling with me, determined to save my soul and to save my ministry. I took some real battering from people who cared enough for me and for Christ's church that they made me face the truth about myself. Two years. Along with my minimal real estate sales, those two years took all the savings Marjory left me. The presbytery's commission finally rehabilitated me, provided I'd always be under direct contact — meaning monthly face to face — with the executive presbyter, only serve small congregations, and always wear this confounded clergy collar out of the house." He stuck a finger under the collar and slid it back and forth. "The matter of the collar lets you know that every ecclesiastical group has its quirky individuals.

"Everyone knows that I ran away from my wife in her greatest need and abandoned my ministry. I'm now serving in the role of the Apostle Peter. He fled his master; yet Jesus granted him a second chance. So I've also been painfully reinstated. Peter wouldn't be able to choose his attire. Neither do I. He wouldn't be able to choose where to go. Neither do I. Yet I share the same grace Christ gave him."

Phil threw his hands out to the side, "That's it. That's who I am and why I'm here. Now, Jeff," Phil said as he clasped his hands on the table and pursed his lips, "do you want to worship in a congregation whose pastor is a well-advertised sinner and only here because he's been granted a painful, special second chance?"

Preaching point: *All Christians, as did the Apostle Peter, live by Christ's grace granting a second chance.*

ABC Ascension Acts 1:1-11

Chapter 61: The Soles Of Jesus' Feet

As Missy ran toward the house from the school bus, she saw her grandfather at his usual place: dozing in his rocking chair by the window. She slammed the door to wake him up and ran to him, taking off her backpack. If he stayed asleep, or kept his eyes closed pretending he was asleep, she'd braid his beard. His eyes opened as she neared him and his smile was immediate, "Well, how's my favorite first grader?"

"I'm good Grandpa." Then she said with a lilt, "How are you this fine afternoon?"

He carried on their ritual, "As accurate as I can tell, I adjudge that I shall not again engage in bungee jumping. My days of sky diving are over, and I swear I will never again sail solo around the world. But," he said as she joined him word for word, "I will still tell stories."

They laughed and their afternoon was off to its usual start.

Missy had spent the last hour of her school day thinking about getting home to her grandfather. Fifteen years before, he'd been a farmer and a preacher. Now, she thought, he's only here to tell me stories. She often asked for her favorite taller tales, as he called them. She requested the one about the bull as large as a house. In order for the cowboys to manage it, four got off their horses and each grabbed a leg and hugged it like holding a tree. The bull would step around — one cowboy on each leg — with a thump, thump. Then Missy asked for the one about the snowstorm that covered all of Canada and the United States except for his hometown of Clarkesville, Arkansas.

When he finished each tale, they laughed and his rocking chair squeaked with each chuckle. Today he abbreviated a couple of stories by saying merely: "The old spinster and the seven brooms," and they laughed, each picturing it, no need for words.

He added, "The preacher and the sarsaparilla," and he laughed the most, being a preacher himself, he said, making his rocking chair squeak like he'd stepped on a mouse's tail.

The two had to catch their breath after that recital. Missy pulled out a paper from her backpack and showed him her work for the day, practicing printing upper case letters. He admired it, then she turned it over to show the drawing she'd made of her teacher and he complimented the green hair.

"I just followed your rule of trying to show things a little better than they are."

He sat nodding at the drawing and she said, "And I've got a question. You said to bring you my wonderings from the Bible. In Sunday school yesterday we heard the story of Jesus going up to heaven, and I kept listening, but the teacher seemed to leave out something really important. It mentioned, "two men in white robes stood by them." What they said was important, so why don't we hear more about them?"

Her grandfather took in a deep breath, "Oh my. Oh my. You've drilled to the story's oil. Those two men, yes, yes. Famous in the church. Legends abound." He stroked his beard to make sure it wasn't braided and put on his serious voice, "Most people, I think, settle for the theory that it was Enoch and Elijah. Yup. That's what Christians in old Antioch thought. Lot of thinking going on back there. Probably because Enoch and Elijah had both already gone up to heaven. So after they'd instructed the immobile disciples and the disciples had gone off and got busy obeying Jesus, the two men just quietly went back to where they came from, to heaven again."

Missy cocked her head sideways and said, "Mmm."

"But," her grandfather said, after a gentle chuckle that barely squeezed a sound from his rocking chair, "another story goes that the two were fairly young, a little younger than Jesus. They came from Persia and each was a son of an original wise man who'd arrived years before, bringing gifts to the baby Jesus. They'd been raised on only goats' milk and persimmons all their lives in order to grow up to be priests like their daddies."

Missy laughed and continued to giggle as her grandfather said, "But neither of them had listened well in Persian priests' school; because, all they wanted to do was to draw pictures of their teacher with green hair and travel back to Judea like their daddies and see what became of Jesus. As it was, they arrived at Jerusalem right after Jesus' resurrection and got to join for forty days in all the reverse funeral parties. They were especially glad, because now they could eat and drink something other than persimmons and goats' milk."

He had to stop for a while to chortle and shake his rocking chair into a splendid series of squeaks. Missy nodded to what seemed to be a sufficient end to the story. Grandfather, however, continued, "but the legend that I hold to," he said as he leaned closer to her as if to tell a secret, "is that these two were Egyptians, pretty old, old enough to be Jesus' parents age; because they were Jesus' parents' friends in Egypt when they fled there with him. They were Joseph and Mary's Egyptian neighbors. Although Egyptians didn't cotton to all the Hebrews who kept tumbling into Egypt for thousands of years, these two were different. They were identical twins and for that reason they were shunned by their family and neighbors. They looked and sounded absolutely the same. No matter who met them when or where, they soon didn't like the boys because they were confounded that they could never identify which was which. The only way their mama and daddy could tell them apart was when they were eating. One grabbed the knife with his right hand and one with his left. And as all children can be naughty, so they sometimes changed hands to fool everybody. Because the two men never felt accepted in their village, their whole lives were spent looking back to the few months they received genuine friendship from gracious Mary and that dreamer Joseph.

"Their journey so many years later to find Jesus had been a sudden decision and it proved difficult and painful. The twins were so bent by age that when they finally stood next to the disciples who were gazing upwards, they couldn't even look up as Jesus went to heaven. But they got their message across. You understand their message, don't you?"

Missy nodded, "Jesus is now in heaven."

"Yes, that's the first of it. That's the message to everyone. But I mean their instruction to the disciples."

Missy screwed up her face, showing she was trying to think. Grandfather continued, "Consider what the disciples were gazing at. Can you see it? A moment ago Jesus is right here next to them, and then zoom, up he goes. What do they see? The bottom of Jesus' feet!"

Missy laughed. Grandfather said, "Well, am I right?"

"Guess so."

"That's what those two old, stooped, right-and-left-handed Egyptians were telling the disciples. They meant that the disciples were focusing on trivialities: Jesus' feet. Are Jesus' feet real? Yes. Are they important? Well, when he was alive someone's washing them showed devotion, but not after his resurrection, as he's heading to heaven. See what that means?"

Missy couldn't come up with an answer. Grandfather continued, "Christians have spent too much time concentrating on things like the soles of Jesus' feet, things that aren't important anymore. They grab a slice of the faith and miss the whole pie, just looking at the soles of his feet. These two fellows remind us to listen carefully to Jesus' whole message. If it's important, the Bible will tell us it's important. So, you know what? People, be they old or young, who investigate unnecessary things in the Bible — like concentrating on these two men in white robes — are just wasting time ogling again at the soles of Jesus' feet."

And grandfather laughed so hard that his rocking chair seemed to play a tune.

Preaching point: *Concentrating on the center of the biblical message.*

A Easter 2 Acts 2:14a, 22-32

Chapter 62: A Way To Meet Jesus

Stuart's head felt like a full balloon, throbbing with each step as he jostled up Ben Gurion Airport's jetway. He gave up trying to walk and reset his watch at the same time. Jet lag was enough, but the added irritation of decompressing a head cold was almost disabling. After ten hours of flight he'd gotten to sleep 45 minutes before landing, only to be awakened then every five minutes by the speaker directly above him blaring out these gagging sounding messages that didn't make sense when the message was repeated in English, smothered with the same language. He stumbled out of the jetway feeling as if he was being vomited into all the people in Israel.

The ceiling lights hurt his sleepy eyes. Nonetheless, he had to look around carefully. Someone would be holding a sign with his name on it. He was on a different flight from the rest of the tour; yet, at least he'd managed to land on time. His best friend EJ had won a tour of the Holy Land, but his wife just had their third child. Three weeks before, he'd entered Stuart's office. He placed a hand on Stuart's desk and leaned toward him, "Lynn and I've deliberated who to give this tour to. We think it might be what you need. It's been a year since...." He let his voice trail off. He leaned down and placed his other hand also on the desk in front of Stuart. "We've been wanting to do something for you. Please take this tour and see if it offers you some... some comfort," he said as though embarrassed to speak the word.

A young woman in a blue blazer held a sign outside the baggage area: "Mr. Prentice." In twenty minutes, Stuart was led to another blue-blazered young woman who grabbed his heavy suitcase and surprised him as she hefted it with a perfect swing into the maw of the bus's storage. While Israel's scenery slid by the bus's window and passengers exclaimed about each rock, bush, and building, he tried to sleep. Seven or eight minutes after he'd finally nodded off, the bus emptied at the hotel in Tiberius. The hotel staff smiled as they spoke their strange version of English, having to repeat most statements twice and herding him to his room. His legs buckled and he collapsed onto the bed.

First thing the next morning, he took cold medicine. He walked into the breakfast room, placing each step gently in order to cushion the pain in his head. At the buffet he selected cheese and sardines and recalled EJ's advice, "Face each day with hope and prayer." So he held his aching head erect and figured that in these circumstances, one out of two wasn't bad.

Most of the tourists were couples and assigned to a corresponding couple for their meals. He, however, was alone, as he became more aware every day. He found a smaller table with his name along with two others and sat. Wait-staff fluttered by floating their strange Hebraic sounds after them. He glanced at the next table and the couple bowed in prayer over their salads and pastries. He thought, "Well, EJ, does their prayer count?" He looked back to see a man and woman standing with full plates across his table. They wore identical khaki safari coats. They grinned. The woman was husky, maybe sixty. The man, thin and tottery, appeared twice her age. Stuart thought that if his cold pills would release the pressure in his ears, he'd be able to hear a creak with the man's every movement. He half stood and aimed an upturned hand to the table. The two sat. Milt and Nancy would be his partners for ten days. Stuart blew his nose, excused himself for doing so, and welcomed them. The three exchanged home cities, families, and professions. Nancy was Milt's daughter and they lived together in northern Minnesota.

After a few minutes of introductory chatter, Stuart pointed to their identical jackets with a question on his face. Milt said, "So if one of us gets lost the other can describe what she looks like," and he laughed so hard his upper dentures nearly fell out. "Oh Daddy," Nancy said, and slapped him lightly on his shoulder. Stuart laughed also and coughed. In the months after Patsy's death he'd laughed a few times for the sake of others, so he'd look as though he were recovering from mourning. This was one of the few times he'd laughed because he was genuinely amused. He'd wondered what partners he'd get in the luck of the draw; but these two should be tolerable for the duration.

The tour met Stuart's expectations as a whirlwind. The first two days were fuzzy because of his cold, but he recovered. For five days their gargantuan bus negotiated tortuous roads and survived suicidal traffic to shuttle its tourists to sites from the Mediterranean coast to northern Galilee. The sixth day was into the southern Jordan Valley, ending with the tour disgorged at a Jerusalem hotel. At the evening meal as the three toasted with their Maccabee beer, Stuart asked his "mates," as he called them, "You two don't go into the churches and shrines. Are you hanging around outside for a smoke?"

They enjoyed Stuart's joke. "Fifty years ago," Milt said, "I'd have given anything for a cigarette. But we didn't come to learn legends or admire fourth century architecture."

"It's our adventure," Nancy put in. "Don't get many of them in the winter. We planned to stay outside here as much as possible, especially in this lovely weather."

Milt said, "We want to see the lay of the land and at least glimpse some of what it was like in biblical times."

"I'm a little like that," Stuart said. "I enjoy the archaeological digs more than the shrines."

Milt said, "Noticed you left the group at Elijah's Spring."

"I was turned off," he said, as he scanned their faces for signs of a disapproval. Most of the conversations between travelers had been exclamations of religious astonishment if not ecstasy. Stuart didn't think that his fellow tourists spoke seriously to one another. Especially no one expressed doubt. And Stuart, except with Patsy, wasn't in the habit of sharing his deeper thoughts and feelings. He leaned across the table and said softly, "The leader lost me in his obsession with Elijah's miracles." His statement brought nods from Milt and Nancy. He continued, "Throwing salt into a spring to *purify* it, cursing 42 boys so they'd be mauled by bears, floating an ax-head on water…."

Fragments of Good News

Milt and Nancy didn't show disapproval. On the flight home, he recalled that evening's meal and assumed that what he said was partially prompted by grief at Patsy's death. He was still emotionally raw. But he'd also been ready to tell the truth. Whatever motivated him, without forethought, he let loose more of his life.

"When I was thirteen or fourteen, I thought about being a pastor. That faded. But when I got to college, I took a course in the history of Christianity. I already had my quarrels with the Bible: Killing witches, that's murder. Judging people by their parents — back a thousand years. So Jesus was descended from King David? Did anyone calculate — all those kings, wives, and generations — how many hundreds of thousands of men were also descended from David? Slavery then as common as the internet today. Lottery for church leaders. The prof was an atheist and he had a chip on his shoulder. Pointed out the negative more than the positive: Christians' slap hazard method of finding predictions of Jesus in the Old Testament; divine right of kings; saints' bones like lucky charms; he especially enjoyed noting that in 1974 the Vatican exonerated the Jews collectively from crucifying Jesus."

Milt made an "mm" sound and listened courteously. A group at the next take shrieked their chairs on the floor as they rose to leave. Nancy raised her eyebrows and said, "You've thought about this a lot."

Stuart took a deep breath and continued. "It's not just the past that bothers me. Some of the Christians I've been around. My cousin Donna. Couple years older than me, quotes the Bible like it's magic words. Swings it like a baseball bat. Our family call her 'knock 'em Downa.' Other religions to her are demon worship. Christian views other than hers are tools of Satan. Especially Catholics. Those old boys are hell on wheels. I watched her one Thanksgiving, shredding my aunt's faith in an impromptu inquisition. All in sincere concern for her immortal soul of course, and all in the name of Jesus. 'Jesus this and Jesus that.' I'm not sure Jesus is greatly concerned about her this's and that's. Makes me sick of the name 'Jesus.'"

With that, Stuart had said his piece to the world, to the church, to God if God cared to listen. Strangely, he wasn't angry now. He'd become angry as he'd gotten into the flow of his gripes, but now he sat quietly, almost contritely in front of these two Minnesotans across his table who seemed to accept him complaints and all.

After a few moments Nancy said, "We've been around Christians like Donna." Milt blew out a deep breath and said, "Can't say *I* haven't copied some of your cousin's antics. I'm not proud of it. Also not proud of what Christians have done across the ages." He shook his head, and began speaking toward the table between them, "We've seen some interesting things these last few days, heard some Bible stories retold, listened to some legends. We believe the Bible," he glanced to Nancy to complete what he wanted to say but couldn't formulate. Nancy gave a grim smile, "We believe the Bible is as human as Jesus. Kind of scary, huh?"

Milt tapped his hand on the table a few times and looked right and left, getting his thoughts together. "It's not hard to notice that the early Christians grabbed anything in the Old Testament that looked like Jesus' life and declared it a prediction. That's okay. Made sense to how people thought then. Human book. What was God supposed to do, communicate with them in ways that only make sense to us a couple thousand years later? For two millennia — no matter what gets plastered onto it — the center of the Christian faith is living with the risen Jesus. It's a relationship, a forgiven relationship, but a relationship always, never a doctrine first or even morality first. And God won't always grab your collar and shake you. Sometimes God starts the relationship in a gentle way with your honest questions."

A waiter came to clear their dishes. They sat quietly again. The old man gave a little gasp along with a wide smile, "Got an idea. I can't blame you for what you associate with the name 'Jesus.' But 'Yeshua.' What the guide talked about today, Jesus' Aramaic name. Try relating to Yeshua before he got mixed up into all the stuff we Christians have been so busy layering onto the faith from our own personalities and prejudices. Excavate through what we've done to Yeshua and see if you can view him without the problems we've added to the faith. Call him 'Yeshua.' It'll make him feel at home. See if that changes your opinion of him, like the first Pentecost that happened a few blocks down the street. When the Holy Spirit came on people, Yeshua was the same, but the people were changed. That's still what the risen Yeshua does — changes people."

Milt began slowly getting up from his chair and Nancy stepped behind him to help. Stuart thought they'd have more to say. His cousin Donna would have more to say; but, they wished him a good night's sleep and teetered off to the elevator.

Four days later, Stuart sat by a window on the bus to the airport. His cold was gone and he didn't dread the flight. As Israel's countryside slid by, he mulled through his scattered thoughts, memories, and feelings about Yeshua and the Christian faith. The daily shuffling to different sites and hotels made the ten days seem half a lifetime. He wondered which sites Patsy would have liked. He recalled EJ's concern for him and Milt and Nancy's friendship. He thought again of his teenage faith.

When his flight was called and he joined his fellow passengers lining into the jetway, his mind was on Yeshua. Nothing outwardly dramatic occurred while edging forward; but, he quietly placed his faith in Yeshua, so that, when he exited the jetway into the plane, it was like leaving a birth canal into a new life.

    Preaching point: *Yeshua/Jesus remains the same; but his Holy Spirit changes us.*

B Easter 5 Acts 8:26-40

Chapter 63: Helena's Touch

After she survived childhood cleaning stables in her father's inn, after she united with Constantius and conceived Constantine, after Constantius divorced her, after Constantine became Emperor, after she and Constantine became Christians, after her name and diademed image were stamped on royal coins, after Constantine killed his wife and a son, Helena was hustled off to the Holy Land. Now a year later, Helena rode in her royal caravan returning from there to Byzantium.

The year was 327 and, over seventy years old, Empress Helena was returning to Byzantium not feeling as a saint felt — supposedly drawn between life on earth and life in heaven. She'd been ensnared between demands of empire and church. Her son had sent her to further unify his empire, drawing those now declared heretics into the church which defined itself as Christ's true church. Her visit was also to help this church outstrip paganism. Helena ingratiated the inhabitants of the Holy Land by conspicuous spending: empire financed, strings-attached charity.

In the Holy Land with Bishop Eusebius she'd inspected the construction of the Church of the Holy Sepulcher and confirmed the locations of the caves where her son's wealth would build churches on the Mount of Olives and in Bethlehem. All this was before Byzantium became Constantinople and before the legend grew (sprouting fifty years after her death) that, while in Jerusalem, Helena found Jesus' true cross. This was also before she was declared a Christian saint.

Beyond the tangled politics that sent her on her mission, as a convert she yearned to see where Jesus lived and to stand where he walked. She ached for an earthly touch with her new Lord. But now that she'd accomplished her mission, she still hadn't sensed the completeness she expected from the pilgrimage.

"Excellency," her chief bodyguard spoke tentatively as he rode next to her coach. Helena, lulled into near slumber, didn't respond. "Excellency," this time from the priest Father Markus, whom she classified as irritatingly proper. She glanced out to see both men riding beside her window.

"What is it?"

"We're approaching another settlement," Father Markus said. "A chance to demonstrate again your royal favor."

She nodded in response. This made the daily drudgery tolerable for Helena. Never thought she'd be in such a position. Helping the poor. She'd never gotten used to being able to spend the empire's money on the needy, even though everything about her retinue demonstrated the opposite of need. So many soldiers, she thought, detachment after detachment escorting her. Yet her son's chief advisor insisted she travel with 400 soldiers along with numerous priests, deacons and servants. Their baggage train trailed them a mile and a half. One reason for so many soldiers scattered before, beside and behind her was her jewels. Brigands knew the caravan carried coins, in that she distributed them to the poor. Even more obvious was that every day Helena wore royal garb with jeweled diadem, royal necklace, and rings on six fingers. "You must show yourself and your mission as royal," insisted Constantine's chief advisor.

Although more than ready to end the daily toil of the journey, Helena was reluctant now to return to Byzantium and the ripples of violence still ringing through the palace precincts. Yet she was tired and had earned the right to rest: bounced through fords, rattled over rocks, and twisted up and down switchbacks. And her royal highness was not allowed to spit. Constantine's advisors warned that common people spit but royalty didn't. The soldiers, who breathed as much dust as she, could spit. Helena had to swallow the dirt. She figured she'd gained half her weight in swallowed soil.

The coach shook her as it rattled over a rough patch. The labor gang strung out before the caravan and couldn't adequately fill every hole in time for the royal passing. She settled herself in the slight comfort of the pillows but she was more than physically disturbed. In another week they'd arrive at Byzantium. She'd again take up residence in her palace. More luxury. Even grander (and weightier) wardrobe. More servants as well as more supplicants. Also, the nearer memory of her favorite grandson's murder by her own son. And her daughter-in-law murdered by her son, although he also was a convert to Christianity.

She'd departed Byzantium expecting to find the peace of Jesus in the Holy Land. To pray where he prayed, that was the touch she sought. But it was not to be. For whatever reason, she never achieved the spiritual encounter she craved.

"Excellency." Again her chief bodyguard and Father Markus. "Paupers waiting ahead." Again she ordered distribution of alms. Strange, it wasn't just from habit. She'd gotten used to the poor again, having grown up poor. Giving to the poor and worshiping Jesus always revived her.

Suddenly she raised her arm and pointed. "Stop that soldier," she yelled. The chief bodyguard immediately trotted to the coach.

"What, Excellency?"

"Stop that soldier," she screamed, pointing to a horseman nearly out of sight in a ravine. He was switching his horse, obviously one of the unruly replacement mounts they'd exchanged at the last staging post. "Stop him immediately," she ordered. "You can beat your soldiers, but don't beat your horses. You can't tell the horse why you're doing it."

The chief bodyguard quickly galloped to convey the command to the surprised soldier.

She was now fully alert. No matter what awaited her in Byzantium, here she was in charge and gave the orders. She waved her hand to Father Markus, "We will stop here and celebrate worship with these poor."

"Excellency?" He gazed at her with his well-worn scorn, as much to say, "Pretentious woman." The soldiers nearby stared at her, puzzled. They hadn't traveled far after their noon meal, and, as they drew nearer to home, they usually traveled longer into the evening. The chief bodyguard said, "Here, Excellency? The scouts tell us we're three miles from a staging post and supplies. There's water there."

"We'll first meet our risen Lord at his altar here, now," she said. "And include these poor," she gestured to the mob congregating near the coach. "Father Markus, prepare for worship immediately."

Father Markus spoke slowly, "Out of the ordinary, Excellency."

"Here. Now," she said. "As quickly as possible. Bring the altar here." If she couldn't use royal power for this, what could she do? Her command issued from a long-forming desire. She'd performed her official mission. She'd do now as she felt led. Outside the coach she assumed her regal posture, directing servants where to arrange the worship paraphernalia.

She took her position nearest the altar as the priests scurried to question the growing crowd of poor to certify they understood Jesus adequately. She cut them short and motioned them to their duty at the Lord's altar. Her longings to touch Jesus led her to this decision. In her arduous travel and managing of the emperor's wishes, with hundreds of soldiers, the noise, the competition of the officers and priests — and the dust! In all this, where did she most feel the presence of Jesus? Where did she have a touch of the divine? In the bread and the cup, and when serving the poor. Nothing crossed her mind about other visitors to the Holy Land before her or those who'd follow, but she understood enough to lead the poor with her to Lord's altar.

There, between staging posts, far from the Holy Land, not yet near Byzantium's palaces, she knelt surrounded by the poor at the altar and Father Markus gave her the cup and the bread. There, continuing her pilgrimage into eternity, she touched Jesus. Perhaps this was a reason she was declared a saint.

Preaching point: *Jesus is known not by visiting the Holy Land, but by sharing his meal and caring for the needy.*

A Proper 6 (11) Romans 5:1-8
C Trinity Sunday Romans 5:1-5
A Lent 3 Romans 5:1-11

Chapter 64: Patternless Suffering With God

Lacey kept her eyes low, trying to keep herself out of the discussion as long as possible. Finally, to her relief, after everyone had passed twice, Buddy responded to Eleanore's question, "I'm here because pastor wanted me to come." Lacey looked at the others, and they all agreed. Lacey was confirmed in her opinion of what was happening. She continued her silent litany, "If anyone had known anything, if anyone had any experience, if anyone had sought out a competent leader...." She continued her ifs, her mind swirling with possible stratagems for how to flee from this mournful group.

They sat in a small circle. Eleanore had set up the room before they arrived. No table between them to emotionally hide behind or to defend themselves. Across from Lacey Eleanore sat, maintaining her beatific smile no matter what anyone said or, in this case, didn't say. Eleanore's suggestion that "everyone should share a little about how you got here," had fallen flatter than Lacey's energy level. Besides acknowledging that a loved one had died recently, Lacey and the four others managed to choke out the unanimous information that pastor encouraged them to attend the congregation's new grief group. The operative term was "new," started only because Eleanore reported that other congregations "ran" such groups and — as they all knew — pastor went along with anything Eleanore proposed.

Lacey was the only teenager, a senior in high school. Her mother died eleven months before. Buddy Elgin sat across from her. He managed to squeeze out the information that his wife died three years, two months, and twelve days ago. Beside him Tammie took her fist out of her mouth to say, "Oliver, my husband, passed a year ago November." Sharon was on Lacey's right. Her eight-year-old daughter died of a slow cancer two years before. Her eyes were dripping tears when she walked in the room and they hadn't quite stopped. On Lacey's left, Barbara acknowledged with clipped speech that she'd been a widow for a year. And, of course, Eleanore perched next to Buddy, leaning forward eagerly into the group. Eleanore, Lacey's lifelong neighbor and her mother's lifelong annoyance, always wanting to fix people, Eleanore whose incompetence was blazingly obvious even to a teenager. Lacey thought, "One of these adults should take the lead and get us out of here. Eleanore doesn't know what she's doing to us, no matter what psychology magazine she says she reads cover to cover."

With that, Lacey's chest constricted. She had to concentrate through each breath. All she could consider was how to escape. Her mother's death had been the worst that could happen to her, instantly deleting two thirds of her days' energy, at times nearly preventing her from uttering a word. Now this? A handful of people drowning in grief and numbskull in charge.

Buddy squirreled in his chair, cleared his throat, and said, "How we doing so far?" Everyone laughed nervously. Eleanore, chuckled longest, and said, "Just being here with others is a great start. Don't you think? Anymore feelings to share?"

"Pretty painful," Barbara said, to which others nodded. Sharon was looking at her lap. Eleanore gazed around the group, face by face, to coax further responses. In the street outside a horn honked, helping Lacey realize there really was a world beyond this horribly confined feeling that pressed in on her. She looked above Eleanore's head, acting as though she was engaged. All she saw was two cobwebs on the white hospital-like wall of the church's conference room.

Eleanore tried three more invitations to share feelings or experiences, didn't wait long for answers, and then said, "Pastor tells me his favorite scripture concerning grief is Paul's fifth chapter to the Romans: 'we also boast in our sufferings, knowing that suffering produces endurance, and endurance produces character, character produces hope, and hope does not disappoint us, because God's love has been poured into our hearts through the Holy Spirit that has been given to us.'"

Most of them nodded politely, obvious to Lacey they weren't agreeing, but acknowledging the scripture from pastor. No one spoke for a few moments until Barbara, sitting rigidly, said in a thin, hopeless voice, "Hasn't worked that way for me."

Eleanore's eyes opened wide. She looked around quickly, bringing her thoughts together, but before she could respond, Buddy said, "Me neither."

Eleanore said, "Well, I'm sure —."

"Not much for me, either," Tammie said.

Sharon reached over and placed her hand on Tammie's. "I sympathize. Nothing's happened in my grief that was like lock-step to healing. If anything, I've gone back and forth leapfrog. Think life's smoothing out, then I see a commercial for Cabela's and cry. Oliver loved Cabela's. Had the catalog in the bathroom." She was able to laugh when she said that, although her tears were flowing.

Buddy said, "Still bothers me to drive by JoAnn Fabrics," and he shook his head to stop himself from crying.

Sharon spoke while she looked at Buddy, "It's a back and forth. I've had longest here to push through grief and mourning. I've heard Paul's words more than once, as well as some ridiculous advice about God having reasons we'll never understand, and at least we had Mitzy for as long as we did, and …" She stopped and everyone thought she would break out in sobs, but she grit her teeth and spoke quickly. "I prayed for her. I guess," she said as she looked at the four other bereaved facing her, "that we all prayed for our loved ones. And I keep praying. Sometimes it helps, sometimes it doesn't. What I've decided is that what I'm going through is different from everyone else's. You feel that way?" She said as she looked around at her fellow mourners. Everyone nodded their agreement.

"My suffering hasn't worked the way Paul's did. It's taken a while to not feel guilty because of that. A person threw Paul's words at me a couple years ago, like if I were a true Christian, my suffering would follow his steps. Only lately I've begun to understand that Paul was talking about him and others then and suffering for their faith. Doesn't mean God commands we will follow that pattern. But it does comfort me at least to know that others have survived suffering and that God was with them."

She looked at Eleanore as though her statement was a question. Lacey noticed that everyone in the room was now turned to Sharon. At that moment Lacey wasn't thinking about what pastor or Paul said. If she were to stay in this group for another minute, it would be only because of Sharon's statement. She'd have time to make it up to Eleanore later, as well as to think about Paul's writing. For now, she spoke up for the first time, "We done for today?"

Preaching point: *Paul's experience of suffering isn't a pattern for everyone's suffering.*

A Lent 1 Romans 5:12-19

Chapter 65: One Man

Frederick pulled his foot from a muddy hole, nearly losing his boot, and swore. He flung his left arm out wildly to gain his balance so he wouldn't drop his musket. Solomon put out a hand and steadied him and half dragged him up. Frederick swore again, "Dust yesterday, mud today." Frederick had an almost perfectly round face and the whites of his eyes were visible around his pupils, giving him a look of constant surprise. A couple of other soldiers marching beside him grunted. They were too tired to speak. Only few of them were Revolutionary War veterans. Their small contingent of militia trudged with a hundred other grim soldiers on the road back toward armed conflict.

The September skies had brought a boiling sun for a week, yet now delivered stripes of rain clouds sopping them every hour, always enough to make the top of the mud shiny slick. But it stayed hot. The track stretched before them muggy and muddy. Horses thudded up and down the lines as officers encouraged the troops and directed the squeaky wheeled cannons and wagons that strung behind them for a mile.

The sergeant ahead called, "Ten minutes rest!" The soldiers melted onto the grass beside the road, disregarding the water as they lay down because everything was already wet. Some stacked their muskets, other irregulars just laid where they were and balanced their muskets out of the damp. Two brothers immediately pulled out their miniature game board and continued their homemade competition that they'd extended for six days.

"I can't help what I think," Frederick said, continuing a conversation from their last rest stop, "that 1794 is the beginning of the end of our experiment with democracy."

Frederick, Solomon, and the half dozen soldiers near them

were farmers drafted into the militia from the Virginia Tidewater. They knew Frederick well. As Solomon said, "Frederick complains all the time. He does, however, fight like the devil's own spawn when round pieces of lead whizz by like hail stones." Most of the militia members hadn't fought in the revolution and they always gathered to listen to Frederick and Solomon jab with their different opinions about war and the things that made for peace.

"Shays' rebellion was just the start. Now this," Frederick said. "The land's in ruins, the government's in chaos. Back in '76, Washington might have had a chance for an armistice, some kind of peace. Should have taken it. Accept the king and negotiate. One leader instead of mob rule. All the blood, the dead, the suffering, now more taxes. Should have kept George the Third instead of George the Washington."

The others hadn't heard such a suggestion before. Solomon laughed, "You're disproving your own argument. If we had a king, you couldn't say such things about the government. We get to disagree without risking our necks or our family's welfare. That's a mighty difference."

Lightning flared ahead, but the rain had stopped and the only dripping was from the trees lining the road. The sergeant called, "Fall in!" and the soldiers were soon back in their groups, plodding ever northward. Frederick and Solomon were refreshed enough to continue discussing the country's situation.

"Both countries tax us and draft us," Frederick said, "and we're fighting among ourselves again. We're marching to battle because we have another debt of a past war to pay for. Another civil war over taxes! Yet, those back country farmers we're going to face are desperate over taxes. My wife's cousin lives in western Pennsylvania where the roads are as bad as here. He raises a good crop of wheat, but by the time he lugs it east to market, he's lost his profit. So the farmers distill their crops because whiskey's a hundred times easier to transport."

Solomon said, "I don't presume to outthink the new government; but I was with Washington's army for the last two years of the conflict, right to Yorktown. I'm not saying we've got the best government or leader just because the French sailed in and guaranteed Yorktown's victory. But I'll tell you what: For me, Washington will always be my leader and example, no matter what happens to our country. He's leading us today. I'll follow."

Solomon spoke louder now and soldiers around him moved closer until he was the center of a bundle of marchers listening to him. "I know the mistakes Washington made and the battles he lost. For me his most important leadership, his pinnacle, came right at the end of the war. You knew that for the final year I was aide-de-camp to the colonel."

"Yes," Frederick said, in a level voice, now very politely listening to Solomon; but the others knew that when Frederick spoke without emotion, it was only so he could pull together his thoughts to rebut Solomon.

"After the war, in the months waiting for the signed peace settlement to arrive from France, the officers were ready to revolt. We almost had peace, but also desperate poverty. They hadn't been paid, years! The Continental Congress had promised wages and pension and some of their families were starving. Pretty much like the rest of the soldiers and the whole country for that matter, except for the speculators who bought up soldiers' warrants at pennies on the dollar.

"My colonel was among the officers at Newburgh, New York, in March of '83 when they were ready to mutiny. Washington got wind of the growing plot and dashed there. Showed up with a speech. Just walked up to the officers and spoke for five minutes. Pretty strong speech, encouraging them to hold on after all they'd sacrificed for the country. I was with my colonel and watched the faces of men hardened by years of battle. I saw tears in their eyes, if not while Washington spoke, when he ended. He had a letter then to read to them from Congress and so he reached into his pocket and put on a pair of glasses. No one had seen him with glasses before. But, as he put them on and prepared to read, he said softly, 'Gentlemen, you will permit me to put on my spectacles, for I have not only grown gray but almost blind in the service of my country.'

"Here was our leader humbly stating what he'd given up for the country, and they knew he'd given it up for them and their families and a future they hoped for. That moment, that one man, at that one place was like the focus of what democracy could be. Not dominating, but serving." Solomon let his voice hang in the air, but picked up his pace.

Those around him stood up straighter now as they marched on with him. Frederick was with them, but in the three minutes Solomon spoke, half a hundred ideas flitted through his mind. His swirling thoughts swept away his attention to a greatness beyond President Washington or democracy. While Solomon praised the "one man" Washington, repeating the one man at one moment of obvious sacrifice, Frederick, without his conscious will, felt the staggering impact from the Apostle Paul's teaching about what God had accomplished through the "one man" Jesus. It was as though his attention had been captured. He couldn't draw his mind away from Jesus, his one sacrifice that mattered infinitely more, eternally for everyone.

Frederick marched on speechless. For no reason the others understood his eyes were wider and his silence profound.

Preaching point: *The eternal impact of the "one man" Jesus.*

A Proper 9 (14) Romans 7:15-25a

Chapter 66: Paul's Innards

In ancient Corinth, just before dawn, Dathan raced from the slave quarters to be first to arrive at his master's shoemaking shop. He was waiting on the sidewalk when his master waddled toward him swatting at slaves who bustled by him. Dathan thought: It used to be every other night and thus every other morning. Now he drinks every night and we suffer every morning.

When the master met Dathan outside the shop, he said, "Where's lazy Lucius?" They looked down the street and Lucius appeared around the corner and sauntered toward them.

"Hurry up," the master yelled.

Lucius yelled back, "I could walk faster if I had shoes."

"Hurry," the master shouted, "or I'll have you whipped!"

Lucius sidled jauntily toward the shop.

"You get here at sunup tomorrow or I'll sell you into the mines. Now hurry!"

"Why? You need me to fetch your chamber pot?"

This caused the master to shake violently. He was about to scream again when he looked as if he would faint. He turned and fiddled quickly with the large key to the stall. Dathan and Lucius, knowing what he needed, tugged out the wooden panels that opened their shop to the street and the master ran into the back room to vomit.

Dathan and Lucius wordlessly grabbed their work and set about supplying the empire with 300 pairs of military boots for legionaries stationed near Corinth. Nothing fancy here, Lucius claimed, just slip shod in this cobbler's shop. The master said nothing as he staggered back and then into the street. Dathan assumed he was going next door to the wine shop to get morning help for his hangover.

As soon as he was out of sight, Dathan said, "Well, what did you think of Paul last night?"

"Don't get excited, young man," Lucius said. "I kept my part of the deal. You covered for me, I went to hear your favorite lunatic."

Dathan's hands fell to his sides. "You didn't like Paul?"

"He delivered an earful, this short social nothing, hardly better than a slave — in fact talking with us slaves — pretending he knows the secrets of life and eternity."

"He's a Roman citizen," Dathan said.

"A Roman citizen, so? He's a tentmaker, hardly better than us. Such a smooth line, his being the slave of all. So pious… just God's tool… as we're just our masters' tools."

"Can't you tell," Dathan said, "he's teaching us for our sake, not for his?"

"Sure, gives us a slice of the letter he's writing to Rome, like that's supposed to impress us." He made a snorting noise. "You latch onto him because he's a Jew and you were sold in Judea. You two have much in common. You're both trying to make up for being so insignificant."

Dathan squinted and said slowly, "You sold yourself and your family into slavery to pay gambling debts. I'd think you'd want to hear what he has to say about true life."

Lucius pointed to him with a boot in his hand, "You think this little guy brings good news, talking about sin, sin, sin everywhere? About as good news as me smashing your face with this."

Dathan squared his body toward Lucius to defend himself if Lucius became violent. "That's not the center of Paul's message. He's not saying we're only sinful, just that we're never good enough to be right with God."

"He sounds as if *he's* full of sin — all through his innards and right up to the wafts of hair on his bald top," he said as he patted his head.

"That's not what he meant. Everyone else gets his meaning. He isn't talking about just himself."

"He was certainly talking about *you*."

"He describes each of us being unable to do the good we

choose," Dathan took half a step backward, "like your being unable to stop gambling, although it ruined you."

"You're going to get this boot down your throat." Lucius stepped into Dathan's work space. "As for your bandy-legged Paul, he'd better guard his words. If he keeps jabbering about another lord fixing us, he's going to find out why Rome's been around 800 years. It's not going to put up with dust like him."

Dathan cringed. The discussion could go no further, but he said, "Rome's power is past. Christ is now and forever. Time will tell — about God and each of us — who's *right*."

Lucius raised his arm to strike Dathan, but he glanced to the door and under his breath said, "Master." They both appeared busy as the master entered.

"Right?" The master stumbled as rushed in the door. "Right? Now what are you two arguing about. Right? Who's right about what?" He suddenly looked sicker and started again for the back room. He said over his shoulder, "If he says that Lucius is a donkey's rear, he's right." The master didn't make it to the back room in time.

> **Preaching point**: *Paul describes the internal struggles of humans in order to portray our futile good intentions, our ultimate moral deficiency, and our need of a Savior.*

B Pentecost Romans 8:22-27

Chapter 67: Honest, Not Courteous, Prayer

Pastor Mel had asked her several times. Bebe remembered three precisely. The first was three days after the funeral when he and his wife brought a casserole to her home and commented on the well written obituary and the courtesy of her grandchildren. The second time was at the door of the church as he greeted parishioners after worship. It was Bebe's first time back in worship. She'd survived the funeral by four days, then fled to her daughter's for a month. On that first Sunday back in worship she'd fought tears that she feared could burst into a loud bawl. The third time was hardly a request. She was crossing from the Christian Education building to the parking lot when he came behind her, placed his hand under her elbow with a little lift, took a couple steps with her, and said quietly but firmly, "You really should share with others your experience of God through this ordeal."

Bebe faced him and spoke each word distinctly, "I'm not ready to talk about it yet."

"I realize there's some pain in this," Pastor Mel said, "but so much victory. I'd really like you to speak at the next Conquerors meeting. You'll have two weeks to prepare."

Bebe didn't remember clearly how she'd finally shed him, but she definitely didn't agree.

On Monday the eighteenth he phoned, pleading for her to speak for the Conquerors. Her indefinite response brought a call the next day. She held the receiver, listening to the pastor implore her as she looked at her favorite photo of Roger on their wedding day. Her mind was a muddle. She was flying in a fog. The only reason she could remember for having agreed was that he suggested, "Maybe you could narrow in on prayer."

So "prayer" it was; and even though Bebe had five days to

seek, grab, and organize her scattered thoughts, she made little progress beyond weeping, "God, how can I do this?" Until then, each step she took had necessitated a conscious decision and more energy than she thought she possessed. Nothing had granted her relief from what she named "terminal grief." Roger — her husband and friend, father of her children, playmate, counselor, business partner. Roger — she still couldn't sleep in their bedroom and, as she stepped around each corner in the house, she expected Roger. Roger — flopping back his stringy hair with a reckless twist of his neck. Roger — shuffling in his thirty-year-old moccasins. Roger — with another knock-knock joke.

The Conquerors adult group met on the last Sunday evening of each month. Bebe and Roger had joined the group for outings to special restaurants and for the regular monthly meetings — always a magnificent potluck, plenty of friends to socialize with, and a speaker.

Now, during this Conquerors dinner, Bebe's mind alternated from dust storm to blizzard to earthquake, but mostly dust storm. She found herself nodding in agreement toward anyone who was speaking as she breathed through her mouth in order to remember to breathe. Her one consistent action was to look at the clock. Nothing could help her now. The hands kept turning. When Pastor Mel stood, she knew what had arrived. She felt as though two clock hands as tall as a house slapped together with a bang that everyone around her must be able to hear. Pastor Mel was speaking and pointing toward her. She didn't register a word he spoke, but rose from her seat and walked to stand beside him while he held his hand on her shoulder, reviewing Roger's tragic, much-too-early death, and how Bebe's faith had drawn her through, and that she wanted to share with them a few things about prayer.

When she went home that night, she remembered staring at Pastor Mel's brown cardigan sweater as he walked away. Roger had a blue one like it.

"I had to learn the Ten Commandments when I was a kid,"

she said. "My parents taught me — 'Thou shalt not bear false witness' — meant to be honest." She pointed down to her piece of paper on the lectern. "I wrote on my notes: 'Be honest.'

"I've never been a great pray-er. Regular, yes. I've tried. Rog tried. We even prayed together sometimes, but he'd usually make a joke to God and we'd start laughing." She looked over everyone's head and said, "I miss his laughing."

She clamped her teeth together and stamped her foot gently like a child's weak tantrum. "I'll tell you what I think about prayer. For me, prayer has been an angry scream, inside me or outside me." She frowned. "When the EMTs loaded Rog in the ambulance, a well-meaning neighbor hugged me and said, 'I'm sure he'll be okay.' Inside me I yelled to God, 'Really? How does she know such things?' I could say that to God, whereas I didn't want to hurt her feelings. We're all taught to be courteous, aren't we? I did better in the hospital where, even though the staff said there was hope, they didn't lie to me. And I screamed inside me, 'Help him, God!'

"And Rog wasn't okay. And I'm in a hollow house now, echoing with Rog's phantom movements and I scream to God asking 'Why?' And this is what I think, being as honest as I can: I don't believe we have to be courteous with God. Jesus' scream on the cross! In his dying breath, he wasn't nicey-nicey with God. And my screams and whimpers to God say more to God than any gallant thoughts I can shuffle together to share with you. I wish I could tell you more...."

Bebe looked at her friends, desperately, courteously, trying to think of more to say that would help them. After a few seconds she shook her head, walked to her chair, and sat with a limp thump. Everyone knew Pastor Mel had to get up and close the meeting. No one could guess what he'd say.

Preaching point: *God's Spirit invites and inspires our absolute (not necessarily courteous) honesty in prayer.*

A Proper 12 (17) Romans 8:26-39

Chapter 68: Too Deep For Words

Dear Mom and Dad,

As I told you a year ago, my mentor at seminary suggested we always put off a thorough report to our parents about a congregation until we had been there a year. Over this year, I have had lots I could say — interesting, confusing, even ghostly. Only a few things one would call "extremely out of the ordinary." I am going to smooth over some details, round some rough corners, and withhold identities. The delay for you in a detailed summary of these twelve months has proven wise (or lucky), because yesterday was a special congregational meeting called in order to fire me. Now is the perfect time to tell you about my first year here as pastor.

First: Most interesting in the congregation is that the church custodian (which the committee told me was a disabled pastor) had been *this* congregation's pastor 33 years ago. The things that a calling committee won't tell you! I found out about him on my first Tuesday here. He's still on his pastor's old schedule. Takes Mondays off. My first Tuesday morning in the church I'm wandering downstairs to orient myself room by room to the building. I hear this "aawww, aawww" coming from the basement chapel, like the sound track of a horror movie. I push the door open slightly to peek in and an old guy with tousled white hair is on his knees in the front pew making this sound. I dash up to tell Gladys the secretary to see if she knows anything about him. She laughs and says, "Dear Old Pastor Bob."

She told me that he had served as pastor here nearly seventeen years and at 49 had a stroke. He does not speak. After thirty years, nobody is sure he can. Later that morning he came to my office and stood in the doorway, as though I should know who he is. No expression on his face. No offered hand to shake. He just motions for me to follow him to the custodian's closet. The closet walls are draped with upside down antique carpet sweepers, like props for a science fiction movie. He points to this large wall calendar. Scratched day by day is the month's schedule. He points me to the note above that states he must (I repeat, "must") have instructions written and posted on this calendar a day before anybody needs something special, like a room set up for a meeting. Do I understand? I acknowledge "yes," and with a slack face he brushes by me with a large broom to start on the halls. His calendar states: Tuesday, sweep halls. He vacuums the sanctuary at one-thirty PM on Sunday. I watched him begin his work and wondered what goes on in his mind.

Gladys is waiting for me when I get back to my office. She is grinning. "You've now met DOPB." She laughs and says, "Dear Old Pastor Bob." She tells me as much as she knows about him, which isn't a lot. He was here before she was hired but she doubts that many people hold him dear. "Fewer and fewer people were even here thirty years ago. But he does his job," she said. "Never asks for a raise. And, as you can see, never argues with anybody, because he doesn't talk. People write him notes, leave them in the custodian's closet and stay out of his way."

"What about that noise he made in the chapel?" I asked.

Gladys became serious, "That's the only sound I've heard from him and the only place I've heard it. I think that's his prayer. Every morning when he comes to work. Some days louder than others. No matter how early that is. By the way, you'll be glad in the middle of summer he shows up at four to open all the doors and windows to cool the place.

"He fixes everything. Wouldn't let anybody touch the dishwasher when it went out. Took it to pieces, parts strung all over the kitchen, then back together and nobody better mess with it again! The carpet sweeper is from the 1950s. Forty pounds at least. They don't make them anymore. That's why he scavenged so many for parts."

As I said, old Pastor Bob is definitely the most interesting thing about the church; but, a few other matters run a close second.

David O. Bales

One lady has been able to prevent the choir's swaying as they sing. You read that right. I am told it was four or five years ago the choir was singing a spiritual and they swayed together right and left. Makes sense to me. However, this particular church member said that it made her seasick and had to leave quickly or she would vomit. So, we have what I call a "rigid choir."

A special Sunday attraction is that several bring dogs to worship. Over a decade ago, a pastor agreed to a "blessing of the animals" service. The congregation liked it so much some continued to bring their dogs. If others aren't pleased with the practice, they haven't gotten around to forbidding it. An interesting consequence is that during worship, a half dozen grade school girls sang, "This Little Light Of Mine" and did a really good job. However, every time they hit a particular note, one dog whined. No one dared an embarrassing chuckle. I experienced how much energy it takes to keep a straight face and not break out hysterically in laughter — which, by the way, people did outside the church immediately after worship.

On the less than hysterical side: A panoramic view of the congregation holds three obvious attractions on the horizon. This is the matter that the couple of pastors who guided me to this congregation warned me about.

They told me of three families. No mentioning of names. They are three farm families who have anchored the congregation for generations. And, they have constantly quarreled over irrigation rights for their farms. They do not show it at church. All nicey-nicey. They might want to quit attending so they would not have to relate civilly to the others, but they fear if they did the other two families might garner community support against them.

For the last twelve months, various members have spoken out of the corner of the mouth or came right out and stated it: They are tired of these families upsetting the ministry here. One older lady even guessed that years ago it was the tension of dealing with the "terrible three" that triggered Pastor Bob's stroke.

I made sure in the first three weeks here to visit one of these families each week. Word got around fast that I had appointments, who with and when. Consequently, each of these evening calls were transformed into family dinners and I mean family. Dining room bursting with all ages. Each generation had a token at the table and each family curried my favor — without saying it, of course. It was slightly comical. I have done my best in every way to maintain an even-handed relation to these three families — equal access to any need, as I do for all members. I must, because sometimes in the past two families have allied against one, then back and forth against one another as their legal actions trickle through the courts.

I have attempted to do my ministry and not be much distracted by those families' problems. Until....

A middle-aged mother in one of the families became ill. Hospitalized and undiagnosed. Don't ask why she wasn't transferred to a major hospital complex, but she was hospitalized here for ten days. I visited every day and sometimes twice, especially when I knew that other family would be with her and also needed my ministry.

That did it. Seemed like favoritism. The situation grew quickly into two families against one and I was linked with the one-out. Consequently, a quick call for a congregational meeting yesterday, dogs and all. Somebody brought in a guest speaker and I had to sit in the congregation during worship, powerless and weak with worry over nothing I had done wrong. Trying to pray, yet with no clear sense of what to pray for. After worship, the meeting started at twelve-thirty and I was exiled to my office to wait. Took a layer off my stomach lining.

At one-thirty-seven, Gladys dashed into my office holding her sides as she burst with laughter. She kept hiccupping with giggles as she told me what had happened. In the meeting no one really spoke openly against me. The families would lose face if they seemed vindictive because of my ministry to a hospitalized member of their enemy family. They haggled about procedure and *Robert's Rule Of Order* for over an hour. A lot of ho-humming about my not being quite the right pastor for this congregation ... until one-thirty.

David O. Bales

I heard it from my office: The carpet sweeper winding up, sounding like a road grader, and then, "aawww, aawww, aawww." Gladys nearly fell over telling me. She had been up front taking minutes of the meeting. One-thirty sharp and on goes the vacuum and with it DOPB (Dear Old Pastor Bob) making a sound that no one other than she and I had heard for thirty years, "aawww, aawww, aawww." People are twisting their heads around. Some are gasping. All are soon looking at the old custodian making this strange sound, and an antique machine like an animal angrily gobbling down the center aisle.

In the confusion, an older man in the center of the congregation stood with a broad grin and said with a voice of doom, "I move the meeting be adjourned."

Before anyone could take another breath, a person across the aisle shouted, "I second," and a third said, "I call the question." At which any semblance of Robert's Rules had gone out the window. Someone then said with a cheery voice, "All in favor." The congregation spoke in unison, "Aye," and stood to flee, stumbling over their dogs and exiting quickly out the side aisles. Dear Old Pastor Bob charged forward with that impassable face, yanking the carpet sweeper down the center aisle left and right, and who knew what thoughts shrieked out in his sighs too deep for words?

Preaching point: *All sighs in prayer — with our many feelings and motives — are acceptable to God.*

A Proper 19 (24) Romans 14:1-12

Chapter 69: A Christian From Nowhere

For Megan, Tiffany fell into her life from nowhere. The twenty-something young lady simply came to the church one day, crept around the door to Megan's office, saying "I need some help."

Tiffany's need wasn't the usual: a meal, a voucher for a night in the motel, a bus ticket to Topeka.

"I need help being a Christian," she said, leaning against the door jam, looking as though this was exactly, and perhaps only, what the Lutheran church and its pastor were there for.

After introductions, Megan asked Tiffany to clarify what she meant.

"I became a Christian over my back fence. Clara rented behind our house for a month and the first thing she wanted to know was if I was a Christian. I knew people who probably were Christians and I'd caught glimpses on TV. But no one talked to me about faith, let alone asked me to become a Christian. Clara told me I needed to be washed in the blood of the lamb. Didn't make sense to me. Blood stains clothes pretty bad. But I repeated the prayer Clara said, asking Jesus to forgive me and help me live for him, trusting I'll be in heaven with him forever."

"Never attended church?"

"No."

"And never had instruction in the faith, except your neighbor's helping you pray to become a Christian."

"None."

"In other words," Megan smiled, "you're at zero in the faith." They laughed and Megan saw worry releasing from Tiffany's face.

Then Tiffany shifted around in her chair. "There's a problem. I told my husband and he got really mad. Doesn't want any of that religion stuff. I didn't know what to say, but Clara told me Jesus helps us love others. That's what I'm praying about." Tears formed on cheeks, "I'm alone in this. Who am I talking to up there? What's he like? If this is forever, what am I supposed to do now?"

Megan had never faced anything like this, in its seriousness and simplicity. She gulped, offered a silent prayer and said, "Tiffany, you're in exactly the spot as the early Christians, say, in Rome around 50 AD. That's when the faith reached Rome. Jesus was born before 4 BC in Israel," she stood and pointed at the map on her wall, "and was killed around 29 AD. That's what started Christianity: Jesus, raised from the dead to eternal life. He's everything we need to see of God's heart. The church started here, east of the Mediterranean Sea." She moved her hand upward on the map. "Within a generation the Holy Spirit spread Christianity all across Asia Minor and finally to Rome."

Tiffany's eyes were intent on the map.

After a long discussion about Tiffany's life and family, Megan said, "Here's a Bible for you. I'd like you to start reading here," she opened to Matthew's Gospel. "Skim the first half chapter, then read about Jesus' life and teaching."

Tiffany took the Bible and held it reverently.

"Will it be a problem having a Bible in your house?"

Tiffany smiled. "Doug never looks in the kitchen cupboards."

"When can we get together and talk about what you read?"

She gave Tiffany a bookmark with the Apostles' Creed and they agreed to the next day at the park. Thus began Tiffany's journey, the "Christian from nowhere" as she described herself to Pastor Megan Norquist. They usually met twice a week. When the weather was too cold in the park, they walked to a coffee shop or to a corner in the library. Megan brought others from the congregation to share their faith with Tiffany and to build a group to pray for her. Worship on Sunday was out of the question with Doug's opposition. But they prayed about it, and one wonderful Sunday, Doug was out of town. Tiffany attended worship and was baptized. More than one person claimed that her face glowed.

Tiffany promised to pray and to read a chapter in the New Testament every day. She always brought questions for Megan, some of which Megan couldn't answer. But she answered enough. Tiffany finished the gospels and read through Acts, seeing the early church form and realizing how much she was living as did those early Christians. She was stumped by much of Romans, but continued to read for all she could understand.

Four and a half months into her new life in Christ she came to the church to tell Megan two things which she communicated with equal seriousness: She and Doug were moving away and she had decided to become a vegetarian.

"I'm sorry you're leaving, Tiffany. You've been wonderful to be with."

"Doug says we need to if he's going to get a better job. He's rented the truck."

"We'll miss you; but... ah... is becoming a vegetarian connected with your leaving?"

Tiffany gave a shake with her whole body and was ready to cry, "I'm so weak. I'm so weak. It's what I'm supposed to do."

"I don't understand."

"Paul to the Romans. The weak eat only vegetables."

"Oh, you must be to chapter 14. That's not about you. You're in a different world than first century Rome. Meat was butchered in pagan temples and offered first in sacrifice to their gods. It really bothered some Christians to eat meat from those shops. You can take more seriously what Paul says about being convinced in your own mind."

"Really?" Tiffany laughed, slapped her hands, "what a relief. Doug and I really like hamburgers." They laughed and hugged and prayed. They saw one another once more and Tiffany was gone. She left with the determination to find Christian friends and to pray for Doug and to be able to worship on Sundays.

Megan regularly visited the park where they'd sat to study and discuss the faith. It became her place to pray. It remained the closest she'd ever been to the New Testament world and the deepest she'd ever lived within the Christian faith.

Preaching point: *Christians today can still receive (most of) Paul's instructions with desperate seriousness.*

A Epiphany 4 (4) 1 Corinthians 1:18-31

Chapter 70: God's Weakness

On the morning of January 8, 1919, the wind off Rio de Janeiro's Guanabara Bay was particularly strong, but Rodrigo and Dimas didn't realize it was out of the ordinary. The two soldiers had arrived by different trains three days before and neither had ever visited their nation's capital. They'd met in the chaos of the army's staging area where veterans and recruits milled together, waiting to be formed into half of a new company. They believed they'd found one another by God's leading and because they were devout Roman Catholics, each wondered if God wanted him to become a priest. Because they were veterans, they were able to finagle leave this morning to seek a church for worship.

As they wound through Rio's crowds, a woman threw her hand up to catch her hat as it was blowing away. Dimas pointed to a steeple a few blocks to their right, Rodrigo turned to his left. "Here," he said, and started walking away quickly, against the direction of the crowd. Dimas looked after him but didn't see sign of a church that way. Rodrigo, however, was approaching a news stand. Dimas caught up with him and saw he held a newspaper with a headline "ROOSEVELT BURIED."

"I heard about it on the train," Rodrigo said.

"The American president?"

"Yes, a very great man."

Dimas jerked his head back, "Wasn't he always interfering in South American nations?"

"Yes," Rodrigo laughed, "but those were Spanish speakers. Never Brazil. He was here on a scientific expedition — 1913 into 1914. Got a river named after him. Didn't you know?"

Dimas shook his head, "I've been stationed so deep in the jungle six years that the whole world could be speaking Portuguese by now and I'd never know. About the only news we received was new army manuals."

Rodrigo folded his arms around the newspaper. He said quietly, "I was with him."

Dimas almost expressed disbelief, but caught himself and changed his statement into a question of wonder, "You were with President Roosevelt?"

"He wasn't president then. Had been out of office four years. His son Kermit was an engineer working in Brazil and the colonel, that's how he wanted to be addressed, was on a speaking tour and seems he'd agreed to do something scientific or expedition-like in Brazil. Ended up being with Colonel Rondon."

Everyone in Brazil's army knew of Rondon's surveys.

"If it weren't for Colonel Roosevelt, I'd probably not be hunting for a church this morning."

The two men turned back toward the church, Dimas listening and Rodrigo speaking almost reverently. "A few years before that, when Rondon had been extending telegraph lines into the jungle from the south, he lit upon a stream flowing north, but no one knew where it went. It must have emptied into the Amazon, but probably a thousand miles of jungle lay between where Rondon discovered a northern flowing stream and where it emerged.

"So the government, this same government that can't get its soldiers to the right place at the right time and sort them into companies, ends up sending Colonel Rondon, Colonel Roosevelt, his son Kermit, a naturalist, and a doctor upon the search for where that river went. There were more explorers with them at the start and I was one of the original 150 hands. We endured a long trek just to reach the stepping off point, over two months with pack mules and ox carts. The going was so rough we ate some of the oxen and I wonder to this day if there's not still a trail for a few hundred miles of junk we tossed out to lessen the loads. Always going north, just to meet the river's source, and there they split the expedition so that one group continued on a different river while sixteen of us conveyed Roosevelt's expedition down the unknown stream."

Rodrigo raised his eyes to look above the packed street and

spoke against the wind, "The two colonels didn't know one another's language, so they spoke together in French, which, obviously, neither was good at. Kermit needed to be there to translate between them. But the language wasn't important. Didn't take the colonel long to communicate with us with gestures and we with him. And communicating became supremely important the farther we went. We found out that the fellow who put together the river supplies was an idiot. Tons of what we didn't need and not enough of what we did. Then, when we finally split from the other group and arrived to start north on the river, we had to navigate these heavy dugout canoes without enough room for all the baggage. Too late we found the vessels weren't suited to the rapids we met again and again."

The two men arrived in the crowd outside the church. Rodrigo stepped out of the breeze near the wall. He was going to finish his report before he entered. He stared at Dimas with a desperate look.

"We lost canoes. We lost men. We didn't find much game for food, and almost no fish. Figure that out, on a river? People were getting sick, including the colonel and Kermit. As I said, we didn't have to know English or French to realize what was most important to the colonel. After a few months his mission became not so much finding the river's goal as keeping his son safe. Clear to everybody. The worse it got, the more he was concerned about saving Kermit. Week after week we splashed into catastrophes, nature whittling us down, as we had to drag those heavy canoes, cutting our way through the dense jungle in portage after portage around the cataracts. Even had to stop for days and hack out trees to make a new canoe. Finally we wrecked so many canoes we didn't have enough space for everyone to board even in gentle currents. Half of us had to traipse the shore, hacking through the vicious jungle. We were near starvation, ill and injured workers having to ride aboard the canoes. The colonel was incapacitated — bad heart, malaria, and his leg infected — when word from his tent came that he wanted us to go on without him. However, Kermit wouldn't leave him.

"So, the colonel's rubbing shoulders with death, but the life he so dearly wants to rescue can only be saved by allowing his son to save him."

Rodrigo clutched the newspaper to his breast. For a moment unable to continue, he shook his head to control his emotions. He turned to the church door whispering, "The powerful weakness of love…. Seeing what the colonel did and why he did it has come to signify for me Christ's love. The colonel saved his son through his suffering weakness. Year by year it means more to me." He spoke wide-eyed to Dimas, "Through his own suffering weakness he set out to save his son, as God through the weakness of his suffering son set out to save us." He crossed himself and stepped into the church. Dimas crossed himself and followed.

Preaching point: *Redemptive weakness*

(Candice Millard, The River of Doubt: Theodore Roosevelt's Darkest Journey)

B Epiphany 2 (2) 1 Corinthians 6:12-20

Chapter 71: Wired

Before he got drunk he'd made up his mind to be hyper-attentive at the hearing. Now, suffering from terminal hangover, he strained to be alert as the door opened before him. They must have arrived late because some official ushered him and his mother right in. The room was larger than he expected and he blinked at the bright lights. He looked around to see tiny clusters of three or four people, obviously family groups. They resembled a photo he'd seen of defeated American Indians waiting to be carted off to some far away reservation. The only person with a head up was at the back wall, a man who seemed intent upon him, with a smile as huge as a cartoon character.

He fought with nausea as he tried to clear his mind. He and his mother were led to stand in front of three people sitting behind a table. He struggled to focus his eyes. Nothing extraordinary about the three at the table. A few papers in front of each. A man on the left with a droopy eye. A younger woman in the middle. He assumed she was the chief judge, her hair waxed like wings. A really old woman on the right kept trying to smile then forgetting to do so.

"Randall Schute," the winged hair lady eyed him and spoke his name.

If his mother hadn't elbowed him, he might have gone to sleep standing up: "Say, 'Yes, your Honor.'"

The lady didn't wait for him to respond. She spoke first to his mother as though she'd said the same thing dozens of times. "We are not judges and you are not in court. We are the Citizens' Juvenile Council." She turned to Randy, "You are here after your first arrest. Our council is in lieu of court. No judges, no attorneys, we are just citizens serving the community. We are here to help you so that you never must be charged with a crime.

We are giving you a chance to make up for your mistake. Do you understand?"

His mother, with her head down, nudged him. "Yes," he said.

"You have been apprehended for underage drinking and driving under the influence. Do you have anything to say?"

Randy made a moan that sounded like, "Wellll," when his mother spoke up, "Randy's a good boy. My baby," she said, as she held onto his arm. Randy knew the tone and could hear the tears coming. "Randy's a good boy, O Jesus help us. My baby. His father was an alcoholic." Tears splattering all over. "My baby. He was a good student. Freshman year an A in history. Have mercy on him." More tears. Her hands in front of her face now, muttering into a mashed handkerchief. "My baby. O Jesus, help us." Randy wondered what the people in the room thought of her, thought of him! The three behind the table waited until his mother gained control of herself. The droopy-eyed man said, "Your mother has suggested a plan to our council."

Randy looked at his mother in astonishment.

"If you accept it and remain satisfactorily under the supervision of Mr. James Clements without abusing alcohol until you are eighteen, you will be beyond our help, which is to say out of our jurisdiction. You will be considered an adult and any infraction of the law by you then will be prosecuted as an adult crime."

Randy's thoughts were spinning: What? Who?

"Mrs. Schute," he aimed his droopy eye at her, "explain your plan."

She stood erect and spoke clearly, "Mr. James Clements, from my church." She pointed to the back of the room and the man with too many teeth stood. Everyone looked at him. Randy had never seen him before. "He will employ Randy three afternoons a week, pick him up at school and bring him home after work. He will get him to and from youth group on Sunday evenings and be his advisor."

Who is this man, and who is this woman he thought was his mother? A minute ago she was crumbling in grief, now she sounds as though she could organize the defense of New York City.

The droopy eyed man was signaling toward the back of the room. The smiley man came to stand beside his mother. The droopy eyed man addressed him, "Mr. Clements, you heard Mrs. Schute. You will give Randall a job?"

"Yes sir," the smiley man responded. "I own an electrical business. We're non-union, but licensed and bonded and we pay well. I'm a recovering alcoholic. I've helped others. I'll supervise Randy."

"Randall," the droopy-eyed man said. Randy drifted uncertainly from his contorted thoughts and faced the council. The lady of the staccato expression was holding a fairly solid smile now. "Do you agree?"

His thoughts ricocheted through his mind; but he managed to say, "I guess so."

"That means 'yes, you will'?"

"Yes," he mumbled.

The difficult problem in the first weeks was Leroy, his supplier. Each time he saw Randy, he said he could get a bottle of weapons-grade vodka. For two weeks Randy held him off. He'd settled into the routine of working six hours a week. He didn't mind the labor. Some of the fellows on the crew were interesting, some hardly sane. By now he was calling Mr. Clements 'Jim,' as everyone in the youth group did. The youth group was different for him; but he knew a couple of the kids from school. An hour of fun and food and then talking Bible and faith and each Sunday's group ending with a prayer circle with Jim praying for each by name.

On his sixth Thursday of what he called "probation," he was in front of the high school with Leroy offering to get him a bottle as Jim drove up. He didn't talk much on the way to work and an hour later he stood absently in front of a junction box, running a wire back and forth through his hand as though trying to polish the insulation. He must have been talking to himself, because Jim came and stood in front of him.

He asked, "How's it going?"

"You mean staying sober?"

"At least that."

"I'm sober, but…" he thumped a fist into a palm, "but it's hard."

"I'm with you on that."

"Still hard for you?"

"Sometimes, but less all the time. And I know I'd be safer drinking transmission fluid than alcohol."

Randy nodded and grinned.

"You haven't asked," Jim said, "but when you're tempted, my advice is that you grip onto the faith that you're wired in to God."

Jim had his attention.

"You believe in Christ, right?"

Randy curled up the side of his mouth and tilted his head, "Some."

"Then you're wired in. That's how I think of it as an electrician. We aren't alone. You're in the grid. We're wired in to God and other believers — like your mom and I are wired to God and into the church. The good thing about being wired to God is that you're on a two way switch." His smile nearly exceeded his mouth, "Turn him off and he turns you right back on."

"I get that," Randy said.

"God's inside you invisibly, the way electricity is. It's another way to say what the Bible does that your body's a temple of the Holy Spirit because God's inside you. Something that I grab onto real hard when I'm tempted. Make sense?"

"Uh huh, a little. I'll be running that over in my mind."

"Sure enough. We owe that help to one another, in that we're wired together. Now, get those 10/2s pulled to the box because I agreed to have this hooked up by Friday night." He gave a big smile, "then the lights come on."

Preaching point: *Christians are united in the most intimate and energizing way with God and other believers.*

C Epiphany 6 (6) 1 Corinthians 15:12-20

Chapter 72: Blissful? Agnosticism

If ever (and it was seldom) anyone asked Sean or Lizzy about their belief in God, they had their answer prepared: They were blissful agnostics. Their glib response meant that generally they didn't know and didn't care whether there was a God or not. No offense to God or to believers, they just found little reason to care.

As children they'd both known nothing other than a secure upper-middle class home, with safe upper-middle class schools, clubs, athletics, and friends, all who had little awareness of a less sheltered or predictable world, let alone the suffering of the greater world. If they'd glanced evidence of a harsher life than what surrounded them daily, they'd taken little notice. The advantages they'd enjoyed led to university degrees only twice as difficult as high school. And not only were jobs waiting for them after university, recruiters came seeking them on campus. Four years out of university they and their friends were charging ahead in life's race. They'd abandoned an apartment for a starter house, certain it would be the first of many steps up in the only kind of life they knew.

Lizzy's family was in the majority on the west coast. They might have professed a nebulous belief in a supreme being, but Lizzy had only been in a church for weddings. All she knew of Christianity was a story passed on from her grandfather about when he was a boy. His mother was dying and the preacher came. Her young grandfather was in the room as the preacher sat by his mother's bed, asked embarrassing questions about her illness, offered a prayer using a good part of an hour, and requested fresh coffee. Then her grandfather heard him in the kitchen joking with the men.

Lizzy and Sean had been married in Sean's church. For Lizzy, it was a legal procedure they must complete in order to continue living together. She never understood "all this religion business." Sean's religious views were more complicated, in that he'd been raised in the Christian faith. He'd discarded the faith immediately after high school but whenever he returned home from university, his parents assumed he'd attend with them to Sunday school and worship.

Until now he'd skirted this problem with Lizzy by making sure they didn't visit his parents on a Sunday. The couple once had been caught at his parents' at Christmas, but Lizzy could brush off any religious meaning of Christmas Eve worship because everyone celebrates the snow, family, and gift season. This time was different. They were visiting on a weekend. "I don't want to disappoint them," Sean said. "It's always been this way with them. Weird, I know. But they believe it and I don't want to hurt them."

They sat in their car in his parents' driveway, yet to get out and greet the in-laws. Lizzy wasn't upset. She just didn't see any reason to rise early on Sunday and get dolled up for three hours with strangers when they could, as usual, lay in bed, read the newspaper, and catch the new YouTube posts. But she'd attend with the rest; and so she did, along with Sean in the back seat of his parents' car as her mother-in-law pointed to the houses where Sean's friends had lived, his high school and dentist's office.

Sunday school was at ten and Lizzy and Sean fit into the younger adults class. Lizzy whispered to Sean, "Why's the leader of the younger adults nearly eighty years old?"

"As far as I know," Sean answered, "Mr. Menon has taught the class as long as I've been alive. Probably started teaching it after the war."

"Which war?"

No place to hide. Everyone sat around one large table and Sean recognized only one person. Because Sean and Lizzy didn't have Bibles, the couple next to them slid one over from the center stack. They also helped them find the text for the morning.

"We're going on with First Corinthians," Mr. Menon stood and said. "Let's pray: Lord Jesus, risen and triumphant, loving and merciful, be present with us now to teach, inspire, and guide us in your ways. Amen."

The old man continued talking, while lowering himself as if by stages into his chair, "We're in the theological center chapter of First Corinthians. Lots of people think the love chapter 13 is the theological center. It's not. It tells us how to live as Christians. Chapter 15 tells us why.

"Why should we believe or live differently than anyone else? Most in our community consider God as a cloud at best. Impersonal, a haze around us that maybe got us here and might find us a seat on the subway if we beg for it." He received some snorts and sniggers.

"We're surrounded by people who view the Christian faith at best as good feelings, at worst as deeply instilled prejudice. People might have the constitutional right in the United States to believe such things, but don't go spreading it around or offering it to others.

"Is our Christian faith merely vague or misty? What've we got? What's this Christian life founded on? Feelings, wishes, denial? The apostle Paul dealt with the same questions. He and his folk were real and they give evidence for us to believe they had as much intelligence to navigate life as we do. They just didn't have all our modern gadgets. Paul tells us the event that our faith is based on. Not something made up, not a mistaken identity, be the motives for suspecting such ever so sincere. Paul knew from Jesus' earliest believers — and the experience of his own life — that Jesus was alive. He'd been resurrected. That means 'to live again.' The resurrected Jesus also, then, lived again in Paul. If not, Paul says, there's nothing." He cleared his throat, sounding like a car whose engine wouldn't start.

"I don't know if you all have thought of that: Nothing. Not just that nothing is lasting beyond this life, but that nothing is important enough now to live for. Why do we live? Chapter 15 is the 'Why Chapter.' What propels us day to day? Just our survival? Just being able to buy the newest gizmos? Just the goodwill of our tribe? What will get you out of bed in the morning when you really don't feel like it? That might seem easy when you're young and strong. I'm here to tell you that's not all of life." He gave a big grin. "For everything that gets easier by growing older, something gets harder and eventually the balance tips. One thing gets easier, three get harder." People chuckled as he nodded.

"Our faith balances on Jesus' resurrection. Might seem like way back then, but it stretches till now. It's for each of us now, something real beyond what we see and feel and wonder about day to day, something from outside this world that crashes in to each of us to start us over from a new beginning — so important that God would actually come to earth to suffer for us. Not everyone knows it and not everyone believes it. Younger people don't always think about what life's built upon and what we can trust, what's lasting. But for the New Testament faith, if Jesus' resurrection isn't true, not only is our faith empty and useless in this passing carnival of life but *everything* is empty and useless. And in the end, death will vacuum life of any meaning.

"Much better to learn this when you're young. Much better to base your life on something that won't tip sideways when you meet those roadblocks and tragedies and downright evil situations that ambush us all. So much better to trust deep, deep down with Paul that God did something wonderful that changes everything."

He looked to the wall on his left, shook his head, then looked to the wall on his right to spot the clock. "Now, time for discussion."

The class offered comments and some slicing questions, which Mr. Menon didn't always answer. Lizzy was about to ask a question but the man beside her spoke first. "For me, if it weren't for faith in Christ, there'd be nothing lasting to plant my life on. Without Christ, I take a step and sink. If I reach for something alone, it crumbles in my hand." The discussion didn't hold tightly to the subject, but Lizzy was bothered. She'd never truly realized what started Christianity, and she hadn't contemplated a life with no meaning. When class was over she was almost dizzy when she stood.

Sean grabbed her arm and looked in her eyes, "You okay?"

"Yeah," she said slowly. She took a few steps, leaned into him and whispered, "You were raised in this faith. I've got a *bunch* of questions for you."

Preaching point: *If Jesus has not been raised from the dead, faith is futile and life is meaningless.*

C Lent 4 2 Corinthians 5:16-21

Chapter 73: Everything Has Become New

In the initial year of Jayne's first pastorate, the pastors' cluster provided her most important instruction in how Christ's grace was applied in the real world. Every month the seasoned pastors listened, counseled, and prayed for her. At the end of her first year she acknowledged what she would never have guessed when she began: Her second most important source of learning was preparing for funerals. In meeting with loved ones before funerals, she bumped into more convoluted life situations, tortured relationships, and families' destructive varieties of grieving than she ever imagined: a man whose aunt was disclosed as his mother, a woman whose husband had hidden two previous marriages with five offspring, a man who found that his wife had been ten years older than she claimed, and a woman who had to face another woman claiming she was currently married to the deceased. Each situation needed a massive infusion of Christ's grace. Yet, Jayne's meeting with one family to prepare a funeral was like no other.

During that first year, Archie Taunton and his wife Evelyn had been able to attend worship only a few times. Archie needed a walker and Evelyn had suffered a stroke which prevented her speaking. Jayne visited twice in their home and she prayed with Archie three times in the hospital before he died. All her encounters with the Tauntons heartened Jayne with their faith. Now their two children Tanny and Graham had arrived and helped Evelyn into Jayne's office to plan Archie's funeral.

Jayne greeted the family and seated them and expressed her condolence. She asked a few questions about where the children lived and when they'd seen their father last.

"Have you thought about favorite scriptures to be read or people to share memories of Archie?"

"First thing," Tanny said, "his name wasn't Archie."

"Archibald?" Jayne asked.

"His given name was Graham Paul Taunton," Graham said. "I'm actually 'Graham Jr.'"

Evelyn nodded to Jayne. Her children seemed smug.

Jayne was puzzled both with the difference in the name and in the way the children told her. She plowed straight ahead, "Sooo….," which brought a broad smile from the children and a slight grin from Evelyn.

"Archie Bunker," Tanny said.

"Television," Jayne said. "Before I was born. He was kind of a loveable bigot?"

"More or less," Graham said.

"It was when we were kids," Tanny said. "We watched it every week, right Mom?"

Evelyn nodded, a pained smile on the corners of her mouth.

"We'd only seen it a couple weeks," Tanny said, "and Mom just started calling Dad 'Archie.'

"It fit. We grew up hearing him slam Jews, Poles, Italians, and Asians; and he had all kinds of terms for blacks. When boys started wearing long hair, he blipped off about it all the time. Thus, 'Archie.' Mom saw the similarity and basically called him on it, but in her nice way."

"He didn't see the program the way we did," Graham said. "We were in middle school and high school with all different kinds of kids. We accepted one another and that's what school taught and encouraged. It's the US Constitution. Dad was thinking like the group he grew up with. It's all he knew. He pushed back against the belief that every human being is equal and others don't have to think, act, speak, and believe the same as we do in order to be fellow citizens."

Jayne listened with awe. "You've considered this a lot."

"I teach constitutional law," Graham said with a laugh.

"We kids goaded Dad," Tanny said, "letting him know racism wasn't acceptable to us and, as Graham says, un-American. Mom did it by calling him 'Archie.'

"That was the early '70s and Pastor Lummer was here. He was a really great preacher. Week after week he preached about what Jesus says to our world. He spoke a lot about racism and anti-Semitism, because it was a problem in this city. Dad had always believed in Jesus and the Bible, but slowly his thinking was sharpened and his heart was warmed. Over the decades, instead of denigrating people who were different from him, he began to tolerate them and — not always wholeheartedly — to extend Christ's love to them. We watched Dad slowly move, slowly being pushed."

"In a way Tanny and I feel he grew up with us," Graham said. "We discussed these things often and sometimes argued, but it's not just that he was losing the household vote of three against one. He really came to understand. Right, Mom?" Graham said to Evelyn. Evelyn mumbled a positive response. Tears dropped onto her blouse. She shook her head to chase them away.

"Dad kept the name 'Archie' as kind of a badge," Graham said, "a statement that Jesus can change people. Others began calling him Archie too. His grandkids only know him as 'Grandpa Archie.' You've probably never heard him called 'Graham' or 'Gray' have you?"

"Sure haven't," Jayne said.

The three younger people became silent. Evelyn was quietly weeping. Tanny stepped to her with a handkerchief and helped dry her tears. Evelyn nodded her thanks. Tanny turned to sit back down and said, "That's why we've chosen the scripture we want read for Dad: 'So if anyone is in Christ, there is a new creation: everything old has passed away; see everything has become new.' In Dad's case, he even got a new name he claimed and rejoiced in."

Jayne told her pastors' cluster that this was the first funeral she'd performed where the biblical text as well as the sermon was supplied by the family.

Preaching point: *Christ changes each believer more and more into a new creation.*

ABC Ascension; A Reign of Christ Proper 29 (34) Ephesians 1:15-23

Chapter 74: Enveloped Into Jesus' Life

"Jesus' view of life is okay, mostly... inspiring; but, I don't go much for his church." Haley said. She had small, close together dark eyes, set so deep she appeared to be looking out of two small tunnels.

"The Buddha states all life is suffering," Lyle said. His blue eyes protruded almost like a fly, and he spoke as casually as if his statement was a response in an evening long conversation among old friends. It wasn't.

The subject of the conversation had slipped up on Clare. Her anxiety distracted her and she wasn't attentive to the two who'd been parked with her in this less than comfortable waiting area. She suddenly realized that her two fellow PhD candidates were speaking seriously. She wondered: how did we get to this? Three graduate students in philosophy, strangers and thrown together, seldom speak of faith, unless one plans to spring religion like a trap on every new acquaintance. Some dimwit, however, had plopped these three to await the committee's decision to which of them the fellowship would be granted. Their lives hung on what an apologetic messenger would announce to them; yet, after five minutes of fidgeting together Haley and Lyle were taking off on faith, their faith.

"I do my yoga every day," Haley said. "Although I admit that sometimes," she giggled, shaking her head at her own contradiction, "I'm thinking about Kant or Wittgenstein... and reviewing for class discussion."

"Sounds more western than eastern," Lyle laughed and turned his blue eyes to Clare as though it were her turn to acknowledge some philosophical or religious stance toward life. She gave a small clearing of the throat (how did this conversation come about?) and said, "Thomism, basically, kind of at the crossroads of philosophy and theology."

"Mmm," Haley said, slurring the word into a statement and a question.

"Go on. Go on," Lyle said, rolling his hand in front of Clare, his eyes seemed even more open as he urged her to continue.

Really, what was happening here? Come to apply for a PhD program and her two competitors seem like her allies, students like her who are interested in life and thus very interesting people.

"It's a long story," she said, looking down, then glancing hopefully toward the hall that led to the professors' conference room.

"Yes?" Haley said, her tiny dark eyes awaiting Clare's statement of personal truth.

"I went to Austria for my senior year."

Haley and Lyle nodded for her to continue.

"That's where I got into philosophy. German can really string together the philosophical words."

Lyle and Haley laughed. Haley said, "The Greeks compounded some pretty lengthy words too."

"I met an Austrian philosophy student, Nela, and we became very close. She already had her master's. She's where I learned everything important about Austria's German side of history and culture. She loved to tell me anything I asked. Had the kind of a memory that retained everything she'd ever seen, heard or read."

"Like Professor Pilsen," Lyle said. "Amazing that people have such brains."

"Nela was Christian. We hadn't been friends long when she told me about the passion play at Oberammergau. She flittered the ditty off her tongue about Unterammergau and Oberammergau forward and then backward. That was a year ago. She insisted we go to the play because here I was in Austria in 2010 — it's only performed every ten years. I should go.

"I didn't know much about the Bible, and some of the play about the Old Testament was lost on me. But, all those scenes of Jesus' last week portrayed with the pomp, music and the flood of costumes. Hour after hour. My German was good by then. Didn't miss much. I was taken in, taken up, enveloped, embraced. Nothing like a philosophy lecture."

She looked quizzically at her companions, not wishing to offend them. They waited with their friendly, intelligent faces. She leaned forward to confide with them, "It's like in those few hours I was told barely enough about God and Christ, yet it included me. I realized that day, although I couldn't put it in words, that no matter what else happened, this would shape my life."

Clare paused and took a breath. Lyle and Haley were genuinely involved in her story. She was flooded with affection for them. At the same moment, the thought flicked through her mind that only one of them would be granted the graduate position. It included a teaching assistantship with a stipend large enough actually to live on.

"I told Nela about it. 'It can happen,' she said. 'Straight from the stage to your heart,' and she started talking about Hitler. I thought, 'What's this got to do with Oberammergau and what's just happened to me?' We Americans had been instructed to be courteous about Hitler and Nazism. Only mentioned it if someone else brought up the subject. But Nela could explain whatever I wanted to know and in this case what I didn't even ask. She plunged right in. 'Hitler came to Oberammergau to the special performance in 1934 — the 300 year anniversary. But this wasn't the performance that changed him. He had an experience like yours when he was sixteen. He and a friend attended Wagner's opera *Rienzi*. He was enraptured. He felt himself encircled and included in the plot. He said at the moment he'd been given his destiny to lead his people out of servitude. Well, the world knows what he dragged it into.'"

Clare was relaxed now. She leaned back. "Nela with her Christian heart put her hand on my shoulder and said, 'God created us to serve a grand cause. Depends which one we surrender to. If you've experienced being enraptured, folded into Jesus' story, it means you'll now be formed by our Lord Jesus.'

"My thinking was like all ten bowling pins tipped over at once... before the bowling ball got to them. Mental chaos. I had six weeks before end of term to scramble around and question profs and fellow students and read philosophy and theology all night, and, of course, write papers. I came back from Europe determined to live for Christ. That's about all I know, the minimum understanding of Christianity. Certainly don't know where I'm going next." She spread her hands to her companions and asked, "Know what I mean?"

Haley opened her mouth to speak, but at that moment the three saw a professor step from the conference room and walk toward them.

Preaching point: *The eyes of the heart enlightened.*

B Proper 16 (21) Ephesians 6:10-20

Chapter 75: Those Who Know What Armor Is For

"So," Tychicus said, "Rome's recruiter didn't exactly snatch you?"

"No," Patrobas said, looking down as he shook his head, "my father made an agreement."

The two younger legionaries were sitting on stools in their tent. New enlistee Patrobas had just arrived to camp and been assigned to this squad. Tychicus was putting on his armor. To Patrobas, it looked like a sad puzzle was being assembled over Tychicus's body. But at the moment everything looked sad to Patrobas. Tychicus said, "You're now in 'Rome's Fighting Mules and Moles': A few days fighting, half the time training, the rest digging or marching with all your gear."

Fortunatus, an older veteran, stood at the tent's flap. His face was like leather and a crooked scar ripped under his left eye. He said, "Don't forget, that's *all* your gear. You carry it wherever we march. Never leave anything lying around. If you do, only trust your tent mates. Well, at least the two of us." He and Tychicus laughed. "Get used to us," the older man said. "You'll be with the seven others in this tent — or in a small room when the barracks are built — for your 25-year stint. After a while you'll be able to identify each of us by our coughs, snores, or farts."

Tychicus finished putting on his armor. "I'm off to guard at the granary." He looked down at Patrobas. "More advice: buy the best gear. Couple peddlers around the camp with special deals. But get the best, and not a bronze helmet. Get a steel one if you really want to save your head from a mashing. Those Dacians have long swords and they love to swing from the top down." He put on his helmet and left.

Fortunatus was still at the tent flap. Patrobas didn't move from his stool. Fortunatus regarded the new recruit, whose shoulders slumped like a worn mountain. "Father, you say, *sold* you into the legion?"

"Almost," Patrobas said. "I had to sign freely. He needed my signing bonus."

"Desperate or despicable?"

"Desperate," Patrobas said. "Can't say I blame him much, though blame him I do."

"Well, you know what? You're feeling bad now. But it's temporary. Wait till your training starts tomorrow. Then you'll feel really rotten!" When Patrobas didn't respond, Fortunatus said, "So tell me. Every recruit has a story of what got him here."

Patrobas glanced up at Fortunatus's kind expression.

"Financial disaster."

"And...."

Patrobas hesitated, then uttered, "The whole rest of our family drowned. My father owned four ships shuttling grain from Egypt to Rome. My mother, brother and two sisters were on one when the fleet went down in a storm. Left my father and me and a load of debt. Sold our house, slaves, livestock, warehouse, even our clothes. Didn't come anywhere near covering the debts. He made me enlist, took the signing bonus and lit out for Spain — I guess. He didn't tell me exactly, so I couldn't testify under oath or, more probably, under torture where he went. Said he'd pay me back somehow."

"Fathers, what can you do with them?" Fortunatus's humor didn't work. "Come on," Fortunatus said, offering his hand down to Patrobas. "I'll take you to the settlement beside the camp and introduce you to an honest armorer. He repairs for our squad. He'll fit you. Might have some used pieces he's fixed up. He accepts recruits on credit. He knows you can't get away from the legion."

Patrobas' first weeks were grueling. No one gave him sympathy; yet, Fortunatus was always the one who gave him any care he truly needed. One night in the tent as Patrobas was anointing his bloody shins he told Fortunatus, "I was going to be a philosopher, not Rome's marching gladiator."

"That include faith?" Fortunatus asked.

Without a blink, Tychicus said, "I make my yearly offerings to the gods and the emperor. Never miss."

"But do you trust the gods out there in the spiritual realm to care about you?"

"The gods? Are you kidding? They're too busy tearing around fighting and fornicating. I agree with the philosophers: Perform the rituals, but don't bet your life the gods will help us. Best to take care of ourselves."

Fortunatus dropped other phrases over the following months that made Patrobas think he might be an adherent of Mithras, a favorite religion of soldiers. Yet Patrobas didn't perceive him becoming either more pugnacious or more detached. If anything, this older veteran was becoming kinder. As Patrobas struggled with learning the brutal skills of a legionary and tried to come to some peace with his fate, he noticed that Fortunatus traded duties in order to have the Sun's Day off. So at dawn one Sun's Day, he trailed him into the settlement beside the camp and saw him meet others. The folk greeted one another like pensioned legionaries at a reunion. They hugged one another and, after they entered a large house, he heard their singing. Most amazing was that each person, when leaving, performed a drama of putting on invisible armor. It was quick but obvious: First a belt, then breastplate and shoes. They hoisted an invisible shield and put on a helmet. Finally, they slid an imagined sword into its invisible scabbard. Patrobas had seen nothing like this. He ducked around the corner and was alone and waiting in the tent when Fortunatus returned.

"I followed you this morning," Patrobas said.

Fortunatus stepped back in surprise, "You going to turn me in?"

"You planning a revolt?"

"No," he said quietly, and then spoke each word distinctly, "I am a Christian." He stood as though at attention.

Patrobas said, "You look like you're ready to be executed. Don't worry. I'm not going to turn you in. What's this you do?"

Fragments of Good News

Patrobas had heard of Christians and some of their strange rituals, how they drank blood and destroyed families and many wouldn't serve as soldiers. Fortunatus suggested they go for a walk where they wouldn't be heard. They spent half the day hiking the countryside with Fortunatus recalling how Christ's followers had shown him kindness when he was recovering from battle wounds. "Maybe three, four times I'd bought supplies from them in the settlement. I didn't know or care who they were. Yet they came to see me every day after I was carted back to the camp hospital. After a month of attending to my wounds, they explained that the Spirit of Christ led them to care for others.

"I've been a believer in Christ for a year. I don't regret it. I'm only concerned that if we have to march away to battle again, I'll miss the Christians here in the settlement. They've taught me what Christ said and did and how the church started and what the apostles wrote for us."

"And what in the name of all the gods was the little act you each performed when you departed?"

"That takes seriously what the Apostle Paul wrote. It's remembering that Christ protects us from the invisible evil powers around us. I suppose it looks strange to outsiders, but I repeat the ritual to myself everyday as I put on my armor. Christ helps me live for him. He loved me enough to lay down his life for me. In our profession, you'll find that means a lot.

"Never before has something from the spiritual realm actually helped me. The love and power of Christ have proven to be what I always needed but didn't know I lacked. I'm trusting Christ's armor right now, because if you turn me in, I can be executed."

Patrobas didn't turn in Fortunatus. Within a year, he also was one of the settlement's group meeting to encourage one another in the Christian faith and learning to put on the kind of armor that prevailed against anything truly harmful in life or death. Then Fortunatus was transferred to detached duty in Gaul. He and Patrobas parted as brothers. The last thing they did was to share the ritual of putting on their spiritual armor.

David O. Bales

Preaching point: *Christ's powerful defense against spiritual enemies.*

(Philip Matyszak, Legionary: The Roman Soldier's Unofficial Manual)

C Advent 3 Philippians 4:4-7

Chapter 76: A Freshman Experience

Reina tossed clothes into the suitcase on the bed as fast as her shaking hands could move.

"I think you really ought to give it a better chance," Jessyca said. "Three days of orientation aren't enough to make a decision. Give your classes a try for a week."

"Riiight," Reina said as she picked up her second suitcase and thumped it on the bed. "Okay for you, maybe. Not for me." She realized that her shaking had increased — from her hands to all over her body. "I'm getting out of here. Don't know why I let anybody talk me into it. I'm straight out the door and a taxi to the bus station. Don't care how long I have to wait."

Jessyca stepped in front of the door. "Okay. I'll be assigned another roommate, or I'll have to move to another room; that's a real pain. But, just one thing. For your sake, if you dash away, you'll have failures in all your classes. At least go to administration and drop. Simple. Ten minutes now could save a lot of trouble when you enter another college."

Reina stood for a moment, trying to stop shaking. "All right. Thanks. Be right back." Jessyca moved aside and Reina reached for the door knob. She realized she'd nearly lost control of her hand. It was almost vibrating.

When she left the dorm, she felt guilty for dumping Jessyca; yet she felt trapped in this college. She'd already had enough of the "freshman experience" she'd heard repeated so often. A Calvinistic college — although self-described as "progressive!" Where else would you find buildings named Oecolampadias and Zwingli? The fall breeze that swept maple leaves into her path didn't slow her. She couldn't remember which building was administration. They were all so plain. She rushed into the first one.

She didn't see signs over the doors, although maybe at the end of the hall. She saw a door partly open and heard speaking. She crept toward the door and saw an arm fling up. A lot of loud talking. She stepped nearer and saw the arm pitch up and down again. She figured this must be the first class of the term, so why the excitement? She slipped quietly beside the door. The instructor was speaking loudly enough for a person across the hall to hear.

"We're freed from sin's shackles and shackled to freedom. Freed from our over self-concern, we're enslaved to love. Others are liberated by our freedom. That was Paul's message. It was his life. We're not talking just ideas. Paul *experienced* this. He ate, drank, and breathed the Spirit of the risen Christ. You read his works and you realize that only when he's done talking about the risen Christ does he mention those minor things we need to be concerned about, like our doubt or fear or anxiety. These are being solved as we live right now. The big problems of sin and death are settled. Death is overcome in resurrection. We're acquitted of our sin and bonded with the risen Christ.

"That's why the Christian faith isn't based on a bunch of rules but the energy of love, the motivation of gratitude. That got Christianity started and that's what keeps it going."

Reina leaned against the wall. She might as well wait until the class finished.

The voice continued, "Some of you have only heard the Bible as representing the Christian faith. Our college wants you to understand that the dynamism of the faith didn't end 2,000 years ago when the last apostle died. The message and experience of the risen Christ has continued, not always with the same words and concepts, not the same understanding and emphases. The faith has progressed and expanded. We're linked not just to the New Testament believers, but also to those second-century and third-century Christians persecuted in Rome's arenas. They out thought, out lived, and out died the adherents of the non-Christian religions. We're family with Augustine of Hippo, who held the world of faith together with his writings as the Roman

Empire fell. We claim fussy Jerome in his cave who translated the Bible into the language of the people. Anselm too. He believed so that he might understand. Francis of Assisi understood enough that the followers of this troubadour for God would preach the gospel at all times and, when necessary, even used words — and friend Clare chose to love and serve God the same way.

"You've heard of Martin Luther and his struggle against superstition and corruption in the church — while fighting his own demons of doubt and sin. And that wonderful Bible teacher John Calvin, and I'm sure you all want to learn about people named Zwingli and Oecolampadias." The class roared with laughter. Even Reina chuckled.

"Thomas More: his prison was a milestone for our faith. Held there because he wouldn't compromise with the blatant evil of England's Henry the Eighth, he suffered martyrdom as the king's good subject, but Christ's subject first. There's John Knox the ex-galley slave who believed it was against God's law for a woman to govern. For all his narrowness, this Scot Presbyterian brought about one of the least bloody revolutions in history.

"Our Christian faith claims Vincent de Paul who prayed every hour and talked royalty out of their jewels to feed the poor. The brothers Wesley both touched our continent: Charles, the sweet singer of hymns, and John whose heart was strangely warmed. They tipped England back from the edge of civil strife and their efforts grew beyond them to give the world the Methodist church."

As Reina listened, she punched on her smart phone to the college's website. Room 115 she noted was "Christianity 101."

"David Livingston healing people, preaching and exploring Africa and Dwight Moody who planned to make a million dollars selling shoes, but traded jobs for the profession of evangelist. There was the family of Beechers, including theologians and preachers, and Harry Beecher Stowe, the little lady who started such a big war, and Abraham Lincoln who made that comment to her. Even in that war he had malice toward none and charity for all.

David O. Bales

"The Presbyterian Jane Addams with her Chicago Hull House served immigrants in every conceivable way. Albert Schweitzer gave up brilliant academic and musical careers to go to Africa to practice medicine and his reverence for life. Dag Hammarskjold, the international civil servant, struggled to bring peace to the planet. Martin Luther King Jr., whose non-violent ways shall someday overcome. And Mother Teresa of Calcutta ministered to the poorest of the poor as though caring for her Lord himself.

"This is a glimpse of the Christian faith. So much more. Broader. So much more. Deeper. The faith is always more than what we know. It's also more than what we understand or live. Our course will look at the Christian faith from the beginning to the present, from the top to the bottom and from the bottom to the top, from the inside out and the outside in. It's not the subject of this class in order to be inspected, but to be entered, not just to be understood but to be experienced. I can't imagine any other way to adequately study the faith."

The waving arms halted. The instructor said, "I've written your week's reading assignments on the board. If you haven't purchased or rented your textbooks, do it yesterday. Come to class with your questions, always questions. The Christian faith isn't pre-packaged, so you have to accept it whole. It's a living thing because it's living with God. You get to question and even doubt it. Yes, that's in the Bible. If you've never doubted, then you can read other people's doubts in the Bible. We've time for a few questions now."

Reina looked at her smart phone in her left hand. It was still as a stone. She realized that her right hand was also motionless and she was holding it on her chest. Her breathing, however, was rapid and shallow. She heard the students shuffling as they stood to leave the room. She thought, well, I could at least try this place for a week.

Preaching point: *A view of the spacious, historic Christian faith can be positively overwhelming.*

C Proper 20 (25); B Thanksgiving 1 Timothy 2:1-7

Chapter 77: First Of All

Ariel and Angelica's deepest memory was their parents telling them no one was sure which of them was born first. As children they asked their parents to repeat their birth story to every new person who entered their home.

"Your Mama was quite occupied," their father said, "and you can't accept her version of the event."

"Right," their mother replied, "like you could be objective while fighting the fire?"

Their births began in a hospital delivery room jammed with people. Because of the expected condition of the twins (not quite to term), two gynecologists, two pediatricians, and a handful of nurses attended the delivery — along with student nurses as well as the girls' father and grandmother. When one child was almost out of the birth canal, a flame burst from a computer monitor beside their mother and spewed sparks like a berserk Fourth of July sparkler.

"It was all jumping, screaming, coughing, running, and swatting hands at the smoke," their father said. "Someone grabbed the newborn and, as they got your Mama onto a gurney to roll her into the hall — dragging behind a drip pole still attached to her — someone else pulled the second of you from between your Mama's legs. By the time the fire was out and you girls were safely tucked into incubators, no one was positive which came first."

So Ariel and Angelica — or "Angelica and Ariel" as Angelica said it — were unique for being "almost identical twins" as they put it, except for their disagreement about which was born first. They always tossed the question of "first" between them.

They'd come running down the stairs before school and one would yell, "I was first to get dressed." The other would follow immediately, "I was first out of the bathroom." All their friends knew the story of their births and the constant "firsts" banter. It was their exclusive intellectual property. Their father and uncle often performed Abbot and Costello's routine "Who's on First." Angelica and Ariel — or "Ariel and Angelica" as Ariel said it — tried to come up with a similar routine for "I was born first, then who was born second?" but their giggling sent them into rolling laughter, never completing their routine.

The girls grew up seldom bored, partly because as twins they always had a playmate, but also they had their game of "First," in which they were not only the players, but the umpire and score keeper. When they were twelve, their pastor visited their Sunday school class and told them, "The time has come to be baptized and live the Christian faith." He asked the class to pray for a week and decide "Who will follow Jesus into his baptized life." Next Sunday, as the students filed into the classroom, Ariel told the Sunday school teacher that she wanted to be baptized. Thus, she declared herself first in the faith. On the Sunday of the class's baptism, however, Angelica was called to the pool first, so she said she was the first in the faith.

The girls' grandmother attended the baptism. She didn't think that faith in Christ and baptism should include rivalry. "You shouldn't be competing about faith," she said, wagging her finger. "As the Apostle Paul says, you should be first 'in supplications, prayers, intercessions, and thanksgivings for everyone so that you lead a quiet and peaceable life in all godliness and dignity.' That means your whole life needs to be in God's Spirit so that all you do is first and always an expression of God's love for others."

The twelve-year-olds smiled and tried to look ashamed, but their grandmother obviously didn't understand her granddaughters. Within the year, the girls' friendly competition continued in diligent Bible study. They hit on how the Bible distinguished each name. Angelica learned that her name came from Greek for "angel." Ariel found that her name was used for "Jerusalem."

So, their life direction was set and continued through school and into adulthood. Even after they were married and with children, they'd talk on the phone every night, beginning each conversation with a variation of another first.

Seven weeks after their twenty-ninth birthday, Ariel phoned Angelica and began the conversation with the news that her viral infection had promoted her to first with kidney disease. Three years of treatment didn't slow progression and the discussion of a possible donor was short, because Angelica was a perfect match.

Before the two were wheeled into adjoining surgery suites for the transplant procedure, they held hands and prayed, ending with their favorite saying: "a real first."

Three hours later as Angelica opened her eyes in the recovery room, she swallowed, coughed, and searched for the nurse attending her. Barely able to push words through her throat, the first she said was, "How's Ariel?"

Ariel, being recovered a few steps away, managed to move her head and gulp as she regained consciousness. With her eyes still closed, the first she said was, "How's Angelica?"

Preaching point: *Putting God first puts others first.*

B Proper 23 (28) Hebrews 4:12-16

Chapter 78: Confidence Corrective

"Looking back, it seems so clear now," Melissa said. She gazed upward over Julia's head, almost with a look of confession. "Not that I consider it my fault — well, not much. I'm getting over that. It's like my daughter Shonda said when our sweet, old neighbor asked her at her birthday party what it feels like to be eight years old. Shonda answered, 'It takes a while to get used to being eight.'" She smiled and returned her look to Julia who held her counselor's smile and nodded.

The two sat facing one another for half a minute. Julia said, "Go on. Tell me anything that seems important."

"Well," Melissa said, "I remember my mother's moving her head around, neither a shake nor nod, kind of a rotation, as she agreed with my father. Mostly I remember his saying to her, 'And you know I'm right.' This also meant that if he was right, others — she, and in this case, I — were wrong. I always felt I had to tiptoe sideways to my father. Obvious to me now, that's what I thought a husband was: someone — like my father — who knew he was right and said so. Consequently, taking a leap of fifteen years, that's a lot of what I saw in Tony that attracted me. Oh, he was kind at the time, even romantic; but underneath I'm sure I was attracted to him because he carried that sense of being right — and he said so. And he was educated and I wasn't. I had fantasized about being a pharmacist, but he convinced me not to go to college but to marry him."

Melissa let out a deep breath. Julia said, "I can tell you've really stirred around your memory with your counselee homework this week. I'm impressed."

Melissa sat up straight in her chair and leaned forward. "Your pages on types of personal transactions and names of feelings were for me like a microscope and a telescope. Opened up how

I'd felt in my important relationships. This week's been like a dozen puzzles falling together — not easily, but so clear now that I'm embarrassed I've lived as I have."

Julia raised a warning hand and Melissa said quickly, "Though I'm not totally responsible for what's happened. Just hard to let that go... the feeling that I start out wrong and others start out right... but I think I understand why I've always felt disfigured."

Julia raised a questioning eyebrow.

"Can't put it any other way. Not ugly. I've never felt ugly, just that something was wrong, like the baking powder was left out of the banana bread and produced banana flavored cardboard." She laughed at herself. Julia smiled, and said, "That's something of what got you married to Tony. Tell me more about how your marriage relationship developed."

Melissa shook her head, breathed slowly, and said, "It went in cycles for eleven years. Tony would get a job and all would be fine. Within a year, or sixteen months, for some reason or other, he'd lose his job. Each time his bitterness and complaining grew — first toward the job and then the community, and that included Shonda and me. It's like his bitterness and criticizing expanded around him like a shock wave: 'Cops should jail that guy for all the car's blue smoke. They should tear down that house; it's a terrible color. Those people wasted their money on snowmobiles, didn't buy insurance, and now the television station is guilting us into paying their hospital bill.' He scattered 'shoulds' and 'oughts' like throwing bricks. At me too. What I wore. He criticized the kind of clothes I like. Sometimes he attempted to be kind. They were like bouts of kindness with Shonda; but, she didn't know what to do. His smile was too broad and his laugh too loud.

"I was in a cloud, thought this was normal. Wasn't until three, four years ago that he criticized the pastor's sermon to the wrong person. I'd met Lisa in Shonda's kindergarten class and discovered we went to the same church. Tony, in one of his rotten moods, mouthed off about the pastor to Lisa's husband, who knew that Tony also complained about *him* — as he did about everyone. So, he told Lisa who told me why Tony kept losing jobs. The word was that he was a good worker — smart, efficient, honest. But after he'd been in a job for a while, he started telling others how to do their jobs and criticizing what he didn't like. Soon he had no friends and the company found a way to release him while giving him an adequate recommendation."

"His job loss, you mentioned, led to the crisis."

"Absolutely. We were almost out of money. I got online and searched for a pharmacy tech program. When he found out, he screamed, kept bringing it up and hassling me about it for weeks as our money dwindled. The day I told him I could get financial aid to enter the pharmacy tech program, he stepped close to me, grit his teeth and said, 'I told you I'd never hit a woman.' Then faster than I could blink he smashed his heel onto my right foot. Two broken bones."

Julia waited as Melissa wiped her tears and blew her nose. Julia said quietly, "That's when you went to Dr. Norrew."

"Yeah. Lisa got me to Dr. Norrew; and Dr. Norrew is so kind. When she asked how it happened, I didn't think about the consequences. Just told her."

"And she got you to me," Julia said.

"No. She referred me to my pastor," Melissa said "He got me to you."

"And how do you assess your life this week?"

"I've been thinking hard; I knew you'd ask me that again. First, Shonda's okay. She doesn't miss her dad, though she sees him once a month, and always with his mother present. For me, I'm two weeks from the end of the course. Yesterday my instructor said, 'For sure in a month you'll be wearing a tunic and rolling pills for a living.'

"What I've been pondering most is that starting way back in my life, I felt that people could see that I wasn't good and I was wrong to start with. But beginning with Dr. Norrew's compassion, I feel strengthened, sputtering, but I feel assured at the same time.

"I'm concentrating and repeating to myself that I don't have to creep sideways into anyone's presence. Dr. Norrew and my pastor have been praying for me." She looked at her watch. "Nearly fifty minutes, I see. But one more thing I want to tell you," she said as she stood. "I've told pastor also. I feel soul-strengthened. Dr. Norrew and you have helped me realize that God is inviting me to stand up straight, like I don't have to creep in sideways to God either."

Julia also stood, acknowledging that the counseling session had ended.

Melissa said, "I don't think I need to meet every week now. How about if I'd get an appointment for two weeks?"

Julia said, "I think that's just about right."

> **Preaching point**: *Christ grants confidence with God and one another.*

B Reign of Christ (34) Revelation 1:4b-8
C Easter 2 Revelation 1:4-8

Chapter 79: Priest For Whom?

Kenny swung the ax with more effort than needed against the large sage brush. His violent swing jammed in the roots entangled around a rock. His next swing hit the rock and pinged off to the side with a splash of sparks. This made him swing harder and even less effectively. After two minutes, when he'd finally displaced the ornery spot of vegetation, he surveyed what awaited him: a field dotted with sage brush. To his right and left, neighboring homeowners labored on this cleanup day of the 25-foot buffer to the hillside nature preserve behind their housing development. *Their* housing development, he thought. Not his. He angrily chopped on the next sage brush.

This? I've survived six years of college for this? I've been dragged through 2,000 years of church history, prodded through my piddly-poor preaching, and immobilized in the Greek language for this? Kenny was the congregation's summer seminary intern. The congregation and Pastor Shleck had never received a seminary intern before, and Pastor Schleck clearly didn't know how to relate to Kenny, whether teach, counsel, or direct him.

On this Saturday, because Pastor Schleck hadn't planned anything for Kenny, how about if he'd help behind the pastor's house as the homeowners cleared the insipient sage brush and skinned the ground with their weed trimmers? What was Kenny supposed to do? Start an argument that might, in a year, prevent him from becoming a pastor? He was here to learn about the church from the inside and to garner hands-on knowledge of ministry. This was not, however, the kind of hands on knowledge he'd expected would teach him Christian ministry.

After half an hour, he'd worked up a sweat and also worked

himself toward the edge of the pastor's property. He could see another young man working toward him, but he kept his head down and hit and hit and hit.

"You're mumbling!" Kenny heard the sounds, but didn't recognize the words. Again, "You're mumbling!" He looked up and saw the young man fifteen feet away laughing at him. Kenny glanced down at his hands, then turned slowly to face the pastor's neighbor. "You're right. One of my bad habits." He set the ax upright and leaned on the handle. It was too low to be comfortable, so he picked it up and held it as he tried to decide how to speak to someone when he was so enjoying being angry. His neighbor just kept smiling, and soon he did also. The young man walked over taking off his glove. "I'm Dean." Kenny smiled and shook his hand. "I'm Kenny."

"Haven't seen you here before. You the pastor's son?"

Kenny used all his will power to respond without anger, "No, I'm the congregation's seminary intern. The incline of this hillside is the beginning of my higher calling."

"Ha," Dean said. "Good. Use that humor in your sermons."

Dean was so friendly that Kenny felt prompted to tell the truth. "I wish I could say my mumbling was prayer. Sorry. I was angry."

"An almost-minister angry?"

"Sure am, or was. I'm pretty well over it. Thanks," he said, and decided to use the moment to share something of the Christian life. "Jesus was angry. Pastors get angry. Anger and grudges are some of my greatest temptations." He took a chance, "You worship?"

"Used to," Dean said with a guarded look. "Raised Baptist. Got some problems with churches. But I'm a priest," he asserted. "Learned that in Sunday school. Don't need anybody else to make the dogmas or decrees. 'Priesthood of all believers,'" he said, clenching his ungloved right hand, "the center of Protestantism."

Kenny was startled by someone who said he didn't worship yet so forcefully claimed the priesthood of all believers as the center of the Christian faith. He responded, "That sounds like the center of the faith for you." And he held his hand toward Dean as an invitation to say more.

Dean bowed his head as he shook it side to side. "Not like the Catholics," he said.

When Dean just stood there, as though his statement should be completely understandable, Kenny said slowly, "Catholic...."

"And mostly my wife. She and her priests and pope. No. Bible says we're all priests. You believe that, don't you?"

"Yes," Kenny said and quickly continued, "What's your wife's name?"

"Emily."

"Know her long when you married?"

"A year."

"She was Roman Catholic when you married?"

"Uh huh, but we kind of slid over that. Now she's got this Legion of Mary thing. Goes every week."

"Mmm," Kenny said, as he stroked his chin with his gloved hand, "does it make her more faithful to Christ and more loving to others?"

Dean made a gulping sound and looked away toward the top of the hill, "Oh, I don't know. Might."

"You guys talk about this much?"

"Not any more. She goes to her meetings. Doesn't ask me to go, I'll tell you! I've quoted the Bible to her about the priesthood of all believers. I've told her we don't need those other priests."

Kenny waited for Dean to continue, but when he fell silent, Kenny said, "You helped me when you spoke to me just now."

Dean took his gaze off the hill and smiled to Kenny, "Good."

"You did for me what priests are supposed to do."

Dean looked confused but interested enough to face Kenny and wait for him to continue.

"Priests serve others, not themselves. You ministered to me, and I appreciate it. I wasn't doing well working through my anger alone. I needed you, another person. We Christians need one another. That's why we're all priests."

"That's what you learn in seminary, huh?"

"That's what I learned in the Bible and in life. They're both necessary and I'm glad you came by. But I wish you'd consider more about who the priests in the priesthood of all believers are for."

Dean pushed a rock around with his foot. Then he turned to Kenny and said slowly, "That's fair." He paused a moment and squinted one eye, "Since you're here learning, you going to write about our little interchange here, like I did in salesman training? A 'he said, I said' thing."

"I'm pretty sure I will," Kenny said with a laugh.

"Change my name, etc.?"

"Sure."

"Okay with me," Dean said. "I'm glad I came by, too. Yeah, I'll seriously roll over in my mind what you said."

After another few minutes' chatting, the two young men went back to their Saturday's toil. As Kenny labored with his ax and weed trimmer he mumbled a constant prayer of thanksgiving for the next door priest and supplication for Dean and Emily.

Preaching point: *Each Christian is a holy intermediary for others.*

C Easter 3 Revelation 5:11-14

Chapter 80: And Under The Earth

The Comstock Lode in the present state of Nevada brought hordes of workers scurrying into settlements like Goldfield with its half dozen structures. Within weeks, the place doubled and doubled again and again. At first, so many hopeful miners arrived that the large mining companies thought the supply of labor was endless. But soon the need for specialists underground led one enterprising company to advertise in Wales for experienced miners who spoke English, offering to pay half their passage to the United States. That's what brought Terrwyn, Ercwlff, and Llywelyn to Goldfield. They arrived with little money left, but they brought the Welsh heritage of mining and singing their faith.

The three now stood in the rowdy group of hopeful hirees clustered in front of Hatfield, a man with a dirty-green hat, seated at a table near the mine's mouth. "I've got your names written here," Hatfield said, shaking his head, "but I won't try to jerk them into American. We gotta call you something we understand. This one," he said, pointing to a name on the paper in front of him.

Terrwyn leaned over to see. "That's Ercwlff," he said with a combination of sounds the boss had never heard before.

"Really?" he said. "Okay, he's now 'Eli.' Which one?" Terrwyn gestured to Ercwlff.

"You're now 'Eli,'" Hatfield said. "You understand?" Ercwlff understood enough English to nod agreement. Next, Llywelyn instantly became 'Lou,' and Terrwyn 'Tom.'

The three looked back and forth warily at one another. Terrwyn, now 'Tom,' raised a hand slowly as if to speak. But Hatfield wasn't looking up. "You've signed your contracts. I've got your Xs here." He plopped his hand on the papers and slid them to his left. "Over there," he swept his hand to the right across the three, aiming them to a man handing out tools. "You tell him your American names and you're the three from Wales and you're getting a nickel a day more. When you get in the hole, tell the boss-man to put you on the shoring." Other prospective workers shuffled up and the three Welshmen had little choice but to move. As they walked away, Eli said something to Lou in Welsh. Hatfield, though not seeming to pay attention, heard it and turned, saying sharply, "American. Speak American. Same as the Bohunks and the Eyetalians." He waved at the others waiting to get into the mine. "You get down in the bowels of the earth only to jabber your funny language, you won't be in the habit of speaking American if there's an emergency."

Tom had the presence of mind to use the opportunity to ask his question, "Can we sing in Welsh?"

Hatfield grunted and tipped back his dirty-green hat, "Sing?" He looked around smiling as though everyone shared a joke. "You talk, you talk American. You feel like singing down there, it's not my problem. No idea what these others will think." He grinned to the crowd in front of him and some of the men laughed, hoping to get in good with the big boss.

From the first day, the three Welshmen worked the only way they knew: hard — but, the foremen soon realized the difference between coal mining in Wales and silver and gold mining in the Comstock Deposit. The Welsh didn't know the new method of supporting huge caverns with square-set timbering. They could offer only a few tips on lifting the timbers into the joints, but they caught on fast and maintained their positions with the shoring crew — and their extra nickel a day. And when they were together, they sang their Welsh hymns.

The sounds were strange to the rest of the workers but no one usually disagreed, except when Hofmeister was their foreman. On their third day in the mine, the three were hefting a beam and singing a Welsh hymn. The first time they heard Hofmeister's shrieky voice was, "Cut out that gibberish." They thought he meant not to sing at that moment, but once again, when Hofmeister caught them singing Welsh, he reprimanded them.

"American," he screeched. "Keep it American."

The next day, when they suspected Hofmeister would be their foreman, they thought they'd solved the problem by singing in English. He startled them by screaming up from forty feet below, "Stop that racket." They knew there was no discussion or possibility of compromise. They could only sing when Hofmeister wasn't their supervisor.

At that time, Lou, Eli, and Tom were the only Welsh in the mine or the town and they were among the few who joined for worship on Sundays. The small group met outside the village for their chapel service led by the town's carpenter, who was a Methodist preacher. That's when the three Welshmen felt they could sing for all the people of Wales who'd arrived to this new world. Their singing in English helped Lou's grasp of the language so the other two didn't have to translate so many of the foreman's orders.

Within half a year they'd settled into the mining routine. Especially they were alert to when Hofmeister would be near. But, as Lou said, "by everything's luck," they were belting out a great Welsh hymn as Hofmeister stuck his head out from behind a beam. "I thought I told you —" as the ceiling crashed down beside them. The shoring swayed side to side. Men screamed as the chamber filled with dust. Miners clung to the shoring and soon realized the structure was secure. Someone re-lit a lamp and shouting served to report that a total of twelve men were now imprisoned in this bubble beneath the earth. The damage seemed to have hit only on an empty space to the south. Their continuing danger was the few rocks that kept falling below them, so their safest place was on the shoring.

When noise of rocks and men halted, Hoffmeister said, "They'll be right in for us," his voice becoming even higher as he tried to sound confident. "Happened before. They can punch through a rise from the north or a drift from the east. We'll put out the lamp, just to save our air. Won't take long."

But it did. All the men could do was sit in the darkness, shouting to those above or beneath them. Sometimes a man told a joke and the others laughed. By the second day, the laughter was only hopeful and not full-bodied.

The chamber was giant but didn't have unlimited air. They calculated they were two and a half days in their dark prison, when Lou could wait no longer. He started to sing a hymn in Welsh. He began tentatively, Hofmeister being only a few feet away. Tom and Eli didn't join right off. Tom, sitting next to Hofmeister quietly recited: "every creature in heaven and on earth and *under the earth* and in the sea, and all that is in them, singing." Hofmeister didn't reply, so Tom and Eli joined Lou in their Welsh praise.

No man made a noise until they'd completed their song. Then beside them, that squeaky voice they'd dreaded said gently, "American. Sing in American."

So they did, and all the years of the praise of Wales echoed in their deadly chamber: "Rough our way and dark the night, Strong our foes but small our might, Prone to droop our faithless mind, Life before, but death behind: Sing we as we journey on —."

"Down here!" the cry split through the song and all their thoughts. "They're breaking through."

The rescue was slow but certain, the rescue crew shoring their improvised shaft as they progressed. In the months to follow, the story was repeated that their rescue was a miracle signaled by the Welshmen's hymn. Some miners, even a couple rescued, claimed it was coincidence. But no one in any language could convince Tom, Eli, Lou… or Hofmeister otherwise.

Preaching point: *Praising God in all circumstances.*

Index
Revised Common Lectionary A

Advent 1	
Advent 2	Chapters 24, 33
Advent 3	
Advent 4	
Nativity of the Lord	Chapter 50
Christmas 1	
New Year's Day	Chapters 13, 47
Christmas 2	
Baptism of the Lord	Chapters 21, 34
Epiphany 2	
Epiphany 3	
Epiphany 4	Chapters 43, 70
Presentation of the Lord	
Epiphany 5	
Epiphany 6	Chapter 28
Epiphany 7	
Epiphany 8	
Transfiguration Sunday	
Ash Wednesday	
Lent 1	Chapters 42, 65
Lent 2	
Lent 3	Chapter 64
Lent 4	Chapters 9, 18
Lent 5	Chapter 30
Passion/Palm Sunday	Chapter 35
Maundy/Holy Thursday	Chapter 56
Good Friday	Chapters 16, 36
Resurrection of the Lord	
Easter 2	Chapters 14, 59, 62
Easter 3	
Easter 4	Chapter 18
Easter 5	
Easter 6	
Ascension of the Lord	Chapters 61, 74
Easter 7	Chapter 23

Day of Pentecost	Chapter 59
Trinity Sunday	Chapter 13
Proper 4	Chapter 22
Proper 5	
Proper 6	Chapters 1, 26, 44, 64
Proper 7	
Proper 8	
Proper 9	Chapters 2, 66
Proper 10	
Proper 11	
Proper 12	Chapters 45, 68
Proper 13	Chapters 3, 37
Proper 14	
Proper 15	Chapter 31
Proper 16	
Proper 17	Chapter 4
Proper 18	
Proper 19	Chapters 46, 69
Proper 20	
Proper 21	Chapters 19, 20
Proper 22	
Proper 23	Chapter 18
Proper 24	
Proper 25	Chapter 12
Proper 26	Chapters 6, 41
Reformation Day	Chapter 39
All Saints' Day	Chapter 43
Proper 27	
Proper 28	
Reign of Christ Proper 29	Chapters 26, 47, 74
Thanksgiving Day	Chapter 54

Index
Revised Common Lectionary B

Advent 1	
Advent 2	
Advent 3	
Advent 4	
Nativity of the Lord	Chapters 25, 50
Christmas 1	
New Year's Day	Chapters 13, 47
Christmas 2	
Baptism of the Lord	Chapter 21
Epiphany 2	Chapters 55, 71
Epiphany 3	
Epiphany 4	
Presentation of the Lord	
Epiphany 5	
Epiphany 6	
Epiphany 7	
Epiphany 8	
Transfiguration Sunday	Chapter 11
Ash Wednesday	
Lent 1	Chapters 19
Lent 2	
Lent 3	
Lent 4	
Lent 5	Chapter 39
Passion/Palm Sunday	Chapter 35
Maundy/Holy Thursday	Chapter 56
Good Friday	Chapter 16, 36
Resurrection of the Lord	Chapter 49
Easter 2	Chapters 31, 59
Easter 3	
Easter 4	Chapter 18
Easter 5	Chapters 17, 63
Easter 6	Chapter 25
Ascension of the Lord	Chapters 61, 74
Easter 7	Chapter 12

Day of Pentecost	Chapter 67
Trinity Sunday	Chapter 21
Proper 4	
Proper 5	Chapter 30
Proper 6	Chapters 8, 15
Proper 7	Chapter 31
Proper 8	Chapter 30
Proper 9	Chapter 48
Proper 10	Chapter 40
Proper 11	Chapter 18
Proper 12	
Proper 13	Chapter 10
Proper 14	Chapter 30
Proper 15	
Proper 16	Chapter 75
Proper 17	
Proper 18	
Proper 19	Chapter 35
Proper 20	Chapters 12, 32
Proper 21	
Proper 22	Chapter 13
Proper 23	Chapters 16, 78
Proper 24	
Proper 25	
Proper 26	Chapter 28
Reformation Day	Chapter 39
All Saints' Day	
Proper 27	Chapters 7, 29
Proper 28	Chapter 14
Reign of Christ Proper 29	Chapters 58, 79
Thanksgiving Day	Chapter 77

Index
Revised Common Lectionary C

Advent 1	Chapters 19
Advent 2	
Advent 3	Chapter 76
Advent 4	
Nativity of the Lord	Chapter 50
Christmas 1	
New Year's Day	Chapters 13, 47
Christmas 2	
Baptism of the Lord	Chapter 21
Epiphany 2	
Epiphany 3	
Epiphany 4	
Presentation of the Lord	
Epiphany 5	
Epiphany 6	Chapters 12, 51, 72
Epiphany 7	
Epiphany 8	
Transfiguration Sunday	
Ash Wednesday	
Lent 1	Chapter 5
Lent 2	
Lent 3	
Lent 4	Chapters 53, 73
Lent 5	
Passion/Palm Sunday	Chapter 35
Maundy/Holy Thursday	Chapter 56
Good Friday	Chapters 16, 36
Resurrection of the Lord	
Easter 2	Chapters 59, 79
Easter 3	Chapters 60, 80
Easter 4	Chapter 18
Easter 5	
Easter 6	
Ascension of the Lord	Chapters 61, 74
Easter 7	

Day of Pentecost	
Trinity Sunday	Chapters 13, 57, 64
Proper 4	
Proper 5	
Proper 6	Chapter 10
Proper 7	
Proper 8	Chapters 11, 14
Proper 9	
Proper 10	Chapters 19, 40
Proper 11	Chapter 1
Proper 12	
Proper 13	Chapter 52
Proper 14	
Proper 15	
Proper 16	
Proper 17	Chapters 27, 38
Proper 18	Chapter 12
Proper 19	
Proper 20	Chapter 77
Proper 21	
Proper 22	
Proper 23	Chapter 54
Proper 24	Chapter 3
Proper 25	
Proper 26	
Reformation Day	Chapters 22, 39
All Saints' Day	
Proper 27	Chapter 25
Proper 28	Chapter 25
Reign of Christ Proper 29	Chapter 22
Thanksgiving Day	Chapters 5, 26